How to Travel FREE as an International Tour Director

By

g.e Mitchell
Author, Tour Designer & Lecturer

*A "Step-by-Step Guide" for thousands of people who Want
to travel FREE and discover the world as a career*

iUniverse, Inc.
New York   Bloomington

How to Travel Free as an International Tour Director
Around the world for FREE A step-by-step guide ion travelling the world for FREE

Copyright © 2008 by Gerald E. Mitchell

All rights reserved. No part of this book may be used or reproduced by any means, graphic, electronic, or mechanical, including photocopying, recording, taping or by any information storage retrieval system without the written permission of the publisher except in the case of brief quotations embodied in critical articles and reviews.

iUniverse books may be ordered through booksellers or by contacting:

iUniverse
1663 Liberty Drive
Bloomington, IN 47403
www.iuniverse.com
1-800-Authors (1-800-288-4677)

Because of the dynamic nature of the Internet, any Web addresses or links contained in this book may have changed since publication and may no longer be valid. The views expressed in this work are solely those of the author and do not necessarily reflect the views of the publisher, and the publisher hereby disclaims any responsibility for them.

ISBN: 978-1-4401-0079-6 (pbk)
ISBN: 978-1-4401-0080-2 (ebk)

Printed in the United States of America

iUniverse rev. date: 11/19/08

The GEM Group, Ltd. Institute of Travel-Tourism

Career Development

The GEM Institute of Tourism and Career Development evolved from the travel professional's demand for unique and innovative material.

Overseen by Mitchell, these publications continue to surpass other competitive literature and are setting higher standards for the travel market.

Mitchell's works are currently in use in the United States, the Middle East, the (former Soviet Union) New Independent States, the Caribbean Basin, Canada, Latin America, Serbia, Africa and Russia.

Continued international growth is imminent as the world's hunger for Mitchell's consulting talents take him around the globe.

The mission of the Institute focuses on preserving the unique history, culture, and ecology of the region that is being promoted to the traveling public.

The promotion of these countries natural resources helps to stimulate the economy while preserving the ecological balance of nature and visitor.

The GEM Group, Ltd.
Established 1976

A company dedicated to helping countries develop
A successful and profitable tourism destination

A full service Tourism and Travel firm, the GEM Group Ltd. Was established in 1976 with the initial purpose of operating as an International Tour Operator company.

Since its founding, the firm has expanded its services from specializing in high-adventure tours to include Hospitality and Tourism Training, Tour Product Development, Marketing and Tour Guiding throughout the world.

Specializing in Cross Cultural Transfer, Rural and Ecotourism product development and marketing, The GEM Group, Ltd. provides the necessary training required for increasing long-range productivity by meeting product demand delivery services while ensuring viable and sustainable economic benefits to the client.

Mr. Mitchell, President of The GEM Group Ltd. and his staff of seasoned travel professionals conduct lectures in t Mr. Mitchell also has authored numerous travel and tourism texts currently in use throughout the world.

The GEM Group Ltd. established the first indigenously owned and operated outfitter and guide service in the Canadian Arctic.

The GEM Group Ltd. Professional Affiliations

- Registered with Who's Who National Registry
- Member of the Society of Travel and Hospitality Executives
- Organizations of American States (OAS)
- World Bank—IMF, DACON
- Lecturer for the Small Business Resource Center
- GEM Manuals registered with the Library of Congress
- GEM Publications are sold through Barnes & Noble, Books-a-Million, and Borders
- US Commerce Department, Washington, DC
- Trainer for Russia and New Independent States of the Former Soviet Union (SABIT)
- Unite States Agency for International Development
- Jordan—United States Business Partnership
- USAID-Booz, Allen, Hamilton, Belgrade, Serbia
- USAID-DAI-Zambia, Africa

Acknowledgments

I would like to express my gratitude to the many students around the world who encouraged me to write this book. They provided important information, and made hundreds of helpful and often candid comments. Too numerous to mention here, they include over 23 countries, NGOs, United States Agency for International Development, the Organization of American States, the Canadian Government, and other Ministries of Tourism and observers.

g.e Mitchell
Author, Tour Designer & Lecturer

"Make detours your Destination"

Note to Readers

In the Appendix at the back of this book, you will find many useful forms for your use as a Tour Director. These include checklists, sample announcements, medical forms, and others. These are samples only, which you can use to adapt to your needs as a Tour Director.

Throughout the text, the term "International Tour Director" is frequently abbreviated as "ITD."

Contents

Chapter 1: *The International Tour Director* 1

- **Introduction to Tourism** 1
  - *Key Facts about the Travel Industry* 2
  - *What is a Tourist?* 2
- **The Role of the International Tour Director (ITD)** 2
  - *The ITD—the "Fulfiller of Dreams"-The Dream Merchant* 3
  - *How Does the ITD travel "FREE"?* 4
  - *What are the Benefits for an ITD?* 4
  - *Who Becomes an ITD?* 4
  - *Attributes of an International Tour Director* 5
  - *Qualifications for an ITD* 5
  - *The importance of an ITD to Travelers* 6
  - *An ITD's On-the-Job Duties & Responsibilities* 6
  - *Problems an ITD May Encounter* 7
  - *Where Your Clients Come From* 7

Chapter 2: *You're Career Options* 9

- **First Choice: Freelancing** 9
- *Success or Failure?* 10
- **Finding Your First Job as a Freelance ITD** 10
- **Second Choice: Start Your Own Tour Company!** 11
- *USTOA-Membership Requirements* 11

Chapter 3: *Preparing Your Tour Group to Take Off!* 13

- **Pre-Tour Departure Rules** 13
- **Meeting and Greeting the "Tour Group"** 14
- **The Pre-Tour Meeting** 15
- *The ITD's Advice to the Traveler* 15
- *Traveler's Trip Cancellation Insurance* 16
- *"Hidden" Hotel Charges* 16
- *Check All Bills Carefully* 17
- *Be Careful With All Purchases* 17
- *Taxi Service* 17
- *Making Money Count* 17
- *Introduction to the Euro Currency* 18
- *Where to Purchase Foreign Currencies* 18
- *International Phone Calls* 18
- *What to Wear For Men* 18
- *What to Wear For Women* 19
- **Before Travelers Leave Home** 20
- **The "No-Show" Trip Kit Mailing** 21
- **Large Group Pre-Tour Orientation** 21
- **ITD's Early Arrival** 21
- *Reviewing the Travel Program* 22

- *Staff Briefing* 22
- *Operational Procedures for Tour Group's Arrival* 22
- *Communications during the Tour* 23
- *ITD's Travel Kit* 23
- *Terms, Liability, and Conditions of the Tour* 24
- *Tour Members' Medical Forms* 25
- *Liability Waiver* 25

Chapter 4: *"Taking Charge" of the Tour Group* 27

- Six Essential Points 27
- Communicating with Your Tour Members 28
- Stops along the Way 30
- Encounters with Unusual Personalities 30
- Travelers' Tribulations 31
- Emergencies and Other Problems 32
- What *Not* To Do As a Tour Director 33
- Multiple Tour Destinations 35
- *Unfamiliar Destination* 35
- *Scenario of a Fully Escorted 8-day Tour to Rome, Italy* 35

Chapter 5: *En Route to Your Destination* 39

- Working with Your Travel Partners 39
- Airline Travel 39
- *Responsibilities of the In-Bound Destination Manager* 40
- The Hotel: "Your Home Away from Home" 41
- *Overbookings* 42
- *Overbooking Policies* 42
- *Luggage Control* 43
- *Coordinating Activities with Hotel Management* 43
- *Opening Hotel Accounts* 44
- *The Tour Group's Hospitality Desk* 44
- *Selling Optional Tours* 45
- *Auto Rentals* 45
- *Shopping: A Destination Highlight* 45
- *Arranging Evening Activities* 46
- Sample Work Schedule for Hospitality Desk Staff 46
- *Free Time* 47
- *Emergencies* 47
- *Great Dining Experiences* 48
- *Pre-Dinner Check List for Group Functions* 48
- Hiring Local Interpretive Tour Guides 49
- *Tour Guide's Responsibility to the Tour Group* 49
- Contracting Motor Coach / Driver 50
- *Tipping Policies* 50
- Travel Supplier Evaluation Report 51

Chapter 6: *Taking the Tour Group Home* 53

- Pre-Departure Notice 53
- *PHASE I: Pre-Check-Out Briefing* 54

- *PHASE II: Checking Out of the Hotel* *54*
- *"Departure Notices"* *54*
- *Airport Check In* *57*
- *The Straggler*.. *57*

Chapter 7: *Closing out the Tour* 59

- **ITD's Post-Tour Responsibilities** *59*
- **The Value of a "Tour Reunion" Party** *59*
- **ITD Field Evaluation Report** *60*
- **Evaluating Interpretative Tour Guides** *60*
- **Why is the Evaluation Form so important?** *61*
- **Sample: International Tour Director's Evaluation Form** *62*
- *Client's Evaluation Report* *65*
- *Welcome Home Letter to Clients* *65*
- *Letters to the Travel Suppliers* *65*
- *ITD's Tour Expense Report* *65*

Chapter 8: *Getting Started as a "Dream Merchant"* 67

- **How Travelers benefit From a Package Tour** *67*
- **Getting Started!** *68*
- **Four Key Elements in Starting a Tour Company** *68*

Chapter 9: *Designing & Packaging Tours* 71

- **Future Trends in the Travel-Tourism Industry** *71*
- *Sample List of Tour Services* *72*
- *Pacing and Balance for a Successful Tour Route* *73*
- *Daily Itinerary Check List* *73*
- *Associating Personality Types with the Tour Program* *73*
- *Five Different Categories of Travelers* *73*
- *"Weaving It All Together"* *74*
- *Creating Tour Highlights* *74*
- *Image and Experience* *75*
- *Sample Tour Highlights and Marketing Features* *75*
- *Promoting Local Resources to Niche Markets* *76*
- **Three Steps to Successful Tour Planning** *77*
- *Avoid These Tour Operator Mistakes* *78*
- *Inspecting a Destination or Cruise Ship* *78*
- **Introduction to "Traditional Touring"** *79*
- **Welcome to the Cruise Industry** *79*
- *Contacts for the Cruise Industry* *80*
- **New Trends in Tourism-"Non-Traditional Touring"** *80*
- *Sample "Non Traditional" Niche Tourism* *81*
- *Introduction to Eco-tours* *81*
- *Adding Eco-Tours to Your Portfolio* *82*
- *New "Non-Traditional" Opportunities for the Tour Operator* *82*
- *Case Study: Agriculture Tourism* *83*
- *Methodology in Developing Non-Traditional Tours* *84*
- *Developing a Agri-Tourism – Business Plan* *85*
- *Become a Niche –Tour Developer*..*86*

- Pricing Tours for Profit! 89
- The Three "Can I" Questions 90
- *Pricing Your Tours* *90*
- *Costs vs. Profits* *90*
- Group Tour Pricing & Foreign Independent (FITs) 92
- Agents/Tour Conductor Discounts 94
- *Tour Organizer Incentives: Free or Discounted Tours* *94*
- How to Market Your Tour Programs 95
- *Finding Clients* *95*
- Designing Your Promotional Brochure 96
- *General Information & Terms and Conditions* *96*
- *Layout of a Tour Brochure* *96*
- *Format* *97*
- *Tour Operator's Company Logo* *98*
- *The Tour Designer Signature* *99*
- Contract between Tour Operator and Client 100
- *Sample Tour Operator's Terms & Conditions* *102*

Chapter 10: *Sample Tour Programs* 107

- Charleston-Awards & Honors 107
- *Charleston's Spa, Culture, and Gourmet Tour* *107*
- Classic Spanish La Rioja & Ribera del Duero Wine Journey 110
- "Eco-Tour"/High Adventure in Canadian Rockies 114
- Sample Study Tour to India 115
- Sample Tour of Nova Scotia 117
- Montreal Spa and Shopping Tour 119
- CROATIA – A HIDDEN GEM 122

Chapter 11: *How to Conduct On-Site Inspection Tours* 127

- *Benefits of Experiencing the Product* *127*
- Visitor's Bureau 128
- Destination Highlights Selection 129
- *Motor Coach Selection / Inspection* *132*
- *Restaurant Selection / Inspection* *135*
- *Hotel Inspection* *138*
- *FAMs: Familiarization / Study Tours* *140*

Appendix 142

- Sample Forms 143
  - CHECK LIST FOR *ALL* TOURS 143
  - ITD's TRIP KIT CHECK LIST 147
  - ITD's Pre-Departure Briefing Check 158
  - Trip Kit Checklist for Mailing 162
  - SAMPLE COVER LETTER FOR TRIP KIT 163
  - Tour Vouchers & Client Instructions 165
  - Sample Hotel Voucher 166
  - Work list of Travel Partners 167
  - Sample Baggage Claim Form 168
  - Sight-Seeing Booking Form 170

- ॐ Airline Change Request Form 170
- Glossary Of Travel Terms.. 175
- Travel and Tourism Resources 191
- Travel – Tourism Periodicals.. 195
- Professional Organizations and Associations 197
- Government and State Tourism Offices 199
- "Know before you go "Sample" Zambian travel information kit for pre-departures 229
- GEM Consulting Services 281

Chapter 1

The International Tour Director

"The Fulfiller of Dreams"

Introduction to Tourism

Tourism in general has already become the most important civil industry in the world, bigger than the auto, steel, electronics or agricultural industries.

Tourism is a broad and multifaceted industry whose complexity is reflected in the terminology employed to describe it. While there are no standard, internationally accepted definitions of many of the terms currently in use, it is important to have at least a general understanding of what they mean. To help you understand the terms you will encounter as a tour director, The GEM Group, USA-Canada has developed a glossary of tourism-related terms, which is located in the Appendix.

Tourism itself has been defined by the World Tourism Organization as "the activities of persons traveling to and staying in places outside their usual environment for not more than one consecutive year for leisure, business, or other purposes."

"*Sustainable tourism*" is "tourism which actively fosters appreciation and stewardship of the natural, cultural and historic resources and special places by local residents, the tourism industry, governments and visitors. It is tourism which can be sustained over the long term because it results in a net benefit for the social, economic, natural and cultural environments of the area in which it takes place." *(Definition used by Parks Canada)* Three general types of travel are identified as tourism, based on the traveler's motivation, the purpose or reason for the trip, along with various sub-categories:

- *Pleasure/Leisure travel* - includes Group Travel and Fully Independent Travel (FIT)
- *Business travel* - includes Conventions and Meetings; Incentive Travel
- *Personal travel* - includes Visiting Friends and Relatives (VFR)

Tourism Market Segments

The past decade or so has witnessed the segmenting of the tourism industry, globally; into a growing number of distinct markets in order to assist International Tour Directors and Tour Operators in developing targeted products and help consumers understand the product offerings. These market segments include:

- Adventure tourism
- Historical/Cultural
- Eco Tours
- Agriculture-Tours
- Soft/High Adventure
- Health/Spa Programs
- Special Events
- Educational Excursions
- Expeditions

Key Facts about the Travel Industry

- Travel-Tourism is the world's fastest growing job profession in creating new jobs.
- Because the industry has been experiencing a boom time, we are in desperate need of qualified tourism professionals.
- Tourism is one of the few industries that can offer exciting, challenging, and varied careers—plus fast promotions.
- Employment opportunities are growing at an impressive rate. In 2005, an additional 130 million new tourism jobs are being created around the world with over 400 different types of employment.
- The travel-tourism profession currently employs one in ten people worldwide.
- Tourism creates jobs and also boosts the local economy. The visitor supports the economy by spending money in shops, local transport, hotels, and restaurants.
- Tourism is a key source of civic pride. Old building sights and museums are rejuvenated and this aids in local conservation and environmental improvements.

> **Special Note:** It is interesting to realize that by 2007, more than 100 million people worldwide will be employed in this renewal of tourism sights. Because of the growth of the industry, travel-tourism is now seen to be of importance to most countries of the world.

What is a Tourist?

Although many of us have been "tourists" at some point or another in our lives, we seem to struggle for the words when asked to define tourism. Here's the dictionary definition:

> **Tourism (tüe(r) izm): n.** the temporary movement of people to places other than work or home. The activities undertaken during their stay and the facilities created to meet their needs.

The Role of the International Tour Director (ITD)

An Old Persian proverb comes to mind for directing tour groups: "Two things indicate weakness: To be silent when it's time to speak, and to speak when it's time to be silent." This proverb should be the Tour Director's credo.

"I like people and want to travel" is so often the opening statement made by candidates applying for the job of Tour Escort/Tour Director. But those are only two of the prerequisites of a Tour Escort. Let's examine the full realm of duties and responsibilities that are, and should be, assumed by anyone who wishes to travel extensively. They will have to be away from their families, work on holidays, and be on call 24 hours a day.

An ITD is a person who loves to travel, has a desire to see, experience, and share new cultures and people with their clients. Sparked by an insatiable desire to maintain this life style, ITDs will either start their own ITD/Tour Company and or freelance under contract with other major tour operators.

The ITD can "make" or "break" the tour. After months or years of planning by the clients and tour company, the participants are now placed in the hands of the escort. Take time to pause and reflect on all the work and expense that went into the creation of the tour program, on the dreams and expectations of the clients. If you do this, you will realize that it is very important that the Tour Escort/Tour Director review the entire tour prior to departure. Make a mistake, overlook important details of the program, and it will be an uphill battle trying to regain the customers' confidence. You will then spend your time in consoling the tour participants and overlooking the harmonious mood that they were in at the time of departure.

The ITD—the "Fulfiller of Dreams"-The Dream Merchant

Making Dreams a Reality is your personal challenge! You have the ultimate opportunity to make each client's dream holiday come true. When your clients bought their conducted tour, they had so many wonderful things in mind. *You* have to help them realize each dream! You will know by now that it can be difficult, even exhausting at times. After all, you are dealing with human nature in its many forms and variations, but only *you* can make each tour a complete success.

Many of your clients will arrive at the beginning of the tour with pre-conceived ideas and prejudices. It is up to you to give them a greater understanding and appreciation, or at least, to help them to be aware of the interesting differences between countries, between people.

How are you going to present yourself, your job, and the countries of this wonderful world to your clients? With this opportunity of expressing yourself on innumerable subjects, *it is important to be prepared*, and equally important, you must avoid becoming opinionated!!

Devote time and thought, as well as study, to the subject which will be covered as you travel in the countries and cities your tour(s) will visit, and you, yourself, will gain a great deal. You will become curious – a note in a guide book about the mysterious "Etruscans" may lead you to explore the Villa Giulla Museum when you have an hour or two free in Rome. Time spent there, plus your travels through the central Italian countryside may awaken your enthusiasm, and consequently, that of your clients, so yet another part of their tour becomes exciting and a highlight for them.

This can happen in so many varied fields! A constant awareness and observation on your part will enable you to give interesting explanations of so many things. . . . The peasant riding his donkey may make a nice snapshot. On the other hand, it will give you a chance to explain the economy of that region. If you constantly keep this attitude of awareness, what you will gain personally will an ever-improving and deepening understand which will enrich you, and which will become a fundamental part of your professional attitude.

Your goal at all times should be to keep your clients informed about what they are seeing, to pass on to them the most valuable and interesting information, not forgetting at the same time that each group is made up of many individuals, and has to be approached individually.

You love Venice, Lisbon, Paris or Amsterdam, or whichever place happens to be your particular favorite. How can you let your clients see it without a similar thrill, the same feelings you had on your first visit?

To sum it up, you cannot give to another your love and your understanding of a place; rather you must help them to come to their own understanding; help them to open their minds to new experiences in different ways of life, of living. . . that is the beauty and value of travel.

How Does the ITD travel "FREE"?

Because a portion of the trip's cost (known as the "prorate") that each traveler pays is used to help defray the ITD's expenses, the ITD travels free for managing the group and is paid a set "daily fee/rate" for time "on the road" along with tips.

What are the Benefits for an ITD?

An ITD can work full- or part-time and provide services in any number of places around the world. Tours and cruises are typically offered in many different areas of the world depending upon the season. Therefore, there are both year-round and seasonal opportunities. ITDs have two choices in deciding whether they want to have their own company and or work for a large tour operator. There are many other benefits, too:

- Traveling and seeing new places
- Establishing a network of friends and colleagues around the world
- Forming a special bond with clients
- Remuneration (tour profits/tips/free travel)
- Being your own boss
- An exciting lifestyle
- Conducting a "flawless" tour
- Earning a good income and seeing the world FREE

Caution! Once travel is in a tour director's blood, few people ever decide to leave the travel-tourism industry.

Who Becomes an ITD?

Doctors, professors, nurses, engineers, school teachers, sales executives, IT programmers, who have either been either laid-off or gone through a life changing experience or have just plain "burned out" in their careers and now want to engage potential customers with a promise of all a new experience. The ITD can promote and celebrate the explorer in people, awaken them to that part of themselves which gets buried in the same old routine --the same drive to the office, the same television shows, and the same beach vacation, year after year. Today's travelers have a sense of wonder and curiosity; they are open and receptive to "off the beaten path" tours.

Your job as an ITD is you choose it is to create, plant new ideas, and grab the consumer's attention by offering a break from the "everyday."

Attributes of an International Tour Director

An ITD performs the role of a "babysitter," ensuring that the clients are enjoying their tour and meet their guests' needs. Their responsibilities can be very demanding -- assuming the role of leader, educator, and being the first to rise in the morning and the last to go to bed at night. They can work full- or part-time, and during the "High Season" they can be gone up to 150 days at any one time. On each day and at each location, the ITD will 'check," "double check," and "triple check" the hotels, airlines, cruise ships, motor coaches, restaurants and local step-on guide services. While the tour members are enjoying a tour or evening activities, their ITD is busy preparing for the upcoming day, seeing that check-out procedures are handled and completing their daily critique and travel expense forms. While on tour, the tour members will form a special bond with the ITD and depend on the ITD to make the "intangible tour" become a reality. In addition, while on tour an ITD plays many roles…

- Educator
- Negotiator
- Problem solver
- Entertainer

Performing these activities can be very taxing, both emotionally and physically!

Qualifications for an ITD

An ad for a tour director might list all the following traits:

- A "people person"
- Excellent oral and written communication sills
- Flexible
- Punctual
- Entertainer
- Able to resolve problems "on the spot"
- Calm in a crisis situation
- Contingency planner
- Meticulous in handling details – must be an organizer, complete daily forms and repots, summarize activities, meals, guide service etc.
- Multicultural skills
- Foreign languages
- Excellent stamina
- Well groomed
- Well read and interested in global affairs
- Able to keep track of all the fast-changing products, prices, and rules necessary to properly advise clients and provide accurate information
- Be current with political issues and situations abroad that might affect upcoming tour programs and the safety of clients
- 'No Problem' attitude! -- a good ITD is a good manager of crises, makes quick decisions, and is prepared to make changes on a moment's notice
- Aware of the common "pitfalls" of being an ITD

- Makes all the intangible aspects of the trip come "alive" and develops a unique relationship with tour members

> ***Special Note***: A background in architecture, art, culinary arts, religion, eco-tourism and foreign languages is beneficial both to the ITD and their clients.

The importance of an ITD to Travelers

Your client/traveler is a consumer who has purchased a product, having first checked on the name of the operator, hotels used, meals, and other services included or not, and the itinerary. You are the "X" factor in the package, which can make this tour a success -- or make it a disappointment. Your client, as the consumer, bought the tour because it appealed to him; and the travel agent who sold it to him assured him it was a good value for his money. The client checked on the tour, but no first-time traveler can realize what a tour is actually like until he has been on one and has realized that he lives with the conditions that he bought, and that there is far more to understand -- or should be -- than he first anticipated.

Every day, being human your client makes mental comparisons among people, their ways of life, and cultural objects, and realizes moment after moment that the people and customs he experiences on tour are vastly different from his way of life at home. Your job as an ITD is to give him/her the confidence and the guidance to be aware of these differences – not that the client should praise or criticize them, just that he does become aware of them and tries to understand them. You can allay his doubts about much of what he sees; after that, he can make his own judgments.

If you care enough to help him to realize his dreams, at least to some extent, to make a success of his tour, then you reach the mind of not only the client, but the human being inside as well. Once an understanding has been established between you and your client, it is far simpler to pass on information and ideas; he feels understood, and will therefore understand you better.

In giving your clients this depth of understanding, small problems which always arise in traveling will not mar the tour, and it will remain an unforgettable and valuable experience for both of you.

An ITD's On-the-Job Duties & Responsibilities

The primary task of an ITD is to ensure that clients have an exciting and memorable experience. The trip needs to be delivered as promised in the tour brochure and itinerary. Taking charge of a group of 40 clients means the ITD has to be concerned about the tour members' welfare and be able to do all the following:

- Keeping the group out of harm's way
- Providing interesting experience
- Organizing optional evening activities, scheduling religious services
- Alleviating emergency situations,
- Interacting with local tour operators, guides, transportation companies, restaurants
- Preparing report form on tour sites, hotels, guide services and expenses
- Being host for the entire tour.
- Educating clients about the upcoming events and sites being visited
- Acting when necessary as an entertainer
- Negotiating group rates, shopping and currency exchange
- Solving problems

- Filling the expectation of knowing "everything"
- Being "24-hour baby sitter"
- Serving as the "bridge over a cultural gap" to clients

Problems an ITD May Encounter

Like a good Boy or Girl Scout, an ITD needs to be prepared to handle any problem that arises – and there can be quite a few unexpected situations that arise during a tour.

- Culture shock
- Illness/death of a client
- Poorly planned tour itinerary
- Difficult tour members
- Airlines going on strike and flight delays
- Political changes in local government
- Terrorism
- Natural disasters
- Currency devaluation
- Negative reviews of the chosen destination/cruise line in the Sunday travel section
- War
- Motor coach breakdowns
- Lost luggage
- Food poisoning

Where Your Clients Come From

Tour groups are traditionally planned for the memberships of organizations and associations, all of which have different interests and backgrounds. Traditionally, a member (President, Secretary) of an association or organization will *travel free* as the "Group Leader" and spokesperson for the group, but that person does not take you place as Tour Director. Some sources of potential clients include:

- International tour operators
- Association directors
- Social clubs
- Incentive houses
- Special interest groups
- University study groups
- Alumni associations
- Church groups and religious organizations
- Travel agencies
- Athletic organizations
- Business and trade organizations
- Chambers of Commerce
- Fraternal organizations
- Fraternities and sororities
- Political organizations
- Professional organizations
- Veterans' and military organizations
- Youth organizations
- The physically disabled

- Senior citizens clubs
- Special events group attendees
    - Olympics
    - Marathons
    - Music Festivals
    - Tour de France
    - Wine & Food Culinary excursions and schools

Chapter 2

You're Career Options

You have exciting choices when you begin your career as an International Tour Director – you can work for someone else, such as a major tour operator, or you can start your own business. Both opportunities offer excitement and the chance to work independently.

First Choice: Freelancing

You can become a "freelancer," working for a variety of international tour operators. The work is varied, and no two tour groups are alike. There are times you will manage large group seminars on tour, provide special assistance to tour members with particular interests, such as wine, food, wild game, high adventure, and the arts.

As a freelancer, your are an independent contractor. You will be paid a fee based on the complexity of the tour. Along with the base pay, a good ITD will be compensated with tips from satisfied customers.

Responsibilities to the Contracting Employer

Your possible employers could include:

- International tour operators
- Directors of organizations and associations
- Incentive planners
- Convention/conference planners
- Travel agents
- Program planners for special interest groups

Here's a typical tour scenario for a freelance ITD:

You have been chosen by an organization or International Tour Operator to be the ITD in charge of their clients. As such, you are viewed as part of that firm and carry the responsibility for their product, just as much as the Tour Operator who planned the tour, designed an expensive brochure to sell it, and advertised it, and as much as the Travel Agent who sat down in his office with the prospective buyer, doing booking details, making long-distance telephone calls, and writing air tickets for buyer, and turned him into a member of your tour group. Even your image has been a part of the Travel Agent's sales approach: "The International Tour Director, the epitome of skill and knowledge if the area, personifies tact and diplomacy." A vast amount of money has been spent on advertising and promotion, planning and operation, and you become *the* focal point, a fulcrum on which the whole tour swings.

Success or Failure?

You are the crucial link in the whole chain of the tour, from its conception our to the client's happy return home. But you are not the most important link -- *ALL* are important; all have their part to play in bringing the client, prepared to travel, to you.

You must give full support and recognition to the preceding work, done long before you appeared on the stage, and *you must not disassociate yourself* from these preparatory operations, even if you feel there has been, or is, a weak point. All your clients return home at the end of their tour, and your conduct of the tour and of yourself will be pre-eminent in their minds when they talk to the person from whom they bought the tour.

You are the representative of the firm as well as being the Tour Director, and the firm has entrusted you with its tour. You strengthen your own position as you protect and support he Tour Company's good name. It is quite simple; you are employed to ensure that the tour group has a happy and memorable experience, which reflects well on the tour company. You will appreciate this more clearly when, after several successful seasons with the same company, they give you better tours, and your position will be strengthened with them.

Remember that your, enthusiasm, dedication, and sincere willingness to serve, combined with the travel company's efforts, make up the degree of success for which your company is known. The genuine feeling on your part that the comfort of the client and the tour participants comes first will go a long way toward proving that the trip is not just another travel program.

Finding Your First Job as a Freelance ITD

Two major sources of jobs are the United States Tour Operators Association (USTOA) and the International Association of Tour Managers (IATM). These are international companies whose tours and packages encompass the entire globe and who conduct business in the U.S.

- ***United States Tour Operators Association (USTOA)***

The USTOA is a professional association representing the tour operator industry and has a list of tour operators at its website: http://www.ustoa.com. USTOA was founded in 1972 by a small group of California tour operators concerned about tour operator bankruptcies. These founding members recognized the need for a unified voice to protect the traveling public, as well as to represent the interests of tour operators. In 1975, USTOA became a national organization with headquarters in New York.

USTOA members number among the top names in travel and represent the entire spectrum of vacation packages and tours available today. In fact, the member companies are responsible for the majority of tours and vacation packages sold by travel agents in the U.S. According to a recent survey, USTOA companies move more than ten million passengers annually and account for an annual sales volume of more than $8 billion. This sales success story reflects the organization's pledge to encourage and maintain the highest standards of professionalism, integrity and service.

- *International Association of Tour Managers (IATM)*

The International Association of Tour Managers (IATM) has a website with listings of over 3,000 members worldwide who work both full- and part-time: http://www.IATM.com. You will find their website filled with resources.

- *Other Resources*

Additional sources:
- National Tour Association: http://www.nataonline.com
- American Association of Travel Agents: http://www.astanet.com

Second Choice: Start Your Own Tour Company!

Your will be self-employed as an International Tour Director/Owner Operator. You can mark up your tours from 25% to 35%, depending on the variability of airfares, volume-based pricing, and marketing. The advent of e-commerce and the Internet makes it possible for a newcomer to reach potential markets in a cost-effective way.

The thrill of starting your own company and specializing in targeting a "niche" market is a relatively inexpensive approach, managed by any or a combination of the following:

1. Direct mail/Local advertising/Television/Radio
2. Group presentations and lectures
3. Internet online marketing

You will grow at the speed of your choice, and you can work either full- or part-time. You decide how many days you want to be away from home, and you select an advertising and promotional budget to match your desired income. A good ITD/Tour Operator should focus on winning the loyalty of clients; i.e., travel agents, association directors, and individual travelers by offering excellent service and well-designed tours and cruise programs.

As a self-employed ITD, it is your responsibility to negotiate hotel rates, block group space with major airlines, cruise lines, motor and coach companies; and design an itinerary that is paced to the clients' satisfaction. Next, you need to find clients! Once the tour has been "packaged," you can market your tour programs to the public and travel industry, generating awareness and brand-name identification.

By using the Internet, you can now narrow your potential client search and design tour offerings to match niche target markets. Being created offers many opportunities for you. Remember that an ITD's goal is to turn dreams into realities, catering to travelers' level of sophistication, special interests, or to those wanting to have an adventure trekking through the Himalayas.

USTOA-Membership Requirements

One of the first things an ITD/Tour Operator should consider is becoming an Active Member of USTOA. To do so, a tour operator is required to have a total of 18 references from a variety of industry sources and financial institutions and must meet specific minimums in terms of tour passengers and/or dollar volume. The company must also be in business at least three years under the same management in the U.S. and must carry a minimum of $1,000,000 professional liability insurance.

Another important membership requirement is adherence to USTOA's strict code of ethics, which is framed by a pledge to encourage and maintain the highest standards of professionalism, integrity and service. In addition to these requirements, all USTOA Active Members must participate in USTOA's $1 Million Travelers Assistance Program.

Resources for contract work and employment:

- National Tour Association: www.ntaonline.com
- National Business Travel Association: www.nbta.com
- American Society of Association Executives: www.asaenet.org
- Adventure Travel Society: www.adventuretravel.com
- U.S. Tour Operators Association: www.ustoa.com

Chapter 3
Preparing Your Tour Group to Take Off!

Pre-Tour Departure Rules

Rule #1 Never take anything for granted.

This rule might well be the credo that an ITD lives by while operating a tour program. In spite of letters of agreement, e-mail confirmations, written contracts, and faxes, things can go awry and will if the ITD doesn't make absolutely certain that every member of the tour staff, as well as hotel personnel, local suppliers, airport skycaps, and airline confirmations agents involved in the program, understand their various functions and what is expected of them.

Rule #2 Check and double check and triple check.

This is the motto of a good ITD. Check, double check, and triple check while en-route about hotel check- ins and informing the tour participants about the local traditions, and do's and don'ts about a destination to what to select from a menu for dinner.

Rule #3 Maintain constant communications.

While en-route, the ITD is in constant commutations with suppliers (hotels, tour guide companies, transportation firms, and restaurants, giving pre- and post-narratives about a destination or cruise.

Rule # 4 do the tedious work prior to taking off!

It is essential that the ITD preview the Travel Program prior to departure. Although each travel program is unique and individually customized to the client's requirements, certain procedures are always the same, regardless of program location or itinerary. The following checklist includes procedures with which an ITD or his/her staff is always concerned:

- Establish billing and accounting methods with hotels and other suppliers, and review costs agreed upon prior to the group's arrival.
- Ensure seat assignments on all forms of transportation.
- Confirm arrangements for the pre-registration of the guests in the hotel.

- Have the participants met at the airport upon arrival and arrange for transferring them and their luggage to the hotel (or ship).
- Establish a hospitality desk to be staffed for the duration of the program at times prescribed by the Tour Director-in-charge.
- Confirm all reservations and establishing guarantees (number of passes), if necessary, for all activities, including dinners, nightclubs, Sight-seeing tours, sporting activities, and cocktail parties.
- Analyze and approve all bills related to the operation of the travel program.
- Finalize instructions to the Tour Guides and to the assistant to the ITD.

> ***Special Note:*** Slides, movies or guest speakers referencing the destination or cruise is a good method in promoting the tour program and having your guest "bring a friend"

Meeting and Greeting the "Tour Group"

Having a Pre-Tour Orientation Meeting is valuable for many reasons.

First, it gives many of the travelers an opportunity to get acquainted before the trip begins. Although not everyone may be able to attend (and some late registrants for the trip may not have reserved yet), the orientation can serve several useful purposes. A pre-tour orientation gives the clients an opportunity to ask questions about the tour, what is included and what is not.

Second, and most important for the ITD …

- Clients to meet with the Tour Directors and Escorts.
- Travelers can be briefed as to what is expected from them, and also what services the Tour Director will provide.
- Clients to meet their roommates and other tour members.
- You to check for the potential problem traveler.
- You to note any clients with physical disabilities.
- You have the opportunity to offer trip insurance (a must for today's traveler's!).
- You can review the trip kit (see sample below).
- You can review the entire trip, notifying clients of any changes.
- You are able to handle any last-minute requests.
- You can discuss the departure gate or meeting location at the airport (ITDs should try to rent a room at the airport for their groups)
- You can recommend airport transfers services for those in need of transportation
- The Tour Operator can market any optional tours. Optional tours can be purchased pre-departure or at the hotel hospitality desk.
- You can check passports and visas.
- Clients can complete necessary insurance and medical forms.
- You can review the rooming list (smoking-non-smoking).
- You can accommodate the single travelers and introduce them to one another. There will be tour members who do not have a husband, wife, or a friend going on the trip, so they will need someone for a roommate. The orientation meetings will give them an opportunity to get acquainted with others going on the trip that also need roommates. Many new friendships are formed in this manner, and often the same two people room together on future trips.
- You can make note of the "no-shows -- clients who aren't able to attend the orientation meeting. If for any reason a traveler is unable to attend the final orientation meeting, contact him in person

so there is no misunderstanding about where and when the group is meeting for departure from your area. Be sure the travelers have received a copy of the tour itineraries, flight schedules, and contact numbers. Sometimes last-minute travelers, and those late in signing up or filling a cancellation, are overlooked.

Special Note: Not enough clients to show a profit? The Pre-Tour Orientation Meeting is an excellent opportunity to have the participants encourage their friends and relatives to sign up and join the tour group.

The Pre-Tour Meeting

The pre-tour orientation meeting agenda will vary depending on the type of trip. Details such as procedures to be followed for pre-boarding planes, transferring luggage, checking into hotels, boarding buses should be discussed. Travelers should be given an estimate of how much money to take. This will depend on what is included in the tour cost, such as meals, sight-seeing, Most travelers appreciate suggestions about tips and gratuities and packing. Remind everyone to place their name, address, and phone number on the inside of all luggages in case baggage tags should be lost.

If a passport, visa, or vaccination is needed, it is very important to explain this at the first meeting. Follow through at each meeting with all travelers and be certain that they have taken care of all those details early. Have all basic information available about procedures to be followed -- for example, in applying for a passport, the travelers must produce two or more passport photos, a birth certificate, and the fee. They also need to know the locations where they can apply and how long it takes to obtain a passport.

The ITD's Advice to the Traveler

During the orientation group meeting with the tour participants, the ITD should review the importance of being prepared for the unexpected. Not everything goes as planned. At the Pre-Tour meeting you must tell your travelers that things can go wrong. There are transportation delays, days of pouring rain, unscheduled museum closures, hotel strikes, an occasional repetitious or even poor meal, and on even the best-planned five-star trips, someone is likely to catch cold or suffer a queasy stomach. Nothing is perfect and imperfection is an integral part of the travel experience.

Persuade participants to purchase trip insurance. Why Trip Insurance? Because it protects:

- The Traveler
- The Tour Operator
- The ITD
- The Travel Suppliers

It will be a convenience for your travelers if you have insurance forms on hand at the meeting and explain what type of insurance is available and the cost. It should be pointed out that most homeowners' policies cover luggage if lost or stolen, but not if it is damaged. Also, Medicare/Medicaid does not cover plan participants if they become ill while in a foreign country. Explain that the type of insurance they take out at airports covers them only while in-flight, while "travelers' accident insurance" covers them from the time they leave home until they return, and that the insurance is relatively inexpensive. The message to travelers is "Don't Leave home without it!"

Traveler's Trip Cancellation Insurance

Trip cancellation insurance offers flight, health, and foreign traveler's coverage, plus travel cancellation insurance, to protect travelers when unforeseen circumstances force them to cancel their trip. The insured travelers will be protected from losing valuable airfare or other travel-related expenses. The traveler has the option to purchase personal travel insurance, family travel insurance, medical travel insurance, and policies that protect them against non-refundable airline tickets. There are plans that provide comprehensive coverage if the client's trip is canceled.

Travel cancellation insurance gives the client peace of mind when a sizable amount of money is spent on a trip. If the unexpected happens, they don't want to risk losing the cost of airline tickets or cruise tickets if the client's trip needs to be canceled for almost any reason, including:

- Sickness, injury or death
- Unannounced strike that causes complete cessation of services of your common carrier for at least 48 consecutive hours
- Weather which causes complete cessation of services of your common carrier for at least 48 consecutive hours
- Employer termination or layoff affecting you or a traveling companion
- Primary residence of you or your traveling companion if it is rendered uninhabitable by unforeseen circumstances
- Burglary of you or your traveling companion's primary residence within 10 days of departure date
- Felonious assault of you or your traveling companion within 10 days of departure or during trip
- Terrorism in a country which is part of the trip
- Hijacking, quarantine, jury duty, or court ordered appearance as a witness in a legal action
- You or your traveling companion are called to emergency military duty
- Traffic accident, substantiated by a police report, directly involving either you or a traveling companion while en route to a scheduled departure point

This plan also offers emergency medical coverage, trip interruption, and delay and missed connection protection, baggage delay, or loss coverage, and much more.

Additional Income for the ITD:

To apply for a license to sell trip cancellation insurance contact

www.TravelGuard.com Travel Guard International 1-800-826-7791 Travel Guard, Stevens Point, WI, 54481

"Hidden" Hotel Charges

Three charges in particular stand as warnings concerning what may happen: laundry charges, telephone calls from the room, and hotel-room "honor bar" refrigerator charges. Frequently all three bear higher surcharges than one would think possible. Telephone calls in France are especially burdensome. Try to call from the post office instead. If calls to America *must* be made from the hotel, place a quick call and have the American party call back.

Check All Bills Carefully

Check all bills *before* you pay them. Frequently, meal prices, unlike in America, include the tip. In France, for example, 15% for service is added to the bill by law. Money on top of that, especially if excessive, makes an American look overly wealthy, foolish, or both. Similarly, ensure that "menu touristique" or "menu du jour" prices include service and wine. Remember also that bread, which in America is considered free with the meal, is often an additional cost abroad on a per-slice basis.

Be Careful With All Purchases

Italian vendors hawk fake Gucci and Vuiton bags; Swiss watches may be more expensive in Switzerland than in America; English paperbacks cost much more abroad (and especially in airports or train stations). Travel packages, too, can likewise be much more costly. If not too inconvenient, it's almost always cheaper to make one's own arrangements. Finally, be careful of prices at duty-free shops. Frequently, prices in town are less expensive. This is particularly true of locally made goods.

Taxi Service

Cab drivers are generally honest but expensive -- a minor fact, but one which the traveler needs to observe. In Italy, for example, the cabbies will invariably ask for more than the meter reads. The reasons range from the legitimate (hour of the day to the number of passengers) to the questionable (rainy weather or special holiday). When in doubt, ask questions. Recommend that clients have the hotel summon a taxi and confirm the rate prior to departure.

Making Money Count

Long gone are the days when the innocent tourist could simply hold out his or her hand stuffed with foreign currency, to be picked over by the market hawker or maitre d'hotel. With travel costs up and people watching their money, it is essential that they get the most from their travel dollar. To help them, the Tour Director might suggest the following, in the pre-departure meeting:

- *Do your homework.* It's very important for travelers to become familiar with the currency of the countries they will be visiting to prevent them from accidentally getting cheated: An unwary tourist might mistakenly leave a tip of $10 rather than $1. Packets of major European and other currencies are available at many major U.S. banks, or they can get some in the departure city and "practice" on the flight.
- *Practice with the currency.* In addition to recognition, travelers need to have some feel for the exchange-rate value of the currency. Try to develop a mental rule of conversion between dollars and the foreign currency.
- *Take some local currency along.* Arrival on a Sunday or holiday or late at night when the banks are closed can be annoying, and take the ITD away from his/her job trying to locate a local currency exchange office. Encourage the clients to purchase currencies of foreign denominations at their local bank.
- *Don't over-purchase money.* Banks will always convert money for you, but there is always a commission and exchange-rate difference to take a little out of your money. If the traveler over-buys a foreign currency, he pays twice: once when purchasing the currency, and again when selling it back and converting it to U.S. dollars. Rather than converting large sums into foreign currency, the traveler is best advised to estimate how much he/she will actually spend in that currency

before converting money. Hotel costs, transportation, meals, spending money for souvenirs and incidentals -- these should all be "guess"estimates and then multiplied by the number of days in that particular country. Then by converting this much money, the traveler should be fairly close on the money exchanging and not be needlessly converting money back and forth.

Introduction to the Euro Currency

The Euro is the currency of twelve European Union countries, stretching from the Mediterranean to the Arctic Circle: Belgium, Germany, Greece, Spain, France, Ireland, Italy, Luxembourg, the Netherlands, Austria, Portugal, and Finland). Euro banknotes and coins have been in circulation since 1 January 2002 and are now a part of daily life for over 300 million Europeans living in the Euro area. Euro banknotes replaced twelve different sets of banknotes in the previous national currencies.

There are seven different denominations in the current Euro banknote series, ranging from the 5 Euro to the 500 Euro note. The designs of the notes are the same throughout the Euro area and feature windows and gateways (on the front) and bridges (on the reverse) from different periods in Europe's architectural history.

Where to Purchase Foreign Currencies

AAA offers *Travelex "Tip Paks,"* pre-packaged foreign currency provided in small bills, which are perfect for tipping, taxis and other small purchases. Members pay $100 per Tip Pak, which provides them with the equivalent of $100 in the foreign currency needed.

Check cards, such as AAA Visa® Travelers Checks, are accepted at more than 24 million merchants worldwide and are the most secure and convenient way to travel. They are fee-free for AAA members. Along with waiving the fee around-the-clock assistance if checks are stolen or lost. Checks are available in U.S. dollars, Canadian dollars, EURO and British Pound Sterling.

ATM Cards, such as the AAA Cash Passport Cards by Visa®, are convenient cards for AAA members who wish to access their travel money at desired intervals. There are more than 800,000 Visa® ATMs worldwide, so you get the currency that corresponds with the country you are in at the ATM you use. Just load the card before leaving home for your trip, and you have instant access to it wherever Visa® cards are accepted worldwide. Visit http://www.aaa.com to order your Visa® Cash Passport, or visit your nearest AAA branch office.

International Phone Calls

You can purchase a Global Phone card worth $5 of free calling anywhere, anytime. After activating the card by purchasing additional call time, members receive $5 worth of free calling. Using this card, members may call from any land-line phone or cell phone in the United States and in over 80 countries, using direct access numbers. The Global Phone card charges the same rate all the time with no hidden fees or monthly charges.

What to Wear For Men

Perhaps the best advice you can give is: *Please don't over pack!* The inexperienced traveler often takes far too many clothes and winds up with excess luggage. At GEM Travel, our motto is "Comfort and Casual!"

The key to minimizing luggage lies in the mix-and-match capability of your wardrobes, as well as quick-dry, wash-and-wear fabrics. One world traveler has estimated he can make up twelve different outfits simply by mixing and matching three jackets and four pairs of pants. This, of course, means you would have to stay with one or two basic colors and rely on your shirts and ties for different "effects." Double knits and permanent press are very good for travel, as they are comfortable and easily packed. Here is a suggested list:

For Men

- A sweater or two and a lightweight windbreaker can be useful.
- A raincoat and a pair of folding boots may also be included.
- Neckties, belt or suspenders, pajamas and robe are sometimes forgotten in the excitement.
- A small first-aid kit, sewing kit (with a few extra buttons and a small pair of scissors), shoe-polishing kit, plastic bags for soiled clothing and damp laundry will be useful, too.
- Suits: Include at least one dark suit which could be used in the evening for semi-formal wear. A tuxedo or dinner jacket is not required, but maybe worn if desired, for parties and dinner in the evening.
- Shirts: Pack wash-and-wear, permanent-press type.
- Shoes One pair of black for evening wear, another pair should be comfortable, well broken-in walking shoes, preferably with rubber or ripple soles. Slippers should be the folding type, simplest for packing.
- Underwear and socks: Drip-dry material is best.
- Swim Trunks should be fast drying Trunks and Bermuda shorts may be worn on shipboard or at foreign beach resorts.
- Hat: If you wish to take one, we suggest a crushable type.
- Glasses: Sunglasses and an extra pair of prescription eyeglasses should be taken. An eyeglass repair kit is also suggested.
- Miscellaneous If you use an electric razor, we suggest the battery-operated type, or take an international adapter for a plug-in electric shaver Electrical outlets and voltage systems vary considerably To be fully prepared, take along a safety razor, shaving cream and lotion Toothbrush and toothpaste, comb and brush, hair tome, deodorant, facial tissues (for various uses), soap powder or detergent (small package) You may wish to include a couple of wash cloths, and also a cake of your favorite soap.
- Camera Include an ample supply of film.
- Medicine be certain to take a sufficient supply of regularly used medicine with you for headaches, sore throat, colds, diarrhea, sinus, anti-acid, and motion sickness.

What to Wear For Women

Again, our motto is "Comfort and Casual!" With so many lovely "no-iron" fabrics available today, packing for a trip is more of a pleasure than a chore! Mix-'n'-match outfits are "the thing." Any of the wash-and-wear fabrics in one or two basic colors will give you many ensembles, but will not require as many accessories. For instance, three skirts, three pairs of slacks, and three blouses or tops in coordinated colors will give you at least eighteen different outfits. Include also two or three knit suits (polyester) or pantsuits, and two or three daytime dresses. Remember, a silk or chiffon scarf can do wonders in changing the appearance of your outfits. Two or three pairs of shoes, at least one pair which is well broken in and is comfortable for walking, possibly with rubber soles, the others for dress. Cocktail dresses or formals are not a necessity, but may be worn for parties and dinner in the evening. Here's a quick list:

For Women

- A sweater or two and a lightweight windbreaker can be useful.
- A raincoat, hat, and a pair of folding boots may also be included.
- Shorts, pantsuits, and bathing suits may be worn aboard ships and at foreign resorts. Many cities frown on shorts being worn on streets, but pantsuits are fully acceptable.
- Handbag: One large enough to carry documents, traveler's checks.
- Lingerie and hosiery: Should be drip-dry nylon, or other synthetic or cotton, as you prefer. Robe, slippers, and shower cap.
- Glasses Sunglasses and an extra pair of prescription eyeglasses should be taken plus an eyeglass repair kit is also suggested.
- Toilet articles We suggest you take an ample supply of your favorite makeup and cosmetics, and plenty of facial tissues You should carry tissues in your handbag at all times
- Miscellaneous: Head scarves, rain bonnets, gloves, handkerchiefs, jewelry and other accessories You will find it handy to have a small first-aid kit, manicure set, a sewing kit (with a few extra buttons and a small pair of scissors), a shoe-polishing kit, dry cleaner, soap powder and detergent, a small travel clothesline, a few plastic clothes pins A couple of plastic bags will be useful for your soiled or damp laundry. You may also wish to include a couple of wash cloths and a cake or two of your favorite soap.
- Camera Include an ample supply of film.
- Medicine Above all, remember to take a sufficient quantity of feminine supplies and regularly taken medicines, plus medication for headaches, sore throat, sinus, colds, diarrhea, motion sickness and an anti-acid.

Before Travelers Leave Home

1. Don't advertise the fact that you will be away from home for an extended length of time. Make arrangements for newspapers, mail, trash cans, etc.
2. Securely lock windows and doors. Leave the window shades in a position which would be normal if you were at home. *Activate your security alarm system.*
3. Make sure insurance policies, taxes, and any other bills are paid up or the company is notified of the delay.
4. Arrange for your mail to be picked up or held at your branch post office until your return.
5. Notify delivery services such as milkman, paperboy, laundry, etc. to suspend deliveries.
6. Arrange for the care of your lawn, garden, and house plants.
7. Arrange for the care of your pets.
8. Check major service installations such as refrigerator, furnace and water heater, to make certain they are in good working order.
9. Disconnect all electrical appliances that will not be used while you are away.
10. Set thermostat at an energy-conserving temperature.
11. Notify local police and firemen that you intend to be away and give them the approximate date of your return. Let them know who has a key to your home.
12. Leave a key to your home, your itinerary, and the telephone number of your Tour Director with a neighbor or relative. In the event that someone must contact you in an emergency while you are on your trip, they should be made aware that the telephone service center is available 24 hours a day and will put them in contact with one of your supervisory personnel.

13. Check the web for climatic conditions.

The "No-Show" Trip Kit Mailing

It is easy to make a mistake and omit certain items from the kit. By using a check list for mailing the "Trip Kit," you will have a record of items that were sent out, when, and by whom.

> Alert! In the Appendix, you will find a "Trip Kit" Check-Off List, plus many other forms you can use as a Tour Director.

Large Group Pre-Tour Orientation

What constitutes a "Large Group"? In general, 75 to 2,000 clients make up a large-group tour. Usually, these groups are part of a convention, seminar, incentive tour, or a series of "Back to Back" holiday programs to the same destination

One individual will be assigned the responsibility for the trip and is designated ITD-in-charge. The successful outcome of the trip will rest with this individual. Other travel staff will be assigned to work with the ITD (e.g., escorts, tour leader, and senior tour guide), based on the itinerary requirements and the number of participants' demands.

ITD's Early Arrival

Normally, the ITD to whom the program is assigned (in some instances, his or her delegate) will arrive at the destination one or two days prior to the arrival of a group of 40 or more. The ITD's purpose in arriving early is to thoroughly check each minute detail of the program. The ITD will perform what is called a "walk-through." This involves precisely what the term implies: the ITD will actually go through the program looking at it from two simultaneous viewpoints - that of a participant, and that of an experienced ITD. Then the ITD will meet with a variety of travel suppliers:

Transportation People

- Transfer Agents/In-Bound Destination Manager should be contacted to reconfirm all transfers, sight-seeing, etc. necessary for the operation of the program.

Hotel Staff

- *Reservations Manager* to go over the actual number of rooms needed: Twins, singles, suites. Verify with the purchase order(s) - changes in rooming list.
- *Front Office Manager* and Controller to verify that the "Master Account" and billing instructions are correctly set up and understood (see hotel accounting letter sample).
- *Food and Beverage Manager* to go over meals and cocktail parties, costs, menus, table locations, special function rooms, dates, and times of the functions.
- *Bell Captain* to explain the method of handling gratuities.
- *Doorman* to give a copy of the social schedule so he will be familiar with transfers for activities outside of the hotel.

Sport Activities (on or off hotel property)

- *Golf.* Name and location of golf course, how far from hotel, number of rental clubs, caddies, or carts. Reconfirm the group number and cost, what is included, when and where to get starting times. Instruct golf pro to keep accurate list of players: names, dates and scores (for trophies). If transfer is required to course, reconfirm with transfer agent.
- *Fishing.* Check number of boats and equipment, dates and times, whether or not transfers are involved (cost); if beer, soft drinks are included in cost; if trophies are included. Make sure captains or travel staff assigned turn in record of catch with names of the fishermen.
- *Other Sports.* Reconfirm with supplier what sports activities are included. In many resort hotels, the water sports concessionaire will "push" group participation. It must be clearly understood by this individual whether or not these activities are included in your land package.

All of this may seem to be unnecessary since file correspondence reflects that the group is expected and that all is in order; but, as any experienced Tour Director can testify, *if this "walk-through" is not performed, more likely than not, something will go wrong.*

Reviewing the Travel Program

There is absolutely no substitute for careful planning and preparation for the tour. Review the entire program. One mistake could develop into a major problem. Prior to commencement of a tour, the Travel Director and staff will have a briefing with the Tour Designer and other office personnel directly connected with the tour. (See Briefing Check-Off List in the Appendix).

Staff Briefing

What constitutes a briefing? In addition to reviewing the background of the preparation of the trip, the following points will be covered:

- Specifics in reference to the hotel property where the trip will operate
- Special room requirements: suites, twins, singles, etc
- Meals (Menus)
- The itinerary, functions, and activities planned, the arrival and departure patterns
- VIPs' names and titles, with special handling requirements
- Special billing instructions, if any (Who may authorize extra billing)
- Local tour guides (Review their duties and assignments upon arrival at the destination)

Operational Procedures for Tour Group's Arrival

The ITD assigned to operate the program will usually arrive with participants. Upon their arrival, a meeting will be held as soon as possible, during which the following staff assignments are covered:

- The entire program is reviewed and alerted to any changes, special problems, etc.
- Responsibilities, by necessity, must be delegated. Coverage of functions will be established and a work-assignment sheet prepared. This will include designating the individual(s) to assume responsibility for activities such as:
- Airport coverage. Assignments of who is to meet participants still to arrive and who is to supervise the transfers
- Coverage of each function inclusive of overseeing all sporting and sight-seeing activities

- Assisting in reviewing all billing and back-up materials for all charges to be made
- Staffing the hospitality desk during the appropriate hours

Other ITD Duties

Confirm Arrangements At the Hotel!

- Arrange for a hospitality desk to be set up and make sure that a blackboard and chalk or a felt board with assorted white plastic letters is available (to remind the participants of forthcoming events and other communications for the group) In the majority of destinations, guests are pre-registered and they will pick up their room keys at the hospitality desk
- Personally check on the VIP suites or rooms
- Make sure room courtesies, when ordered, will be in rooms before the guests' arrival
- Review the complete social schedule with the hotel contact handling this group - General Manager, Assistant Manager, or Sales Manager
- Check all services to be performed upon arrival; i.e., banners, arrival music, welcome drinks, etc.

Reconfirm Activities outside the Hotel

- *Transfers*: Number of cars or busses, dates and times, and length of time for each transfer.
- *Sight-seeing.* Reconfirm dates and times with ground agent. Check with agent regarding alternate plans due to inclement weather.
- *Lunches.* Date and time, number of people, drinks included menus, etc. It is most important that the menus are checked out for each planned event so that the group does not end up with *chicken three times in a row.*
- *Cocktail Parties.* Date and time, number of people, open bar, hors d'oeuvres, location, number of waiters and bartenders, music, etc.
- *Dinners.* Date and time, number of people, menu, location of tables, drinks, etc. It is also important to again check planned menus of entire trip so that duplication of main courses is avoided.
- *Nightclubs.* Date and time, number of people. Time of show, location of tables, and number of drinks included.

Communications during the Tour

- While on-site, the ITD will need to carry out ongoing communications and meetings with support staff. A daily meeting with the staff and suppliers should always be held by the Tour Director-in- charge, who will review and discuss the following:
- Pre arrival of the clients, welcome signs, VIP limo service
- The tour itinerary and make any necessary changes and adjustments
- Sending out notices to all the assigned rooms of the tour group
- Pre-Departure Check-Off List, confirm airport transfers, flights, baggage trucks

ITD's Travel Kit

There are a number of necessary documents that the ITD should have in their possession while on tour:

- *Name badges* These will be very helpful to the ITD and the travelers, because it's much nicer to be able to call fellow travelers by name. Uniform luggage tags should be distributed so it will

- *Rooming List* Copies of the rooming list is excellent means of "control" and checking and re-checking your clients into hotels, keeping notes on special diets for restaurants, optional tour payments, special request, copies of the rooming list can be distributed to:
    - Front Desk
    - Bellmen
    - Local tour guides
    - Driver (Keep count prior to taking off, always a chance of leaving someone behind… it happens!
- *Tour Vouchers* An important part of the Tour Company's responsibility is to issue tour vouchers for services to be rendered while managing a tour. The tour vouchers are used for payment of services, confirmation of services, and advice on service required, client identification, and recognition by the travel supplier.

    Each Tour Company uses tits own voucher system in order to maintain his image and serve the needs of his own internal accounting procedures. These forms of payment usually have no cash exchange value and are valid only for the dates and services shown. The tour voucher identifies the tour group traveling and indicates prepaid confirmation or reservation of the service request noted. Once the voucher has been redeemed for service by the client, the travel supplier will be paid by the travel company.

    A copy of the tour voucher is e-mailed/mailed/express mailed to the suppliers (hotel, outfitter's land tour, guide service, transfer company, welcome /restaurants providing farewell dinner reception. It is accompanied by a letter outlining final instructions:

    - Advising of VIPs' special requests
    - Summarizing any special functions (e.g., Welcome/Farewell Dinner)
    - Billing procedures as to items to go on the Tour Director's account and what to collect from the individual guest (i.e., phone bills, laundry charges, etc.)
    - Changes in rooming list

Terms, Liability, and Conditions of the Tour

The ITD should be conscious of the Tour Operator/Organization/Association terms, conditions and refund policies which clients were made aware of when making their reservation(s), when the client wishes to drop out of the tour program for any of the following reasons:

- Illness back home
- Doesn't like tour members
- Gets sick
- A problem traveler"
- Misunderstanding as to "what was included" in the tour

To avoid potential problems, tour companies provide a statement of liability and conditions on the back of tour vouchers, cast in language similar to the following:

> The Tour Company, whose name appears on the reverse side hereof, issued this travel voucher in the sole capacity of agent for the owners, wholesalers and/or contractors, whose names appear on the face of this document and who are hereinafter referred to as Suppliers of the transportation and/or other services specified. As such, the sole financial liability of the Tour Company is limited to the amount of commission it receives from said Sup-

pliers in arranging said transportation and/or services on behalf of the named Client. If any Supplier shall cancel the specified transportation and/or other services for any reason other than financial insolvency, the Tour Director is bound to refund all deposits received on behalf of the named Client upon advice and/or refund from the said Supplier.

This voucher is issued subject to any and all terms and conditions under which any transportation or other service is provided by the Suppliers. The Tour Company shall not become liable for any personal injury, property damage, accident, delay, inconvenience, change in itinerary or accommodations, or other irregularity which may occur due to (1) wrongful, negligent or arbitrary acts or omissions on the part of the Suppliers, their employees or others not under the direct control of the Tour Company, (2) defects or failures of any conveyance, equipment or instrumentality under the control of the Suppliers, and (3) but not limited to Acts of God, fire, acts of governments or other authorities, wars, civil disturbances, acts of terrorism, riots, strikes, thefts, pilferage, epidemics, quarantines or dangers incident to the sea, land and air.

The Client, by engaging the Tour Company and making deposit and/or full payment for the travel arrangements specified, acknowledges the position of the Agency as stipulated by the foregoing, agrees to hold the Agency blameless in making the arrangements on his behalf provided same shall be made through generally acceptable Suppliers at the time of engagement, and further agrees that restitution or damages, if any are claimed, shall be sought directly from the Suppliers. The Client further agrees to abide by the terms and conditions of the Suppliers of the services to be performed. In addition, the Client acknowledges that insurance was available that would provide compensation for lost or damaged luggage, trip cancellation, medical expenses and Supplier bankruptcy while planning or on the trip.

Tour Members' Medical Forms

The medical form is of particular importance in the event a traveler becomes ill or injured during the tour. The medical form should be completed by the client and signed by the client's physician. This form is highly recommended for physically disabled travelers, senior citizens, and travelers on high adventure trips, although it is excellent ideas to have all travelers complete this form. The orientation meeting provides an ideal opportunity to stress the importance of this form. *The ITD should have a copy of all medical forms at all times—plus a copy of Trip Insurance!*

Liability Waiver

A special medical form, a "waiver of liability" should be required to be completed prior to departure for all the following:

- School groups
- Adventure Travelers (hiking, white water, scuba, mountain climbing etc.)
- Senior Citizens tours

The Tour Escort should have copies of this completed document before the client boards the tour. The signature on the form should be witnessed by a representative of the Tour Company. If the traveler is a minor, the minor's parent or legal guardian must sign the waiver.

Chapter 4

"Taking Charge" of the Tour Group

Six Essential Points

#1 Your primary function is to ensure that the trip occurs as planned.

This means being responsible for the group's safety, covering a destination tour's highlights, providing an exciting and memorable experience, reviewing the tour itinerary and pacing it to accommodate the groups size and age, responding and finding immediate solutions to problems and alleviating emergency situations.

#2 You are on duty 24 hours a day.

Working as an ITD is often referred to as being a "baby sitter". Many tours vary considerably, the typical ITD joins his/her group at the departure point, usually the airport or the association's club house to prepare the clients for departure via airline or motor coach. The group then flies of to meet up with their cruise ship or board a private motor coach to transport them on their tour.

#3 be positive.

Be honest towards the country or the town through which you are traveling; give true value, unbiased value, to the things you see and show and explain to your clients. One could give many examples of the differences in varied European or other cultures, but this must not affect your attitude, which must always *be positive.* Whether you like a place or not, any show of nervousness on your part, any lack of enthusiasm, or any show of disparagement toward any country or part of your tour program, will affect your clients and their attitude, and *you cheat them of part of a product for which they paid.* By speaking disparagingly of an aspect of cultural, social, or other value of a place, because you personally don't like it (or because you feel lazy that day, or tired, or hung over!), you lower your standards, and the clients lose a part of the tour. They are entitled to a fair summary and the chance to decide for themselves whether they like it or not. It will be your fault alone if your clients miss the beauty of a place, or underestimate its true value. They will feel cheated, even defiant; and you will have shown your failure in your job by your inability to make the environment enchanting, mysterious, and interesting.

Your employer included that place in the tour program; your client bought the tour with that place in it. *Be positive in your approach – in spite of your personal feelings.*

#4 Take control of the tour.

There are various ways of controlling a tour, of handling a group, and dealing with the everyday problems which crop up. From the beginning, you must adopt the right attitude, give attention to details, constantly checking to make sure all that has been planned can and will be done during the tour.

#5 First Impressions are lasting impressions!

The initial contact with your clients is of vital importance. The first impressions you project, and their first impression of you, are vital. Those impressions form the basis of their eventual complete confidence in you, and subsequent success of the tour.

Remember that your clients are strangers at first, everything is strange to them, including you, and that they may not grasp everything at once. This is especially true if they have just flown transatlantic overnight, and are tired, confused, and on edge. Make everything both simple and gentle, keeping detailed explanations to a minimum.

Just introduce yourself to your clients, let them know that you will be with them for their tour, that they can rely on you to sort out problems for them, that you are there to help them, to talk to them, to share their interests and to enhance their trip, and only give the immediate details they'll need. Then, as soon as possible in the tour, give them a short resume of the program, important information such as meals, times of departure, etc.

#6 Consider providing Daily Bulletins.

If you use the "Bulletin" system, make sure they understand they can check daily on the various hotel bulletin boards for the latest information about their tour. Explain that they will have different local guides in each city, but that you will be with them all the time to help them enjoy their tour fully, to advise them of their free time, shopping areas, optional tours, gastronomic delights, and so on.

Communicating with Your Tour Members

First, *know what you are talking about.* Careful scrutiny of maps and brochures and consulting with your driver helps. Be prepared to answer questions intelligently. There is no need for a continuing deluge of remarks. Make the presentation interesting by making general comments about native foods and life styles. Alternate information, songs, stories -- there is only so much the tour members are able to absorb at one time. Also, check with the tour participants; have them share stories, jokes (clean), and comments about their travel experiences.

Non-Verbal Communications

Don't stand or sit too close to a client. When talking with two people, be sure to include both of them in the discussion even though you may receive feedback from only one. Deal with couples extremely carefully. Never flirt with tour members of the opposite sex.

Verbal Communication

- Use tact.
- Be precise.
- Speak clearly.
- Be enthusiastic.
- Provide sufficient information to back up your statements.
- Consider the listener's background.

Common Listening Problems

- Viewing a topic as uninteresting
- Criticizing a speaker's delivery or appearance
- Getting over stimulated
- Listening only for facts
- Tolerating, creating or filing to adjust to distractions
- Faking attention
- Letting emotion-laden words interfere with listening
- Permitting personal prejudice or deep-seated convictions to impair comprehension
- Daydreaming

At the beginning of each day, you should review the day's itinerary. This also gives you an opportunity to remind the tour members of any special events which will be taking place and review the daily itinerary and the degree of physical requirements in the event of any walking tours. The more control you have, the better the participants understand their responsibility to each other. Getting on and off the bus during the day should not become a time-consuming and irritating experience. Get to know the tour members by name and see that they get to know each other. A good way for everyone to get to know each other is rotating seats. This should be done daily. Of course, smoking aboard the motor coach is prohibited.

Remember, the participants are eager to learn and participate in the program; however, as the day wears on, and after heavy lunch drowsiness sets in and keeping their attention becomes more challenging. Often it is better to play a series of games, put on a movie, open up the bar or inform the members what exciting experiences they can look forward to the following day. It is up to you to decide how important the information is and when to disburse it to your clients.

> **Special Note:** Keep the stragglers in check! On an extensive tours, the ITD and his/her assistants will soon wear themselves out rounding up the stragglers and herding the group to and from the motor coach. Therefore, if not done once but twice daily or when necessary, remind the tour members how important it is for them to be punctual! If the tour bus is late arriving at their hotel, other tour groups could very well take the pick of the better rooms.

Gerald Mitchell

Stops along the Way

Pace your tour to allow for "Rest stops" along the way. This provides a chance to rotate seats, let the tour members stretch their legs, smoke a cigarette, use the toilet facilities, try local snacks at the refreshment stand, shop, and take some photos.

Encounters with Unusual Personalities

There is the old saying "the customer is always right." You know as well as I do that this is not always true. Sooner or later, you will encounter some unusual personalities. There are those clients who will always complain about problems that don't really exist --or they will cause problems for the group. As a Tour Director, you will have to handle imaginary complaints as well as genuine ones. Your clients come in all different types, with their own idiosyncrasies you will find over and over around the world.

The Perfect Traveler. Most of us would prefer what might be called the "standard client," the one is the least bother. But we know that this world is full of different types of people. We <u>must</u> provide the same service to all our clients.

To be of service to someone means to choose. As an ITD, you have chosen to be of service to your clients -- not just the "nice" ones, but the not-so-nice ones as well. As an ITD, you are putting your expertise at the disposal of your clients. Furthermore, you must give the impression to the client of being always available to cater to their needs.

At times, people may be irritable for various reasons: a succession of bad weather days, overbooking of hotels, different foods, contagious illness, too large a group to offer personalized attention, jet lag, ill-mannered or poorly trained tour guides or outfitters, to name a few.

There are some tours which are clearly unsuitable for some clients: the pace maybe too fast of difficult or the accommodations may be below their expectations. No matter the reason, there will be occasions when you will encounter problem clients. Because you or the outfitters will be destined to live closely with each other on the land, these problems have a way of surfacing within 24 hours of the start of the tour.

The Wanderer This person is always late, lost, takes off on his/her own without giving thought to time or the instruction given by the ITD, tour guide or in-bound destination manager. Whatever the reason, their inconsiderate attitude delays the entire group schedule.

Solution: Pressure from the tour members or a gentle reminder will keep the wanderer in check. If all else fails after several warnings, leave the "wanderer" behind and continue to conduct the tour.

The Expert "Know It All." This person offers advice to the tour members contrary to the in-bound destination manager's; i.e., flight departures, changes in tour plans, currency changes -- or fabricates reasons for changes in tour Itineraries. These people must be stopped as they are harmful to the entire tour program and the members.

Solution: Meet with them in private and tell them to stop misinforming your clients. (*Note:* Always take the problem client aside, away from the group, to rectify any problems.)

The Insulting Client/Chronic Complainer. This person is angry with other clients or services offered by the hotel, restaurant or ITD. By nature they are unhappy and enjoy making other people unhappy.

→ *Solution:* Approach the client and review their problems, making them aware they are ruining the trip for the other tour members. Should they fail to adhere to your warning, kindly ask them to leave the tour or invoice them for an F.I.T. tour which will provide personalized service at an increase in tour price.

→ *The Organizer.* This individual wishes to lead the tour, to be in charge. They will try to challenge your authority.

→ *Solution:* First of all, take the client aside, question them as to their reasons for wanting to take charge and re-organize the tour -- hear them out, take notes, and in conclusion thank them for their concern but assure them you have everything under control; however, should they care to be of assistance, assign them a task such as luggage control, or helping one of the elderly tour members on the scheduled walking tour.

→ *The Veteran World Traveler.* He has seen it all before. While the ITD or tour guide is trying to comment on historical facts, landscape, or animals, the veteran world traveler will try to outdo the guide's performance, telling the other tour members where he has traveled before and how great the attractions were.

→ *Solution:* Simply ask if the person has information which could be shared with all tour members. Alternatively tell the person to refrain from talking during the commentary so that others may gain from the local guide's/outfitter's knowledge.

Travelers' Tribulations

- *Jet Lag:* Possibly the tourists didn't get enough rest or were too nervous to sleep on the aircraft en route to their destination. Upon arrival, the client is now experiencing an adjustment in time zones and entering into another culture.
- *Languages:* The first time they attempt to purchase a cup of tea or make a purchase, an effort on their part will be necessary to understand the transaction and understand the currency exchange.
- *Climate:* The heat or extreme cold will take the client by surprise if he has not been fully advised as to what to wear and is not prepared to dress accordingly. High altitudes and heat will naturally slow the client down and he will have to understand the physical ramifications should he insist on keeping up his regular pace.
- *Food:* Food has always played a very important part in the daily activities of the tour itinerary. What the client might experience could be different hours for dining, seven-course meals, spicy foods, menus written in strange languages when all he is really looking for is a simple hamburger. Encourage the clients to be more adventurous in their eating habits while on tour.
- *Loss of money, passport, or personal items:* The Tour Director can anticipate many hours of "extra time" applying for lost passports, purchasing airline tickets, and filing claims for missing luggage, which certainly could have been avoided if the necessary precautions had been taken.
- *Overbooking or transportation delays:* Even though the hotel rooms have been confirmed and paid for, and the airline tickets written for the proper date and time, the hotel will still overbook and the flights will still be delayed. Again, the clients will have to be made to understand that everything in your power is being done to rectify the situation.
- *Disappointment in the tour:* Sometimes an over-zealous travel agent has promised too much. Where is the deluxe hotel room on the ocean? The free wine with all meals? The dinner with the captain aboard ship? -- and the list goes on and on. Whether it is a figment of their imagination, or from an advertisement on TV or in their local newspaper, or from a salesman representing your travel company, what the client envisions and what he is about to receive may be two

different things. Should this occur, make sure you have a sample copy of the tour brochure to set the client straight on the exact tour features.
- *Not getting along with the other tour members:* There must be a reason for their behavior (e.g., being late for departures, or being loud and demanding). Seek the source of the problem and correct it, as the other tour members paid to go on the tour for enjoyment and peace of mind, not to be disturbed by a client who plans to ruin the trip by making a nuisance of himself/herself.

Emergencies and Other Problems

- *Illness:* Nothing is more upsetting to a tour member than to be ill during the tour. Should this occur, help him receive proper medical attention, and encourage him to rest rather than go on a full-day excursion which could result in worsening the problem, as well as slowing down the tour.
- *Overindulgence:* The person, who insists on eating his way through Europe or being the last one to leave the party, will eventually feel the effects. Do your best to make him/her realize that tomorrow there will be a busy schedule and that it would be best not to overtax themselves, or he/she will miss out on the farewell dinner party.
- *Not physically fit:* That climb along the Great Wall of China was theft main inspiration for taking this tour, and now they are not physically fit enough to make the climb. This could be devastating. The Tour Director should make themselves or their assistant available to assist the person to make a partial climb along the wail to see that dream come true.

Handling the Death of a Tour Member

Should a person pass away while on tour, this will naturally have some effect on the mood of the tour members. You should attend to details as soon as possible so as not to have lasting effects on the tour program. You should immediately contact all the following:

- Your Tour Operator who you are under contract with
- The Embassy which holds their citizenship
- Local police
- Hospital
- Local In-bound Tour Operator. (Ask the Tour Operator for an assistant to take over the 'tour group" so you can deal with the emergency.)
- Insurance company concerning the deceased person's travel insurance
- Immediate family members

> **Special Note:** The numbers for emergency contacts should have been entered in your list of "contacts" prior to leaving on the tour.

If your are traveling overseas, contact the American Embassy along with the local authorities to obtain a death certificate and to comply with local laws and regulations for removal of the body to the home of the deceased. Obtaining necessary permits is usually required, both in the United States and in foreign countries. This can best be handled through a local mortuary. If at all possible, concurrence should be obtained from the immediate family for the expense of returning the deceased. It is not the responsibility of the travel company to return the deceased. Again, use of a local mortician is recommended.

If the deceased is traveling with a spouse or other relative, all efforts should be made to relieve the burden by accomplishing the steps outlined above. Consent for return of the body to the family home should not be given by you, but should be obtained from the spouse, preferably in the presence of another person.

In cases of accidental death, it is usually required that an autopsy be performed. This, in many states in the U.S., is done without the consent of the family because of the nature of the death. It would be best if consent of a member of the family could be obtained.

The travel company/insurance office should be notified so that if this group has been provided with travel accident insurance, the necessary steps can be taken to contact the insurance company for preparation of claim papers. It is essential that, in the case of death by accident, a certified copy of the death certificate be obtained for insurance purposes. The insurance company will assist in the preparation of any claim papers, as required Result of autopsy should be obtained as it will determine whether the death is ruled accidental or not

What *Not* To Do As a Tour Director

Do not overtax yourself.

There will be occasions when you will be faced with a problem at the end of a tiring day and will become impatient or angered at the slightest request. Perhaps upon check-in at the hotel he/she will blow up at the desk clerk for not having the room keys ready or when faced with an overbooked situation. Should this occur, remove yourself from the situation and seek help from management. Don't let the group see you getting upset or angered. They will not be the least bit impressed, and it can only turn the hotel staff and other travel suppliers against you.

Don't be disorganized.

Giving instructions and then changing them at every meeting with the tour participants can only erode the trust the clients will have for the escort. Get your facts straight and confirmed prior to notifying the membership of any changes in the itinerary.

Rooming lists, flight manifests, airline tickets and tour sheets, plus all other documents that are in your possession, should be organized in files or your lap top. Don't be sorting through a pile of papers at the dock or check-in counter of the airport, trying to find a current list of names or the supplier's contract.

> *Tip:* At the end of the day, take some time to bring all records (expenses, re-confirming the next day's movements and hotel rooms) up to date.

Don't assume that your clients are world travelers.

Your job may have taken you through many countries, airports, cruise ships, and hotels. However, the clients have to be directed and assisted through each and every phase of the trip - from baggage check-in at the airport to clearing customs at the end of their tour.

Don't be inflexible.

Learn to give in if necessary. If the group leader asks to make an unscheduled stop or detour en route to their destination, it should be permitted if no added expenses will be incurred and the tour schedule is not drastically modified – and of course, provided the tour members have voted an approval for this unscheduled stop. This, in fact, could turn out to be one of the highlights of their tour (you may want to add this stop in future tour itineraries). It is a good indication that the tour participants are showing interest in the trip, and wish to learn more about the country or state being visited.

Don't over-"party" with the tour participants.

Make the necessary appearances and conduct the tour in a professional manner. When your duties are completed and the tour members have been transferred back to their hotel and continue to "party," offer the excuse, "I have paper work and duties to attend to for the following day."

Don't play favorites.

Everyone should be treated equally. Spending too much time with one or more tour members can give rise to gossip or jealousy in other tour members.

Don't push the tour members.

Observe the participants closely as the tour progresses. Should they start showing signs of fatigue, suggest taking that "nightclub tour" the following night, or slow down the trip, allowing members of the tour to return to the hotel or sit on the bus rather than visiting that last museum which was scheduled in the tour itinerary.

> *Tip:* Any change in the mood of the tour participants requires immediate action

Don't lie or cover up the truth.

If you make a mistake or encounter a problem, consult with the tour leader of the group and let him/her know the true facts of the situation. No "cover ups," as they will surface at a later time and can only cause you and the company embarrassment. Once you have explored all avenues for correcting the problem and have arrived at a solution, then approach the tour group with the situation and alternative plan.

Don't take on a tour if you are not mentally and physically fit.

Should you not be prepared to take on the tour because you are unfamiliar with the destination or have personal problems at home or at the office, it will certainly reflect on your attitude while escorting the tour group. The same holds true to not being in good physical shape. There will be occasions when the escort will have to help unload a motor coach of 40 to 50 oversized and over packed suitcases, run from one terminal to another, and walk many miles and climb stairs to view an historical site, assisting some tour members along the way. You should plan to spend a great deal of the time on your feet. *Stay in shape.*

Tip: Order a special diet on the airline, and watch those late evenings trying new and exciting foods (very rich in many cases), which may make you suffer the following day Take care of your stomach and it will take care of you.

Multiple Tour Destinations

Taking a tour group to one destination for a week's vacation at a hotel within the Caribbean is basically simple. The Tour Director can manage the tour group by operating from their hospitality desk and visiting with the tour members during meals or around the pool. But to take the group on the road for any length of time requires the skills of a professional and well-informed ITD.

The *real* challenge is how to get a group to move in unison from one point to another. While the tour should not be operated as a military exercise, the tour members should adhere to the planned itinerary if they are going to be able to visit and observe everything promised them in the tour brochure. Of course, not everyone is a team player. Some are late to board the bus or just wander around without giving consideration to the other tour participants. Whether the participants like it or not, the ITD must require them to develop a certain amount of discipline. They must be punctual and willing to follow instructions quickly, if for no other reason than for their safety in the event of an accident.

Unfamiliar Destination

Even though most tour programs will include the services of local guides and In-Bound Destination Management firms, as the ITD, you should research and become knowledgeable about the destination and places to be visited scheduled on the tour. The Government Tourist Board, travel agencies, public libraries, and websites provide various resources and reading material.

Upon arrival, your first priority is to get out the maps of the countries scheduled to be visited and familiarize yourself with distant, local tours and points of interest that would be of interest to the clients. It's important to become acquainted with the county's local customs; particularly the taboos, rates of exchange, and areas of the countries to avoid that are not safe for the clients to wander off in on their own.

Scenario of a Fully Escorted 8-day Tour to Rome, Italy

Number of clients: 40 tour members

ITD: Ms. Rose Watkins

Tour Operator: Global International Tours

Day 1- Activities: ITD arrives at airport 2 hours before departure. Check with flight schedules and departure gates. Secures a space or airport lounge to assemble the tour group.

Group arrives: Check passports/airlines tickets and boarding passes. Count heads, reconfirm meet and greet services in Rome.

Problems:

- Two clients arrive late
- Airline oversold
- Flight delays due to bad weather
- One client forgot passport

Day2- Rome- Activities: ITD clears customs with group and collects luggage with local porters. ITD searches for the Meet & Greet tour local tour company, boards coach with group. ITD counts all luggages, introduces group to local guide and reviews itinerary and hotel check-in procedures with guide service.

While en-route to the hotel, the ITD re-welcome the group, reviews the day's activities, answers questions and concerns and facts and tips about Rome. Tour group arrives at hotel, collects key and distributes them to the clients. Confirms afternoon city tour of Rome and Welcome Dinner.

Problems:

- Rooms not prepared
- Group arrives at 11:00 am and check-in is 2:00 p.m. local time
- Group tired and HUNGRY
- Hotel overbooked
- Hotel staff doesn't understand English

Day3- Activities: Tour group scheduled for full day tour of Rome.

Problems:

- Long lines at tourist sites. Some tour members not able to stand in line
- Unable to understand the tour guide (speaks too fast, all about history; group loses interest)

Day 4 Activities: ITD manages Tour Group for all day tour. Tired and wish to cancel scheduled evening actives

No problems!

Day 5 Activities: Tour guide providing further city tour.

Problems:

- Tour member slips on hotel step and breaks foot and ITD spends day at the hospital with the injured tour member.
- Group is left in the hands of the tour guide who hopefully, will slow down their presentation and give less history lessons.
- ITD return late at the hotel tired and behind in paper work and preparing for the upcoming day.

Day6: Activities: Group is scheduled for wine & culinary tour outside Rome. Late return few members 'over indulged." ITD returns to hospital to pick up injured client.

Day 7- Activities: ITD has group meeting with clients to prepare for their departure for home.

Problems:

One client has misplaced passport. ITD spends valuable hours searching for passport. Good news! Three hours later, passport found on tour bus.

Rest of day ITD prepares for "Farewell Dinner" and passes an envelope around to all tour members for tips to be given to driver and tour guide.

Day 8-Activities: ITD has 4:00 am wake up call. Restaurant is closed. ITD orders coffee and rolls for the tour group prior to departing for the airport. Motor coach arrives on time to transfer the clients to the airport.

Problem:

- One piece of luggage is m missing. Bell Captain placed luggage on another tour bus.

ITD directs tour group members for "security check" supervises luggage check in and seat assignments. Group disbands and spends time in duty free shops.

Arrival JFK ITD spend afternoon helping clients claim their luggage and make connecting flights.

Problems:

- Two tour members miss their connecting flight.
- ITD reschedules tickets to depart following day and secures hotel room outside the airport.
- Clients are upset and concerned about staying in New York. ITD calms their fears and bids farewell.

Chapter 5

En Route to Your Destination

Working with Your Travel Partners

When you arrive, you be carrying out operations with the following Travel Partners:

- Airlines
- Destination Management companies/Tour Guides
- Hotels
- Restaurants
- Transportation Companies

Your network of contacts (travel partners) is so important that without them, it would be like starting your travel career over from day one on every trip. It's "who you know" that can make a difference whenever particular needs arise.

In the travel industry, time is of the essence. An immediate response to a situation is crucial to keep people's travel plans from being interrupted and/or revenues from being lost. Knowing the right contact to find necessary information is why your colleagues and clients depend on you. Constantly update your list of new contacts. Keep in touch with former contacts on a regular basis, if possible. Your "network" of business associates and friends will grow over the years – and your credibility and respectability in the travel industry will grow right along with your "network."

List the names, addresses, phone numbers, and other "specialty" information about the many people you will meet within the travel industry while on tour.

Airline Travel

Probably more than 90% of today's group travelers arrive and depart from their tour by air, and often travel many sections of their actual tour by air as well. The various airline companies have long recognized this vast, growing market, and spend great sums of money on advertising tours. Co-operation with them is of prime importance for the Tour Operator; therefore, it is also important for the Tour Director.

> **Special Note:** Prior to landing, the Tour Director should circulate amongst the tour participants and explain to them what will be taking place. Make sure that you have the necessary documents handy to clear customs and immigration, and that all entry forms have been completed.

Group Airport Check In

When you have a group arriving by air, and you are meeting them at the airport, make sure you introduce yourself to the ground staff as a representative of your company, as well as giving the Tour Group name to them so they may direct your arriving passengers to and enable you to assemble your group quickly. Advise the baggage porters of your group's arrival so they will get the baggage all together.

While on the tour, check all of your clients' tickets, passports for their return flight, making sure they are in order, and confirm their flight(s) way in advance. If there are also flights as part of the tour itinerary, these must also be confirmed. When, as part of the tour, you fly together as a group, you collect all of the tickets - if there is a local airport tax, collect that, too, (if not already included by the Tour Operator), in local currency - and make sure that you arrive with your group at the airport on time to process security.

> **Special Note:** When you arrive at the airport, ask your clients to take a seat comfortably out of the way while you deal with the check-in procedures. Remember, too many people clustering around the check-in desk just leads to confusion.

Responsibilities of the In-Bound Destination Manager

Meeting your In-bound destination Management Company/tour Guide Upon landing, you should go ahead of the group and make contact with the ground operator "meet & greet" tour guide who has arranged to transfer the participants to their hotel. It is a good idea for you to wear a name tag—the bigger, the better. The ground operator/"meet & greet service" usually has some kind of sign to aid the Tour Director in identifying him or her.

Sample "Meet & Greet Sign" for Incoming Tour Groups/Individuals

The Global Travel Company
Paris, France
Welcomes the "The Royal Oak Tour Group"

Once the group has identified their luggage and cleared customs, the ground operator will lead them to their bus or buses. Each ground operator/In-Bound Destination Tour Operator has their own system for transferring the tour participants and their luggage.

- *For large groups*, the participants will be transferred directly to the hotel and the luggage taken separately by truck.

- *For small groups*, most likely the porters will put the luggage on the same bus with the participant that is why it is extremely important that the tour director keep an eye on the luggage and maintain an accurate count at all times (use copy of rooming list).

Don't depart for the hotel without taking a head count. If more than one bus is being used, the ITD should make sure everyone has boarded, and then ride on the lead bus so as to be the first to reach the hotel.

For group of forty-five passengers or more, it is recommended that you hire an escort to assist in controlling the group - one leading and the other bringing up the rear.

Previewing the Tour Program

Upon arrival either at breakfast or the "welcome dinner" it is advisable to preview the entire tour itinerary. The purpose is to make sure the tour members understand what is included in the way of meals, sightseeing, rooms, tips, etc. If your driver and guide or assistants are to be with you for some time, introduce them and their duties. Place a sign on the motor coach so the members can easily recognize their bus.

It's happened before! An ITD has taken off with a traveler not belonging to his/her group!

You as the ITD have been "blown up" by the Travel Agent/Tour Operator as an important part of the Tour Package. It is easy to live up to that image for the first few hours or so, as the "epitome and skill and knowledge..." However, you must retain this image for the whole tour, whether it lasts only five days, or forty-five days.

Depending on whether your heart is entirely in your job or not, your clients must feel your enthusiasm, learn from your knowledge of the countries through which you travel, and come to share your "*joie de vivre.*" The possibilities are never-ending. Your aim is to convey your appreciation for life and your love of travel to your clients, as daily changing and ever-exciting! You must always strive for more knowledge. Try to leave nothing out. If you don't know something, find out about it, if possible, in advance. We should never stop learning, never stop trying to understand.

The Hotel: "Your Home Away from Home"

Upon arrival at the hotel, "win over with patience." One of the most important aspects of a travel program is checking the people into the hotel. For it is then that the initial impression is created. In order to prevent confusion and chaos, the ITD must determine from the hotel precisely what the room situation is and he/she *must* continually be checking and rechecking to determine that rooms are actually ready and being assigned to the tour participants. This is critical for travelers who have traveled through several time zones and haven't slept or had a good meal.

En route to the hotel, you should advise the front desk by calling ahead to give the front desk manager the estimated time of arrival and any last-minute changes in the rooming list. You have several choices as to how you will distribute room keys and confer with the tour group members:

- *First Choice:* There will be occasions (lobby is small or busy) when it will be more beneficial to distribute the keys on the coach using the PA system.
- *Second Choice:* Book a Private room or designated area at the hotel, or an area in the lobby away from the front desk. *Any place where you the ITD has complete control and are able to communicate with the group without any outside disturbances.*

No matter where the location may be, you will want to clear up some last-minute details with the tour members such as:

- Location and time of dinner and/or welcome reception.
- Introduction of the clients to the hotel staff or local ground handler
- Information on the scheduled tours or location of the hospitality desk
- What to do m the event they require help
- List of hotel facilities
- Address of hotel and what to visit within the surrounding area.

As the ITD, you should be the last person to leave for your room. Do not grab your bag and go to your room once the keys have been handed out. Wait around the front desk, for reports of any keys not fitting and rooms not prepared, or rooms too close to the elevator -- just some of the complaints that will arise on check-in. During that period, confirm hotel rates, taxes, baggage handling, and other fees previously agreed upon by the Tour Operator. Also, confirm with Food and Beverage Manager upcoming functions and see that the bell captain and front desk have copies of the group's tour itinerary.

> ***Note:*** Overseas clients must have their passports on hand at check-in and are asked to fill in a registration card.

In theory, it's simple! The hotel receives a rooming list, a room is assigned, and the Tour Director gives the key to the guest. However, all hotels have certain *operational problems* which can greatly affect the checking in of a group.

Overbookings

There are times when a hotel has no other choice but to "Walk the Group" to another hotel. The ITD must arrange for transport and set up scheduled functions at the other properties. The ITD will have to assure the tour members that the hotel in question is of the same "quality" (3/4 /5 star) that they were scheduled to check into.

Overbooking Policies

Most hotels have a planned "overbooking" policy in order to compensate for no-shows and last-minute cancellations. Considering these factors, it is apparent that when the hotel is running at 100% occupancy, they cannot assign a room to a tour participant until a room has been vacated. Similarly, when people are checking out of the hotel at the last minute, a housekeeping problem is created. The room must be cleaned and made up for the arriving guest.

What to do while waiting for room assignments? When a problem arises, the ITD must be prepared to do something "on the spot" in order to aid the hotel in alleviating the problem. Here are some possible strategies:

- Attempt to delay the participant en route to the hotel by taking them on a sight-seeing tour, if possible
- Arrange some sort of function at the hotel so the guests may relax and enjoy themselves while waiting for their rooms.

How to Travel Free as an International Tour Director

- Arrange for changing rooms (men/women) to be assigned to the group, allowing them to leave hand luggage in a safe area or change into beach attire, or take a walking tour.

Luggage Control

With tour groups, some pieces off luggage may inadvertently be placed in the wrong rooms, a room may be assigned more than once, or a key may be placed in the wrong envelope, all causing a barrage of questions and complaints from the incoming guests. All of these details add up to pressure being placed upon the ITD.

An important feature of an ITD's personality is their ability to deal with pressure!

Coordinating Activities with Hotel Management

Four people are important in coordinating activities

- Front Desk Manager
- Food & Beverage Manager
- Bell Captain
- Sales Director

Every hotel used on your tour's itinerary is carefully chosen for your particular tour and its category, and should, therefore, be the best for that tour. Your attitude and behavior towards the different department heads of the hotel, from the reception to the concierge to the porters and restaurants, should always be courteous and co-operative, efficient and pleasant, especially when your clients are present. You are the liaison between your group of individuals and the hotel; your job is to handle all relations between them, to keep them pleasant and running smoothly.

Prior to arrival, if you have any room changes, advise the front desk in advance as soon as possible; if there is time, write; if not, make a quick telephone call. *Don't* arrive at a hotel and demand to start changing room arrangements—you will delay your group after a day of traveling, when all they want is to get to their rooms and relax.

The front desk, too, may have had to balance their room availability with the arrival of clients, and if you start making complicated demands late in the day, you will disrupt everything, including what should be smooth and friendly relations.

The Bell Captain. Hotel baggage porters are extremely useful to you, and it is in your best interest to maintain good relations with them. Make their work easier, keep them informed of the group's activities by giving them copies of the tour itinerary, rooming list and never forget the tips to which they are entitled as per your company's policies.

Concierge Services. This is the center for information where the tour members can get directions, recommendations and "where not to go" for restaurants, tourist sites, shopping, walking tours, public transportation-spas, churches, and night spots etc.

Special Note: Should any serious problems arise between you, your group, and the hotel, sort them out quickly and quietly, and if possible, in private. <u>Definitely not in the hotel lobby!</u>

Opening Hotel Accounts

It's important to open a Hotel Master Account to ensure that you can track all charges effectively. This will entail an advance letter to the hotel requesting this service. A sample of such a letter is found in the Appendix. The Master Account is for all charges which were contracted on behalf of the tour in advance. In addition, request a separate "Additional Billing Account" for other charges.

For example, if you contracted for a one-hour cocktail party and you advise the hotel that the party is to be extended one-half hour, the cost of the first hour will be charged to the "Master Account" and the extension will be charged to the "Additional Billing Account." The way to handle this would be to cut off at the end of the first hour, and start a new check for the extension so that the figure would agree with the amount posted to the "Additional Billing Account." The Tour Director will sign an authorization for this additional half hour.

The Tour Group's Hospitality Desk

Why a hospitality desk? The hospitality desk is the center and base of operations. This is the place where participants will come for information, for answers to questions, to seek help on problems, and to sign up for activities. Needless to say, this area must be kept attractive and reflect a neat, businesslike atmosphere.

Who manages the hospitality tour desk? There will be occasions you as the ITD will be behind the desk, however due to a hectic schedule you will normally hire a local representative to service the tour members. They should be experienced in managing tour groups and be knowledgeable about the local restaurants, tourist sites, shopping, and evening activities.

For small groups, your local ground handler will make his tour desk available to the group to be used to purchase optional tours or to act as a hospitality desk. After the trip participants have checked into the hotel, the hospitality desk must be staffed at all times, as the program dictates, generally 8:00 a.m. to 10:00 p.m. The exact hours will be determined by the ITD In Charge. A felt board or blackboard should be set up in the immediate area of the hospitality desk. The board should feature the day's activities and any important messages which should be conveyed to the group—for example, a change of a scheduled function or check-out time.

Sample Sign for Hospitality Desk

Welcome Royal Oak Garden Club
Tour desk hours: 9:00 am-5:00pm daily
Welcome dinner: 7:00 p.m.
Location: Garden Room Suite 2nd floor
Emergencies: contact your ITD Mrs. Rose Watkins Room #323

Sample Optional Tour & Activities Bulletin Board

> Attn Tour Members from "The Royal Oak Senior Club"
>
> Optional tours and excursions (not included in the tour program)
>
> Harbor Dinner Cruise: $75.00 per person
>
> Every night @ &:00pm
>
> City Walking Tour of the Old Town $25.00 per person
>
> Departs hotel @ 9:00 am Monday-Friday
>
> Antique Shopping tour w/lunch $45.00 per person
>
> Departs hotel every Wednesday @ 12:00 p.m.

Selling Optional Tours

Selling optional tours can bring additional income to the ITD (10%-15% commission) when promoting local tour packages. The local destination management company/tour guide service can provide a listing of optional tours for you to offer their clients at the groups "hospitality" desk.

Auto Rentals

Discourage your clients from renting a car if this is their first time abroad and they are not familiar with the road signs, conditions, language, or the fact that they drive on the left side of the road (as in England). Auto rental rates vary along with surcharges (VAT, Taxes, and drop off charges, fuel, and Insurance) your clients will not be familiar with.

Shopping: A Destination Highlight

A daily tour excursion is not complete until the tour participants have had an opportunity to shop. Often your local guide or driver will recommend shops offering good discounts and product value. At the beginning of the tour package, it is advisable to inform the tour members what the good buys are and then they can plan ahead when and where to purchase that tile coffee table or those handmade dishes.

Most tour information bulletins distributed to clients include a note from the Tour Director with the following statement:

We urge you to be cautious and discriminating in your purchases. We regret that we cannot be responsible for any shopping activities and are unable to intervene on your behalf in the event that merchandise does not live up to your expectations or if merchandise that you may ask to be shipped home does not arrive."

Gerald Mitchell

> ***Please Note:*** Local tour guides and drivers are often given a commission for leading tour groups to gift stores and restaurants. The ITD should be aware of this worldwide practice and not allow his clients to be misled for the sake of the driver/guide getting a commission.

Arranging Evening Activities

Because you are not immune to fatigue and needs time alone to prepare for the following day, to complete reports and enjoy a meal without the entertaining 40 tour members, you should use the services of a local tour guide to assume the responsibility of the tour group. This allows you to bring your paperwork up to date, get some rest, and review the forthcoming tour arrangements (hotels, transfer companies, etc.).

During this *down time,* you can recommend shopping, optional touring, or taking advantage of the planned activities the hotel has to offer or have the local tour guide "take charge" and earn additional income by escorting the group to restaurants or nightspots for the evening activities. These activities can be pre-sold through the Tour Groups Hospitality Desk.

Sample Work Schedule for Hospitality Desk Staff

TIME: 9:00 am – 7:00 PM
Agent on duty: Jacques Molin

Day 1 through Day 8
9:00 am - 4:00 P.M.-tour desk
5:00 P.M. - 7:00 P.M. —evening activities

Work Assignment-In Bound

- Airport (meet group and assist in transfer to hotel) Hospitality Desk
- Manage Hospitality Desk
- Organize Welcome cocktail Party - Blue Room
- Welcome Dinner - Sun Room
- Dispatch and go on city tour
- Dispatch fishermen; remain at dock to cover return transfer
- Dinner in local restaurant – organize transfers

Work Assignments-Out Bound

Have departure notices completed and distributed by 3:00 P.M.
Meet Bell Captain to collect luggage for early morning departure
Confirm time for tour group to be transferred to the airport lists by 4:00 P.M.

- Cocktail Party - Location
- Farewell Banquet Location
- Check and dispatch luggage for airport Hospitality Desk Airport (remain until entire group has departed)
- Dispatch participants from hotel to airport

Forms at Hospitality Desk

- *Follow-Up File.* A follow-up file must be kept at the hospitality desk at all times. Any time a participant makes reference to a previous, specific request - an airline change, delayed luggage, lost or damaged luggage, special reservations, etc—the Tour Director at the desk will locate the request under the first letter of the individual's last name, and the information and an answer should be right there. No participant should ever be told, "You will be told later" or "You will have to see the Tour Director who is handling your request." An ample supply of the following forms should be kept with the follow-up file at all times.
- *Airline-Change Request Forms.* When a participant requests that his flight itinerary be changed in any way, the airline-change request form should be filled out by the Tour Director. This form will assist the Tour Director in maintaining an orderly and systematic record of airline-change requests. When properly filled out and kept up to date, it will help to assure that new reservations are confirmed correctly and old reservations are cancelled.
- *Delayed-Luggage Forms.* When a participant reports that he has not received his luggage, a delayed-luggage form should be completed. It provides the Tour Director and the carrier when applicable, with the information necessary to accomplish tracer action and follow-up until the baggage is located or its disposition determined. Again, this form should be properly filed in the follow-up file.
- *Baggage-Claim Forms.* When it has been determined that a participant's luggage is lost or damaged, the baggage-claim form should be filled out to provide the information necessary to process a claim. However, please note that in 99 *out of 100 cases, the airline (carrier) is responsible for delayed, lost or damaged luggage.*
- If a participant's baggage is delayed, the respective airline should be contacted and a tracer sent out on the bag (obtaining information from the delayed luggage form). The airline should be requested to authorize the inconvenienced party to purchase essential toiletries and related personal items until his/her bag can be located and returned.
- Your company is not responsible and should not be obligated to pay out money for lost, delayed, or damaged baggage resulting from careless handling by the carrier.
- When it is determined that a bag or baggage is permanently lost or damaged, the participant should be assisted in filing a claim with the respective carrier while on location. Naturally, there will be isolated incidents when a carrier's representative cannot be contacted and the Tour Director will have to pay out money to a participant for the necessary toiletries. The Tour Director should advise the participant to purchase only those items he will need for the duration of the trip.
- *At no time should the Tour Director assume the responsibility for reimbursing a participant for the actual total value of the items lost.*

Free Time

A good Tour Designer will prepare an itinerary which allows for the tour members to "stay put" at their hotel after three or four days of traveling. This allows the tour participant to take care of personal needs such as laundry, letter writing, and spending time alone to reflect on what has happened over the past few days.

Emergencies

When leaving the hotel for a tour or evening out, advise the hotel of your location and a telephone contact in the event of a serious illness, a problem caused by one of the tour members overindulging, or not understanding the language or customs, etc.

Gerald Mitchell

Great Dining Experiences

There's more to feed a tour group than chicken, beef or fish. You need to turn the meal into a memorable experience. A festive affair described in the tour brochure as a "tour highlight" should offer some of the following memories and opportunities to form new friendships, "photo ops," local entertainment, guest speakers, and, most of all, fond memories. After hours of touring on a motor coach they are now ready to let their hair down and relax and have some fun! You can use the services of local event planners for:

- Folkloric dancers
- Local entertainers
- Professional storytellers
- Group can learn to participate in local dance routines
- Guest speakers on such subjects as; art and crafts, history, gossip, culture, tales of the past

Don't forget to order cakes and photographers for special occasions such as birthdays, anniversaries, and travel awards.

Pre-Dinner Check List for Group Functions

- Check out area or room no less than one hour in advance of the group.
- Make certain you have enough tables, chairs, etc, and that they are properly arranged.
- In a public room or at a dinner show, see to it that the group has the most advantageous seats.
- Make certain the dining area has enough staff to handle this function -- captains, waiters; busboys make sure the menu to be served is in accordance with hotel contract.
- If wine or drinks are to be served, verify with the captain(s) what exactly is to be included, the kind of wine to be served, and how tips will be handled
- When hors d'oeuvres are included, check that they are ready and that the supply will be adequate.
- For birthdays, anniversaries, and other special occasion, you should arrange for a cake to be delivered. This is an excellent opportunity for the tour members to take photos.
- Set up the V I P - Guest speaker's table.
- Make sure the tour members are informed of location and dinner times.
- Greet dinner guests at the door -- assist in seating tour members.
- During dinner be sure the group is served as quickly and smoothly as possible Be sure no participant or group of participants is being overlooked
- In the event of a problem or in anticipation of one, you should immediately contact the maitre d' For the sake of good working relations; do not criticize the employees, but take all complaints to their supervisor.
- You should have a list of tour participants that are on a specific diet
- Arrange for a photographer.

Special Note: The ITD's role in overseeing the group dinning function is to work with the General Manager or Head Waiter. For example, should a tour member want ice water, bring it to the head waiter's attention "quietly". Don't run around giving orders to junior waiters; that's the Head Waiter's job. That's why your company pays extra gratuities so YOU the ITD can "socialize" with the tour members and prepare to take them back to the hotel.

The behavior of an ITD has to be that of a real professional at all times, but first and foremost when dealing with their travel partners, for it is there that the company/ITD maintains its image and prestige. Therefore, it is not professionally acceptable for an ITD to arrive with his group at a restaurant with a delay of over half an hour on a prearranged schedule without previous notice being given by telephone or email.

Even more blameworthy is the ITD who, without giving any notice to the Restaurant Manager, tries to change the menu for an entire group at the last minute. This is not only against professional principle, it also proves that the ITD is not running the group as he should, but on the contrary, they are being run.

After Dinner

- If transfers are required following dinner, check out the buses while dessert is being served
- Review bill(s) very carefully prior to paying them.
- Upon completion of a group dinner, preview the next day's schedule.

Hiring Local Interpretive Tour Guides

These men and women are specialists in their fields and experts in their own particular city or area. The choice of local guides may be made by your tour operator or you, and the guides can be most helpful to you personally, as well as keeping your group receptive and in a happy frame of mind.

A local step-on-guide can add authentic flavor to a trip, and give tremendous insight into people, their customs and cultures. Provide the service of an interpreter and narrative about the many sights to visit, shopping, local restaurants, safety notes and do's and don'ts about the region such as national parks, areas to avoid in a city etc.

Tour Guide's Responsibility to the Tour Group

The Tour Guide should report at least a half hour prior to the departure of the tour. Before local guides take your group off on a visit, make sure they know the specific program promised to your clients, the one they have printed in their itinerary. If there is to be a change, or an unavoidable omission; e.g., a museum or gallery is closed; explain this to the group before they start out, to avoid any later misunderstandings or complaints.

The guide must meet first with the Tour Director to review the tour itinerary, and always introduce the local guide cordially to your clients, it gives them a good start, and they will reciprocate with similar courtesy. He should be neatly dressed, groomed, and set the tone and pace according to the age and physical abilities of the clients.

Both the guide and the driver should work together in selecting routing and rest stops. The guide should not be permitted to solicit optional tours, events, or shopping without first clearing it with the Tour Director. In his presentation, the guide must give more than dates and historical facts. He should keep his clients' interest by providing an interesting "mix" of cultural understanding of a city or country.

Gerald Mitchell

Contracting Motor Coach / Driver

On tours which travel by varied forms of transport -- trains, planes, ships, etc., you will, of course, have many different transfer and sight-seeing drivers. However, many tours still do much of their program by road, the most interesting way of seeing the countries. So you will, have one person driving you and your group for the length of time that the tour goes by road. Your jobs are complementary and interdependent.

Ninety-nine per cent of drivers are professionals, and they may quite possibly have been driving tours longer than you have been directing them. Consequently, these people can be of great help to you, and will understand some of your problems.

REMEMBER: To each his own job. Although both your responsibilities should combine to make an excellent well-run tour for the clients, each of your responsibilities is different. *YOU* deal with the clients and their well-being; your driver looks after the bus, drives it, maintains it and keeps it clean.

Be correct with him, and help him by setting good timing for the day's activities or traveling time; he will help you by being punctual, courteous to his clients, and careful with the luggage, and keeping his bus in top condition. He has a hard, physical job and works hard; always be fair with him. The driver is responsible for:

- Getting the tour members to their various destinations safely, comfortably, and on time
- Removing baggage from the coach for hotel check-in, and doing a luggage count with the Tour Director.
- Having the coach cleaned, and fueled, and assuming that the air-conditioning and PA systems are working.
- Being at the hotel at least a half-hour prior to any departures to review itinerary, maps, and the tour routing for the day with the Tour.
- Counting luggage for hotel check-out and loading on the coach.
- *Not getting lost!*

Tipping Policies

The company you represent will often have a tipping policy for the Tour Director and what is expected of the tour members. Persons normally to be tipped include:

- Baggage Handlers
- Airport
- Hotels
- Motor Coach Drivers
- Driver/Guides
- Local Guides
- Waiters.
- Bell Captains

Tipping can range from 10% to 30%, depending on the level of service. For tour groups, many restaurants and tour guides and hotels have a set tipping policy that is stated in their contract of "service."

For most groups, the ITD will assure clients the tips are built into the tour cost. At the end of a tour, traditionally the ITD will pass an envelope around to all tour members who wish to contribute an additional 'tip" for "outstanding" services rendered by the driver and guide to give to them at the end of the tour.

50

> **Special Note:** Tour members will be given advice on this subject in their documentation kit, such as *"Gratuities to escorts, although customary, are not required. Any such expression of appreciation should be offered on a voluntary and personal basis."*

Travel Supplier Evaluation Report

Comment Sheets should be filled out and mailed to travel suppliers after you have had an opportunity to relax and give the trip some thought. Hasty letters or comments reveal uncertainty and show that you have put forth little effort. All parties concerned are deserving of your "professional opinion." Both compliments and constructive criticism will be well received and replied to if they are formulated with full consideration.

Remember that the suppliers are your peers within the trade. They regard your comments as a means of adopting changes and improving their services in order to continue receiving your business. Be honest, but practice diplomacy if you have a complaint. See the sample "Comment and Evaluation Report" in the Appendix.

Chapter 6
Taking the Tour Group Home

Pre-Departure Notice

Two days prior to departure for home, you should start preparing the tour members for the return trip -- the end of a memorable holiday. In other words. . . *back to reality*. The past few weeks have been great, an escape from reality, experiencing a dream vacation come true, with new friends, exotic sights, culinary delights, and being serviced by a host of travel suppliers always on hand to attend to their needs and demands. For you, this could very well be the most important part of the tour -- "unwinding the clients."

Sample Pre-Departure Notice

Departure notice: "Royal Oak Senior Club"

Sunday June 8th coach to leave hotel at 6:00 am Sharp!
Please have your luggage outside your room at 5:00 a.m. for transfer to the airport
For additional information contact your ITD Mrs. Rose Watkins
Room #212 or cell phone 413-555-2000

PHASE I: Pre-Check-Out Briefing

Anticipate the group's questions and schedule a meeting for tour members to cover the following details:

- Check-out time (hotel or cruise ship)
- Baggage handling pick-up time by bell captain
- Departure time
- Location for group pick-up, transfer to the airport
- Airport, Group check-in, Seat assignments
- Security check
- Duty-free shopping, customs declaration forms and limits
- Assurance that all tour members have the proper documents (passports, airline tickets)
- Departure taxes (pre paid or do your have the clients pay for them?)

PHASE II: Checking Out of the Hotel

Twenty-four (24) hours prior to departure, you should meet with the hotel accounting department to review all billing. This is the time to note charges that are not part of the general billing (i.e., tour members' bar charges, etc.) and to have the tour member pay for his incidentals at the front desk of the hotel.

> **Special Note:** Do not wait until the morning of departure to review the accounting. You will be too busy organizing the group for their transfers and checking the luggage.

"Departure Notices"

These forms are supplied to the Tour Director prior to a trip. The purpose of the departure notice is to advise all participants when their bags will be picked up by the bellman, the time their transfer leaves from the hotel, and their flight time. The forms are filled out with the appropriate information by the Tour Director, after he has reconfirmed transportation (ground and air) arrangements. The forms are then distributed to all participants the day prior to their departure.

Sample Pre-Departure Notice

(To be delivered to each room/distributed at the hospitality desk)

DEPARTURE NOTICE

Room Number _____
Client's Name: _____
Pieces of Luggage:_____
Breakfast: Time: _____
Location: _____
Time of Day: _____ Date: _____

Please have your luggage packed and placed out side your room for pick-up.
Check that your special bag tags are securely attached to your luggage.
Extra tags may be obtained from your Tour Director.
Your transportation will depart from the hotel for the airport.

Your _____Flight No. _____ will depart Destination: _____

Please check with the cashier regarding your incidental account prior to leaving the hotel (no later than two (2) hours prior to departure).

We hope you have enjoyed your holiday and wish you a pleasant journey home. It has indeed been a pleasure serving you.

Please Note!

1. Don't forget your passport and airline ticket
2. All tour members are responsible for their carry-on luggage.

Hotel Departure Procedures

Bag Pull List: In order that the bellmen can pick up the luggage when the group is leaving the hotel, the Tour Director will make a bag pull list. This is a numerical listing of all room numbers of the group. A copy of the bag pull list is given to the bell captain of the hotel the day prior to the group's departure. It should be given to him as early as possible on that day so that he will have adequate staff on hand to move the luggage. The bag pull list shows the time at which bags should be pulled; also from which rooms the luggage is to be moved. The ITD should retain a copy of this list and distribute copies of the list to his travel staff.

Gerald Mitchell

Sample Bell Captain's Check-Out Form

Hotel: Bellvue Hotel
Attention: Bell Captain
Group: Royal Oak Group
Departure Date: May 12th, 2005
Time: 6:00 am
Special Instructions: Motor Coach Company: Global Tours
Date/Time received by Bell Captain:
(Signature)_____
Tour Director: Ms. Rose Watkins
Room #:212

Reconciling Bills with Travel Suppliers

After meeting with the hotel accounting department, billings with ground operators must be audited. If the ITD had been issued tour vouchers for each item arranged with the ground operator, such as airport transfers and sight-seeing, and has instructed the ground operator that final payment will be made based on the return of these vouchers, the final accounting would be fairly simple. There may be some cases where the agent must *"guarantee"* a number to the ground operator in advance. This would usually be in the case of an option that includes a meal or ticket for entry such as a nightclub or dinner function. In such a case, the ITD would be obliged to pay for the "guaranteed" number, even if some persons do not show up for the event. Again it is the responsibility of the ITD to advise the client when there will be no refunds should they pay and then have a change in plans.

Sample Paid-Out Gratuity Form

For Drivers/guides/wait staff/baggage handlers/tour guides

Date: _____ $_____
Account No:
We appreciate the service you have rendered. Please sign and present this form to:
Received:
Tour Director: _____
Explanation:_____

INSTRUCTIONS TO OUR SUPPLIERS
- Please pay your employee the gratuity shown above.
- Please have employee sign and return to us with your - Invoice for services rendered.
Thank your, Rose Watkins, ITD

Airport Check In

Now that the group is preparing for their departure home, they will require assistance obtaining their luggage, clearing customs (if necessary), and making connecting flights to their home towns. On the flight homeward, it is preferable to have each person check in at the airport as an individual passenger for the following reasons:

- Security Check
- Seat Selection
- Confirmation of Connecting Flights
- Baggage Claim Check is in Their Possession
- Customs
- Special meals

You must remind tour members that they will have to locate their luggage and clear it through customs. This should all go quite smoothly, but in many cases they have over-packed, over-shopped, and will be laden with gifts and objects d'art that will slow them down. Naturally, carrying the newly acquired items was not one of their major concerns when purchasing their souvenirs. Indeed, you will be called upon to help "move them along" to they can make their connecting flights and you can get the last client safely home.

Be patient! It goes with the job. After conducting a successful tour and providing a twenty-four-hour "baby-sitting service" to forty tour members, this is not the time for the you to lose your patience. By keeping calm and collected and preparing the clients for the return trip home, you will be rewarded by favorable comments to the home office and repeat clients for future trips.

The Straggler

Always keep an eye out for clients who will need help going through customs and preparing U. S. customs declaration forms, the over-packer, the straggler, and, of course, the person who never listens to a thing that is said during the departure briefing.

Chapter 7

Closing out the Tour

ITD's Post-Tour Responsibilities

Welcome home! Now it's time to complete the following tasks to "close out" the tour:

1. Pay off all outstanding bills to suppliers
2. Pay commissions to sales personnel
3. Note all names to be entered on the mailing list
4. Forward client referrals to sales department
5. Meeting with group leader, tour directors, and/or escorts of the organizations to review evaluation sheets
6. Enter names of new travel partners/contacts made in past tour
7. Complete evaluation reports (field report; ITD and Clients)
8. Prepare for reunion reception
9. Start designing, packaging and scheduling upcoming tours and cruises
10. Schedule and send out invitations to tour members and potential clients for "Tour Reunion" Travel Party

The Value of a "Tour Reunion" Party

Many clients get the "Post-Tour Blues." After coming home, they are restless and ask themselves, "Where do we go next?"

Yes, the tour was successful. Your clients returned home with an enthusiastic attitude towards future trips with your company. Everything offered in the tour program was fulfilled, plus many extra exciting features were interjected into the itinerary as the group proceeded on their *tailor-made* tour. However, the applause is short lived. The past trip is history. Memories, photos, and souvenirs are put aside after they have been shared with their friends and relatives.

What is on your client's mind is . . . *When is our next trip?* Well-satisfied group members will probably sign up for your next trip as soon as you announce it. Others, including those who complained somewhat loudly about the air conditioning, the walking pace, the number of steps leading to the pagoda, or the fact that the guide's speech was unintelligible, will recommend your trips to their friends with great enthusiasm. When the tour has come to an end, we tend to remember the marvelous moments, not the temporary tribulations.

The post-tour reunion is an excellent method of informing the clients of future trips and having them bring their friends to become part of your company's travel club. Throughout the event, the travelers will be exchanging pictures and viewing movies and slides which were taken during the tour. For the reunion, your company should have on hand:

- Brochures for upcoming tours/cruises
- Early-booking discounts
- Gifts for a drawing *(Note* Money gift certificates to be used towards any of the upcoming trips)
- General information on the destinations being promoted
- Films, slides
- ITD's, company staff
- Name Badges
- Refreshments
- Guest speakers

Reunions should be fun. Keep them fresh and exciting. Different locations, such as restaurants which offer a theme or a member's home, guest speakers, and meeting with some of the travel suppliers all help to stimulate a feeling of camaraderie among the membership. They will become your company's number one salespersons.

ITD Field Evaluation Report

Important to the success of your tour is your evaluation when it is over. Your tour group's reaction to the tour can increase your business in the future or cause your career to crash. Pay attention to each person's comments and the ratings of all the guides involved, as well as their assessment of the facilities, attractions, transportation, and overall impressions of the tour. Satisfied customers will tell their friends -- and so will unhappy customers!

It's important to be objective about negative comments -- they can often tell you more about the success or failure of the tour than the positive praise you receive. A tourist may say nothing at all when the hotel is overbooked or the room service is inefficient, and you could be lured into thinking that all is well, when that tourist is really critical of the facilities. If they think you talk too much and your presentations are too long, they might say nothing but you will find out by their comments on the evaluation form. Take all comments to heart and determine which flaws in the tour can be fixed in the future and which were just odd occurrences that can't be helped. Let your tour group know that traveling to strange places is an adventure, and while you will make every effort to ensure their safety and comfort, the unforeseen will occur from time to time.

Evaluating Interpretative Tour Guides

You will want to evaluate cultural, historical, nature, adventure, and special interest Tour Guides because their performance is critical to your success. The importance of having a qualified Interpretative Tour

Guide cannot be overstressed. The interpretative tour guide can plan itineraries to retrace historical links for history buffs or bird watchers, or also plan a program where the client is escorted to areas of their destination which have been "untapped" by other travel companies.

However, tourism works in an inescapable cycle. Guidebooks and tour brochures trumpet the latest so-called "undiscovered place," but like so many places before them, in their turn they too become discovered and mundane. How can we avoid overtaking the environment and causing a destination to become mundane? We can do this through a proper interpretative tour guide training program, thus putting a stop to local city guides assuming the role of interpretative guides, who are more interested in selling transportation and stops at souvenir shops. You can also appoint professionals in their fields of expertise to assist in formulating a series of training workshops (e.g., scientists, naturalists, and travel-industry leaders) acquainted with eco-tourism and the needs of their clients.

Get their input prior to spending money and time developing a series of eco-tourism tours, so that you will not find out too late that the tours that were so well planned on paper cannot be designed, packages and delivered due to the lack of qualified personnel and infrastructure.

Why is the Evaluation Form so important?

The Evaluation Form shows your company is interested not only in selling your clients a trip but also that their opinions are valuable and helpful in improving the tours for future travelers. It may provide referrals — friends or organizations that might travel with your tour company in the future.

Transfer the ITD Field Report onto the ITD's final Tour Evaluation Report to distribute to:

- Tour Operator
- Sales Department
- Operations
- Tour Designer
- Travel Suppliers

How Can the Tour be improved? The ITD, while on tour, look for ways of improvement by critiquing the hotels and restaurants, entertainment, inbound destination managers, tour guides, transportation services and tour highlights for the tour designer back at the home office.

The time to make note of these changes is while on location. Pay special attention to tour costing and tour pacing. Price-out the tour in net rates, preferably in U.S. funds. Take care to calculate the number of hours your clients spend on a motor coach traveling to and from attractions or destinations. The ITD is the "eyes and ears" for the tour designer/tour operator back at the office. Point out of the fact that the clients were "overworked" and that the tour was being run as a "meal-to-meal" program if this is the case.

As you develop tour itineraries of your own, and your notes are recorded in the sample permanent record which follows, you may consider the possibilities and potential of becoming your own tour designer and packager of tours. (For additional information, order the Gerry @tour-guiding.net *Tour Designing and Packaging Manual* ©

Sample: International Tour Director's Evaluation Form

Copy to: Tour Operator/Tour Designers/Sales/Operations

1. Did the tour meet your expectations? ___Yes ___No ___Not sure
2. What was your opinion about the pacing of the tour?

    A) ___Too rushed   ___Too slow   ___Just right

    B) ___Not enough free time   ___Too much free time

3. How did you feel about the balance of activities on tour? (Sightseeing, museum visits, shopping, cultural events, etc.?)

    There was a good balance of activities.   ___Yes   ___No

    Too many of the same types of activities   ___Yes   ___No

    Too many different types of activities   ___Yes   ___No

4. Which parts of the tour did you like best?_____
5. Which parts of the tour did you like least? _____
6. What changes, in your opinion, would have made this a better tour?

_____

_____

Tour features/highlights to leave out:

_____

_____

Keep same hotels or change to a different location:

_____

_____

Recommendations (hotels):

_____

_____

Improve activities:

_____

_____

Delete activities:

_____

_____

_____

New programs that are available that should be included in future tours:

_____
_____

7. What was your opinion about the meals provided on tour?
   (A) ___ Too many meals packaged into the tour

   ___ Not enough meals packaged into the tour

   (B) ___ Not enough variety in the cuisine

   ___ Too many strange native foods

   ___ Too much standard American fare

How was the staff?

_____
_____

8. How would you rate the price and value of this tour?
   ___ Too expensive   ___ Just right   ___ A bargain

   Recommendations for other dinning establishments:

_____
_____

Contacts: _____
_____

9. What was your opinion of the hotels you stayed in?
   ___ Good   ___ Bad   ___ Average

   Comments: _____

   Recommendations for other hotels within the vicinity:

_____
_____

Contacts: _____
_____

10. What was your opinion of the airlines (domestic, international, or both) you flew?

_____
_____

11. Please rate the performance of the tour guides (step-on guides) who met the group
    Local Guides: (fill in name or city)

    _____ Yes/ No   Why: _____

_____Yes/ No   Why: _____

_____Yes/ No   Why: _____

12. How would you evaluate the service you received from the In-Bound Destination Management Company?

    ___Good   ___Bad   ___Average

    Contacts: _____

Comments:

_____
_____
_____
_____

13. How did the clients learn about this tour? (Check all that apply)
    - From the sponsoring organization
    - From other tour members: __
    - Travel agent: __
    - Tour flyer Advertisement: __
    - Direct mail:__

14. When is the best time of year to run this type of tour? Yes_____No:_____

15. What length of time would your recommend for this tour?

    ___5 days ___7 days ___10 days ___2 weeks ___3 weeks ___1 month

Would you manage this group again? Yes:_____ No:_____

ADDITIONAL COMMENTS:

_____
_____
_____
_____
_____

ITD Name: _____

Date: _____

Name of Group_____Group Leader: _____

Contact: Phone:_____email: _____

Address: _____

Client's Evaluation Report

Your clients' evaluation of the tour is extremely important. Without an honest opinion from them, the tour designer will not be able to make changes and improvements in the itinerary. Thus by writing and requesting their input, a dialogue is established between the client and the travel company.

This evaluation should be mailed to the tour participants within seven days after their return, along with a self-addressed, stamped envelope. Allowing a longer period of time to elapse will result in less meaningful answers on the evaluation. Clients will forget important details and put less time and effort into completing the evaluation form.

Welcome Home Letter to Clients

A cover "Welcome Home" letter should indicate how pleased you were with the results of the tour, and that their names have been added to the *"preferred"* mailing list. In the future, they will be receiving a list of upcoming trips along with discounts, free trip insurance, VIP luncheons, etc. If the ITD has taken a group photo of the tour members, it helps to include a copy for each tour participant. Also, mention the planning of a post-tour reception. All replies are private and confidential and addressed to you, the ITD.

Letters to the Travel Suppliers

You should send letters to the people who helped make the trip successful. The hotel personnel, reservations clerks, tour guides, bell captains, food and beverage managers, and motor coach companies are just a few of the people who helped make the trip successful. Should there be any outstanding comments on their services made by your clients, it helps to include a copy of the evaluation sheet to help substantiate the comments made by the client.

ITD's Tour Expense Report

The sample tour Travel Expense Report which follows will provide you with a basic expense report to record expenditures while on tour. Should you have need of additional information about taxable and non-taxable expenses, you should contact your tax advisor.

Gerald Mitchell

Sample Tour Travel Expense Report

Date:	Name:							
	Destination/Cruise							
EXPENSES	Day	Day	Day	Day	Day	Day	Day	Day
Hotels $								
Breakfast $								
Lunch $								
Dinner $								
Other Meals $								
Air/Rail/Bus $								
Local/Cab/Bus $								
Auto Rental Gas/Oil $								
Mileage								
Parking/Tolls $								
Telephone $								
Tips $								
Laundry $								
Entertainment $								
Touring $								
Other $								
DAILY TOTALS								

DETAILS OF EXPENSES			Cash Permanent
Date	Item/Receipt No	Business Purpose	Amount Advanced Temporary
			Total Expense
			Balance Due
			Employee Signature
			Today's Date
			BALANCE PAID
			Approved By
			Cheek/Voucher No

Note: Keep records of all your travel expense:
- Business
- Personal tax

Chapter 8

Getting Started as a "Dream Merchant"

Who is a tour operator? A Tour Operators are better known as "The Dream Merchants" who make fantasies a reality. However, when approaching a organization or association with the idea of preparing a tour or cruise for their memberships, the Tour Operator should always be forthright and inform them of what is really involved in each activity and overall quality of possible activities; and how will their membership benefit: Price; learning experience; companionship; safety; lodging arrangements; and/or myriad of other possible services and of course their "first hand" knowledge of the destination or cruise.

"A Tour Director must be an entrepreneur and love to travel".

Throughout this chapter, the term " ITD" or "Tour Operator" is used. Today tour operators wear many hats and go by many names, some of which include:

- Receptive In-bound Tour Operator
- Destination manager
- Ground Operator
- Tour Wholesales
- Tour Organizer
- Travel Agent

How Travelers benefit From a Package Tour

With only two weeks of vacation to call their own, why do so many people submit to the rigors and the headaches of group travel and run the risk of not liking other traveling companions? Why do they submit to the indignities of being herded around a destination like sheep?

There are many reasons, including cost saving and convenience and the difficulties of visiting certain foreign countries on their own.

These are legitimate reasons, but they are not the only ones to concern us here. As an ITD, you need to understand why certain people prefer traveling with a group to going alone. The group-tour type of traveler tends to enjoy:

- Being with other people of the same age, race, or background

money because the group rates are usually lower than individual travel
common interests
activities for evening and free time
ncing new sights and destinations
tours, meals, guide service, and transportation
safety in foreign countries

Getting Started!

In putting your business plan to together you will need to consider the *five basic* components of starting an International Tour Director's Company/tour Operations.

> *Special Note:* For additional help go to http://www.tour-guiding.com

#1-Staff: How well trained are your reservation staff, tour designers, tour directors/managers? Without a good ITD/Tour guide, your staff can either "make or break" your tour. A tour for 40 clients you have worked on for the past 6/9 months can be ruined by the lack of good staff.

#2-What are your tour offerings? Nature based tours, super deluxe or economy? How well do you know the destination you are promoting? Is it safe, easy to fly into? Can you match and design tours to appeal to your target market?

#3-Promotion and advertising: Establish a realistic budget. What are your channels of distribution? Direct mail, Travel agents, association's newsletters, TV, radio, e-mail or Internet Niche Markets?

#4- Knowing why people want to be escorted on package tour clients are willing to pay the extra money for the convenience of having somebody along who knows a specific geographical area and who is familiar with many details of group travel. Handling the logistics of a weeklong group tour involves quite a bit of work, but the benefits can be great. ITD's meet people from all over the world; serve as cultural ambassadors to their clients and the local residents.

Tour members benefit from the knowledge the ITD provides such as history, geography, and culture. The safety and cost and one price "cover all" puts the clients at ease so they can relax and enjoy the trip under the watchful eye of the ITD.

Four Key Elements in Starting a Tour Company

#1-Ensure that you have unique and/or signature tours to offer.

Seeking niche markets and building a client base is essential to survive in the travel-tourism industry. Who do you plan to tailor your tours for? Senior citizens, Gays, Wine enthusiasts, Students, antique Dealers, Arts & Craft groups? Research the demographic characteristics, such as income and geographic location. Consider departure cities; remember flying to New Zealand is a lot easier from the West Coast than starting out in Vermont. People do not have a lot of time to spend getting to their "vacation spot."

You can increase your opportunities for success by understanding the mindset of your current and future customers. We all make assumptions as to how we conduct business each and every day. Unfortunately, many assumptions are not based on solid research or an understanding of our customers.

The key is to separate fact from fiction. By understanding the decision-making process of leisure travel, you can better equip yourself to address the issues most important to your clients.

#2- You must have the ability to provide the best options and prices.

It is not just about price. Consumers are looking to travel agents to provide the best overall solution to their individual travel needs. We have a tendency to immediately think price is what sells and not necessarily what the customer wants or needs. Qualifying the customer up front can provide you with a relevant needs assessment. This can include dates, quality or location of accommodation or stateroom, cancellation policy, recreational amenities, the ease of doing business, etc. *It may not just be the price.*

No two customers are alike. What works for one may not work for another. Taking the time to better understand your customer, one at a time, can increase your closing percentage. Price is important when it is the only thing you sell.

Your tour programs must…

- Grab the potential client's attention
- Motivate them to make contact with your office
- And leave YOU with a profit for your efforts

Saving money is also not just about price. It is more about value. If the hotel was not the right location, if the cruise line was not the right cruise line, if the golf course was not the right golf course…it does not matter how much your customer saved. They will not come back to you. One can save a ton of money and be miserable. Saving money is important to consumers only after they have evaluated the value equation.

Value is what they are looking for. This is where you, the travel agent, can provide a discernible difference. By properly qualifying your customers up front, you can recommend relevant offerings and also provide cost-saving strategies. Moving a date, changing the location of a room/cabin, being open to flight options, etc., all can save money. Nobody wants to pay more than necessary. In today's environment, it is now fashionable for customers to brag to their peers and friends how much they have saved, whether it is a hotel room, airline seat or cruise. Value perceived and received is critical. And remember, if the customer has a bad travel experience, you will never hear from them how much money they saved.

#3- You must have substantive product knowledge.

Know where are today's travelers going. Top Destinations for 2005-2006:-In a recent United States Tour Operator Association (USTOA) survey, the organization asked their members whether they were planning to add new destination for the upcoming years.

<u>Top three Destinations</u>: Croatia, Costa Rica, and New Zealand were in a three-way tie for the most popular new destinations.

<u>Second Place-</u> Argentina, Brazil, Iceland, the south Pacific, and Turkey tied for second place.

Other new destinations cited by USTOA members are listed below by area.

- Central and South America: Guatemala, Mexico, and Panama.
- <u>Africa:</u> Ethiopia, Rwanda (gorilla trekking), and South Africa
- <u>Europe</u>; Apulia, Italy European cruises, Mallorca, Scandinavia, and Southern Italy.

...ean/Eastern Mediterranean: Egypt, Greece, Iran, Jordan, Libya/North Africa, Malta,

...ope; Russia, Badlands and Slovenia

...Taiwan, and Yangtze River cruises/Mekong river Cruises

...Australia, Papua New Guinea, and Tasmania.

...s; Arizona and Historic Trains of the Southwest

...buy insight. This is the most important attribute next to the offering of pricing and product options. ITD's can position themselves to be travel experts if they have the proper training and knowledge to back it up. This is why continuing education is so critical, whether you are in an office environment or at home. Also, you cannot be expert in everything. It is important to narrow your scope in travel products and experiences. However, the key is being the best in what you choose. Learn about the travel products you are recommending through FAMs, site inspections, collateral, the internet, past customers, etc. Your insight is what your customers will pay for…not a brochure or handout. Insight is your most valuable asset.

In addition, accreditation builds trust and credibility informs the customer they are dealing with a travel professional.

#4 – You need the ability to answer questions about safety/security.

How well are you informed about the destination and cruise being advertised and promoted to potential clients? This is such a strong factor in turning a client 'inquiry" into a "reservation." Safety and security have always been at the top of the minds of leisure travelers. Since 9/11, it has become more important than ever. Consumers are seeking out safety/security information which provides them with up to date information on travel destinations. In the world we live in today, this is critical. One cannot make assumptions about any destination, especially international, without having the insight from up to date information, whether it is political, health related, terrorism, or weather related. And we know how rapidly this can change. ITD's can provide a terrific service to their customers by providing this information on a timely basis.

Many sources are available:

IJET Travel Risk Management, www.ijet.com

www.cdc.gov,

www.asirt.org,

http://travel.state.gov/travel_warnings.html,

http://travel.state.gov/

ITD's who have the right strategies in place to address these top 4 reasons will achieve greater success in retaining customers and attracting new ones.

Chapter 9
Designing & Packaging Tours

Future Trends in the Travel-Tourism Industry

ITD's/Tour Operators should be aware of the future trends influencing the demands of the traveling public in designing their tour packages:

- *Flexibility:* Searching for tailor-made packages and maximum flexibility
- *Concerns:* Increasing recognition of negative impacts and demand for a quality environment.
- *Extension of Life:* In search for authentic or spontaneous experiences, learning and communication with others
- *Nature:* Search for safe sun plus additional nature-based activities
- *Active:* Mental and physical exertion, new skill acquisition, or update existing interests. Products based on entertainment, excitement or education, or some combination
- *Experience:* Tours are more traveled and have become more demanding consumers, unfazed by novelty and in pursuit of individuality
- *Speed:* Less regulations and restriction on global travel, harmonization of currencies, use of technology to speed up the travel process from reservations to the distribution of travel products.
- *Image-based:* Image critical to ability of destination to attract tours. Tourist use destinations as *branded fashion accessories* to help identify themselves from the mass of tourist and to make statement about themselves to others.

In this chapter, we'll cover packaging and designing a number of tour features and highlights (services) that would usually be purchased one at a time, but which, in a tour package, are offered as a single product at a single price.

This requires some strategic planning on your part to develop a profitable tour program. You have some specific goals in this planning:

- Promote tour features and highlights of your area.
- Make sure you offer an all-inclusive package.
- Present the benefits of using your services.
- Price your tour to compete with other destinations offering similar services or experiences.

- Pace the tour with your client's safety and comfort in mind.
- Stress a "quality" package.
- Pay attention to details.
- Allow flexibility in the tour program.
- Keep your customers fully informed of what they will experience on the tour.
- Develop a fair refund and payment schedule.
- Be unique
- Make sure your tour package is profitable.

Sample List of Tour Services

Basic Services

- Airport "meet and greet"
- Airport Limo Service
- Local Sight-seeing service
- On-site representative for a domestic or international tour company
- Escorting and managing the group tour
- Providing well trained interpretive tour guides

Day Programs

- Shopping Tours
- Conference, event planner
- Wedding planner
- Fishing and hunting guide services
- Soft and Hard Adventures
- History, cultural
- Music programs
- Special Events
- Archaeological
- Educational workshops

Evening Programs

- Dine-around program
- Gourmet and traditional cooking classes
- Arts & Crafts shows and "hands on" workshops
- Folkloric performances
- Health/Spas
- Pilgrimages/Religious Conferences

Sample Niche Markets

- Gay & Lesbian Tours
- Student Groups
- Senior Citizens
- Special Events
- Family Reunions
- Physically disabled

Pacing and Balance for a Successful Tour Route

To plan a successful tour route, keep in mind the following - *Pacing and Balance*!

Pacing: This is the exciting, yet frustrating part of tour designing, converting the idea into a practical itinerary that works. Laying out the day-by-day program with tours, meals, and other tour components.

Balance: An important aspect of itinerary planning. Introducing a variety of activities into the tour. Even though a group may be a history tour, no one will want to study or visit historical sites the entire trip. Offer variety to balance out the tour.

Daily Itinerary Check List

One of the easiest ways to plot out an itinerary is to use a daily check list. This ensures that no days or tour features have been overlooked. For example, on Sundays or holidays, are the shops open or closed? Pace the program, considering how quickly or slowly the itinerary moves. Free days allow you and your staff to regroup and plan for upcoming next sequence of events that will be delivered by the tour guide. So often, because of a tour designer's desire to show the group everything, too much is packaged into the trip. Allow free time for your tour members to shop, wander about the community, relax, and take photos.

Associating Personality Types with the Tour Program

First, know your clients. A close liaison with the clients is essential. Find out who they are, where they come from, and their ages and sex, special interests, and the purpose of their visit. A booking form is useful for this, with spaces for all relevant information, including the desired dates and times of travel.

Men are generally a little intolerant of gardens and shopping; women generally like historical homes and shopping. Try to include tour features for both genders. Age limits walking steep steps; this may not be acceptable and could change the mood of the tour group. Special plans to be made for disabled clients; many towns issue brochures and other literature on facilities for the disabled. Keep this reference data handy. Request for your service will come from all sorts of clients requesting unique or different tour services. Perhaps it could be a mystery tour — pre and post conference or archaeology students wanting to discover new sites to dig and research.

Five Different Categories of Travelers

#1-Fearful: About 10% of the populations are very cautious, prefer domestic destinations, and often stay with family and friends. They can be appealed to by offering familiar and safe destinations and by emphasizing security. Their prime destination is home.

#2-Careful: They represent about 25% of the population and comprise half the market for group tour takers. They want familiar destinations they've heard of, worry about foreign travel, are concerned about hassles and do their research so they don't have any unpleasant surprises. They can be appealed to by suggesting escorted tours and cruises. Marketing should emphasize stress-free travel, and offerings should be to domestic and familiar international (never say foreign!) destinations. Careful travelers favor areas such as England, Hawaii, Ireland, Australia, and other areas where English is spoken.

#3-Norm: They comprise about 35% of the traveling public and mix familiar and international destinations. They are somewhat independent and therefore look for some free time on their trips. They want efficiency, low stress, and structured independence. They can be offered independent tour and city stay packages, as well as international escorted tours. They will travel on domestic escorted tours with a pre-formed group, but for camaraderie rather than security. Norms prefer destination like Mexico, Alaska, Holland, Belgium, Germany, Austria and Switzerland.

#4-Adventurers: They are 25% of travelers. They enjoy independence, foreign exotic destinations, new destinations, culture and learning. They will buy escorted tours to exotic places. Special events appeal to them, as do areas such as Hong Kong, Greece and Turkey.

#5-Daredevils: They are extreme and enjoy exotic, dangerous places. They are young at heart.

"Weaving It All Together"

Important elements in designing tour packages include the unique tour features. The objective of many destinations is to maintain their tourist position against increasing numbers of destinations which offer the same tour features and to assist in maintaining tour highlights to be included in a one day tour. To enhance a tour, the following could be included:

- Native and traditional dances
- Arts and Crafts
- Festivals
- Traditional Foods
- Museums
- Experiences "on the land"

The ITD/Tour Operator should include elements of the natural and man-made environment, festivals and events, activities, purpose-build facilities, hospitality and transport services. The highlights can be considering A-Principal Resources or B-Supporting Resources.

A-Principal resources are those which have the strongest pulling power, and usually represent the key motivating factor in the tourist's travel decision process.

B-Support resources are those which supplement a destination's principal resources and contribute to the destination's visitor appeal, but do not on their own represent a prime motive for the visit.

Creating Tour Highlights

You should take advantage of tourism resources and turn them into *Tour Highlights* to be included in marketing a well designed tour itinerary. Planning and designing tours demands researching the popularity, cost, and transportation to a destination. The planning and meals for the tours depend upon your target markets, demographics: age, income, interest and major airports with international connections. To stay ahead of your competitors, consider the Four-Way Development Plan:

- Capitalize on a natural, physical attraction.
- Capitalize on your location (staging area).
- Capitalize on your operation and/or your area's environmental reputation
- Create something out of nothing!

Image and Experience

Will your tours suggest a mental image of what the client will "experience"? The essentials of all tours include air transportation, rail, cruise ship, motor coach. Creature comforts; hotels, cabins aboard ship, well planned meals with focus on local cultures, special events; professional tour guiding; all "hidden" taxes and tipping to service staff at hotels and restaurants. Being able to negotiate rates and block space, coordinate all the intricate details of an itinerary are things that the clients take for granted. Once this segment has been completed, you start packaging the Tour Highlights (activities, special events) along with the Tour Features (transportation from their home town, first class hotel accommodations, all meals, professional local guide services, privates coaches) and last by not least full escorted by you, the International Tour Director.

Sample Tour Highlights and Marketing Features

Highlights

- Bike tours through Europe
- Jungle tours in Thailand
- Glacier and wildlife tours in Alaska
- Bus and mountain bike tours in Australia
- Winery tours to the world's best wine regions.

Features/ Components of a tour

- **Transportation (air/motor coach/cruise/rail)
- Accommodations (2,3,4,5 star rating)
- Meals (all meals included)
- Touring by professional guides
- Attractions (admission included)
- Fully escorted by professional ITD

**How to select a motor coach for tour group

First question to ask a motor coach company …………..

Charges "Am I being charged for distance by miles, or chartering for my itinerary or for a period of time?" "Am I being charged for the driver's meals and accommodations?"

When making the final decision about the transportation for your group, it's important to consider all the factors. A quality motor coach operator is one that is reliable, professional, offers outstanding customer service, meets all your needs, and is affordable. It is easy to select the cheapest option; however, this is not necessarily the best option. I recommend that you meet with the dispatchers and check out the motor coaches and note the number of the motor coach.

Here are some basic steps to follow in selecting a motor coach:

Research the company:

- Average age, type, seating capacity, and maximum
- Height clearance for their motor coaches
- Frequency of cleaning
- Bus driver uniform policy

- Policy in cases of breakdowns
- Most cost effective option for your specific situation
- Cost of additional services such as videos, music, and coach amenities

How much? Get several quotes from various carriers and ensure they meet all your requirements before signing any contracts.

Reliability is very important (get references) in a transportation provider. Look for companies that conduct themselves in a professional manner over the phone and that promptly follow up on your inquiry.

Payment and Cancellation Policies fully understand the cancellation and payment schedules before your charter a coach. Some motor coach firms provide trip insurance program that protect your deposit in the event your tour group cancel.

How safe is the Motor Coach Operator? Motor coach companies must have federal operating authority if they cross state or provincial lines and should be able to offer you proof of that authority, which is issued by the U.s. Department of Transportation (DOT) or Transport Canada. Additionally, many states and provinces require that a carrier obtain operating authority for intrastate operations.

Insurance!! Ask for proof of a valid current insurance certificate that provides a U.S. minimum of $5 million in liability insurance coverage.

Obtain carrier's U.S. DOT number. Carriers are required to have a U.S. DOT number clearly displayed and should be either five or six digits long. By using that number you can view the carrier's safety information on-line at www.safersys.org.

*Annual Inspections-*All U.S. – based motor coaches must be inspected annually. You can call the individual motor coach company to inquire about inspection, bus maintenance, and repair. Alternatively, you can look for a decal issued by the Commercial Vehicle Safety Alliance (CVSA).

*Drivers License-*All U.S. drivers are required to have a valid, current commercial driver's License (CDL), with a "passenger" endorsement printed on the license itself. CDL's are only issued after drivers have demonstrated their abilities through skills and a knowledge test.

Special Note: for long or quick-turn-around trips may require an extra driver to adhere to federal safety requirements.

Promoting Local Resources to Niche Markets

A destination's resources are what appeal to the visitor. The tour features at the core of the visitor's attractions include accommodations, food, shopping, and entertainment. Tourism tour features include natural and man made attractions.

Natural

- Flora: Forest, jungles, farms, wilderness
- Landscape: Beaches, unique land form, glacial, rain forest, mountain, islands, sand dunes, semiprecious gemstones, swamps, volcanoes
- Fauna: Birds, insects, wildlife, marine mammals, rare game
- Climate: Seasonal-spring-summer-autumn-winter, tropical
- Water: Rivers, rapids, lakes, thermal springs, ocean, waterfalls, snow & ice

Heritage & Cultural

- Religious: Shrines, mosques, cathedrals, chapels, missionaries, burial grounds, pilgrimage sites and other religions
- Heritage: forts, castles, historic building, cottages, interpretation centers, battle sites, ghost towns, mansions
- Other: dance, dress, languages, food & drink, music, art, crafts, famous residents, folklore, local traditions, archaeological sites

Events

- Festivals: Music, Jazz, Country, drams, theatre; dance, classical ballet, national folk, literature/poetry
- Tournaments: sports, horses, dogs, cars
- Business: Trade shows, agricultural, boat, spots equipment, conventions, clubs and organizations
- Other: Reenactments, carnivals, rodeos, parades, craft fairs, flower shows, contest; fishing, air, photos and celebrity visits

Activities

- Recreational: Golf course, diving sites, ski slopes, hang-gliding, surfing, whitewater rafting, hunting, off-road driving, bungee jumping, horse-trails
- Services: Retail, winter sports, art galleries, glass factory, health resorts
- Facilities: winery tours, wildlife sanctuary, game parks, botanical gardens, amusement parks, industrial tours

Services

- Transport: access to air, rail, sea, motor coach, other transport while at the destination to include; snowmobile, sail boat, stable, tour busses, mopeds, horse and carriage, bicycle
- Accommodations: Hotels, 2/3/4/5/ star, B&B, motels, campgrounds, guest ranch, farm cottages
- Reception: Information center, maps, brochures, souvenirs, interpretation, town trails, local guides, In-bound tour operators
- Food services: Bars/pubs, coffee shops, fine dining, ethnic cuisine, international cuisine, bistros
- Car rentals, banks, currency exchange, hospitals, telephones, email service, good water supply.
- Government support, political climate; safe, friendly, receptive to international clients

Three Steps to Successful Tour Planning

Step One

- Work out a route, remembering how different the view may be from a motor coach.
- Plan stops-check suitable cafes, hotels, restrooms, viewing location.
- Double check opening times, entry fees, pathways and steps.
- Prepare a list of distances and a rough timetable for your driver and guides. Allow for stops and delays. Time goes quickly so don't try to cover too much.
- Pace the tour according to age and interest of group members.

...tly done the route, carry out a preliminary reconnaissance of the entire route, recording ...ts. If you have recently done the route, this suggestion may not be necessary—but ...kly. There are new roads, new one-way streets, and restaurants open and close and ...ish, so be careful. It is better to be safe than sorry on the day of the tour.

...inary arrangements in person for coffee, meals, entry, etc. Check costs and how the should ...

Is there a parking free? Some tourist attractions charge at the gate before you can park; others allow free parking so that those not interested can sleep or go for a walk instead.

Prepare visual aids you may like to show to the group, perhaps an old photograph to compare with the present view.

If needed, create and duplicate handouts, maps, etc. or collect materials from the local tourist board for distribution to the group.

Step Three

Return home and prepare commentary summaries on cards for reference. If you already have these on file from previous excursions, re-read and update them if you have not done that tour recently. Make a point to inform your staff and drivers of all changes and that they have copies of your routes and rest stops.

Avoid These Tour Operator Mistakes

- Selection of bad hotels, hotel in wrong locations, hotel amenities not conducive to leisure travelers
- Motor coaches without air conditioning, restrooms, or those with mechanical problems
- Step-on-guide rude, indifferent, not knowledgeable about their city/country
- Pacing of tour too fast or to slow
- Meals, restaurant under staff, food poor quality and lack of choices
- No evening activities-(optional touring)
- Too many clients on one tour
- ITD not trained
- Destination not safe
- Airline not non-stop to the destination's hub city
- Cruise line oversold

The list can go on. That is the reason a good designer seeks quality service and that the tours appeals to the customer's particular interests. To avoid the list of "mistakes" and plan a flawless tour, it is recommended that the tour designer/planner conduct a Pre-Tour Site Inspection that they visit the destination to obtain first-hand experience to see attractions and to evaluate the tour features and tour highlights being offering in the tour programs.

Inspecting a Destination or Cruise Ship

Why participate in a FAM Tour-Site Inspection? The Tour Operator who may be responsible for designing their tour programs one to two years in advance should have a thorough understanding of what a destination has to offer. The purpose of the site-inspection is to review what the destination has to offer, without a clear understanding of how these resources fit together or what the destination could realistically hope of offer your clients. The responsibility of assessing the destination tourism potential (i.e. resource quality, accessibility and pulling (marketing) power is often overlooked in favor of the more immediate and glamorous activity of advertising and promotion. Evaluating your travel purveyors is an important step for the tour designer in the development process. Conducting site inspections helps identify weak links in services, accommodations, meal plans, local transportation, and interpretive guide services.

Introduction to "Traditional Touring"

Motor coach Touring: Motor coach touring has a significant impact on the tourism industry. As a rule of thumb, one overnight motor coach tour generates approximately $7,000 per day to the economy. Motor each tour passengers have traditionally been seniors or 50+ but this has expanded recently with the growth in specialized tours like theatre and soft adventure. Indeed, charter passengers are of all ages, usually brought together by a specific event or a common interest (country & western music tour or casino trips). Sample duties of the ITD while escorting motor coach tours:

- Check group in & out of hotel rooms
- Selecting safe /clean rest stops
- Confirm dinning arrangements (other than 'fast foods") while en-route
- Planning festive/theme dinners (i.e., welcome, farewell, anniversaries, birthdays, and folkloric presentations)
- Confirming hotel accommodation
- Carry out tour group hotel check-in's
- Selecting and confirming 'Step-On-Guide" Services
- Review daily itinerary with
- Tour Group
- Assisting motor coach driver with directions
- Inspect the cleanness of the motor coach prior to morning departures
- Providing entertainment (music, videos, "touch down pools" and other forms of entertainment)
- Prepare reports for the sponsors of the group tour
- Conduct site-inspections field reports
- Collect comment sheet from clients

Welcome to the Cruise Industry

A cruise can be part of a tour. Many tours, for example, to Greece will include four- or seven-day cruises to neighboring islands (Crete, Samos, Mykonos, etc.) Land tours can be arranged as pre- or post-cruise tours to include 2/3 night hotel accommodations, sightseeing, and a farewell dinner.

You can relax on a cruise. Your duties aboard ship are less taxing then touring via coach. Your main duty is to enjoy the cruise and make certain that your group is happy with the arrangements and with one another. The tour designer can appeal to virtually ever age bracket, taste, and budget: singles, married couples, families, retirees. An onboard amenity makes it a lot easier for the ITD to enjoy the cruise as well. The clients have a menu of choices; big band music, lectures, health clubs, computer rooms, card games, tennis, golf, bowling. The cruise lines have a very diversified and dynamic product, which makes for an excitement that is distinct from other segments of the travel-tourism industry.

> **Special Note:** Before booking your group with a cruise line, check out their services and ports-of-call by going to www.cruisecritic.com and www.cruiseopinion.com

An ITD's duties will include the following:

- Get the clients to the cruise ship on time
- Assist in the embarkation process
- Oversee baggage handling
- Hold an orientation meeting as to the facilities of the cruise ship, dining hours and other scheduled activities
- Confirm dining "seating" arrangements
- Meet with the group at specific locations and times to listen to any complaints or inform them about shore excursions or disembarkation producers
- Escort tour members on shore excursions
- Inform group about disembarking procedures
- Collect tips for purser, wait staff personnel
- Manage transfers to the coach and airport
- See clients through security and boarding process
- Manage tickets, passports
- Provide physically assist services for those who require assistance
- See that the clients return home safely by air or motor coach

Contacts for the Cruise Industry

International council of cruise lines: www.icl.org

Cruise line links:

www.cruising.org

www.cruises.tgn.com

www.seamax.com

www.travusa.com

New Trends in Tourism-"Non-Traditional Touring"

In the old-fashioned style of touring, the average traveler's perception of an escorted tour was a rush through six European countries, hectic schedules, and being confined in a motor coach with a group that didn't provide an opportunity to "break away" for free time.

Today's tours are an escorted travel experience that combines blending motor coach travel, small ships or river cruises, or trains. Today's traveler wants a more leisurely style of travel with fewer places to visit, but longer stays with local guides to facilitate and help optimize their free time. The term "tour" is slowly being replaced by the travel-tourism industry with words such as "holiday", "excursions," "vacations," "programs," and "expeditions," and "journeys."

Sample "Non Traditional" Niche Tourism

Culinary tourism

The culinary-tourism trend is being driven by the growing number of celebrity chefs in the United States and Europe. Everybody knows that you can eat well in Europe. But why stop there, when you can spend your vacation digesting the fine art of making Italian cuisine? Instead of tramping through churches, museums and shops, increasing numbers of visitors to Italy are enjoying culinary tourism: chopping and stirring, processing olives, learning how to produce wine.

Learning foreign cultures and crafts

Hands-on training is available for people whose passions lie somewhere in the broad field of arts and crafts. A growing number of trips give vacationers hands-on lessons, often with exposure to another culture overseas or in a remote locale in North America. "Art is a way to understand the culture you are visiting." Clients who are pressed for time can take their week-end getaways at resorts in rural areas of North America.

> **Special Note:** According to a study by *Business Quarterly*, travel-tourism receipts internationally, are expected to reach $8 trillion dollars in 2005, employing over 96 million people and accounting for 48% of the trade services. With such a vast income at stake, no nation can be expected to forget the tourism option.

Introduction to Eco-tours

The phrase "green is gold" is indeed true for countries which are safeguarding natural resources that can be turned into tour programs for the environmental minded traveler. Eco-tours (nature-based) are a delicate business—and a booming industry, growing up to 30% annually as natural wonders and raised environmental consciousness draw tourists. The money that they spend helps to protect the threatened wilderness.

Who is the eco-tourism traveler? Eco-tourism, a booming industry growing upwards of 30% annually, will continue to take a fair share of the $3 trillion dollar receipts, as natural wonders and raised environmental conscientiousness draw tourists. This person is an intelligent, curious, adventurous, open-minded person, with an enormous appetite for nature, who selects a tour package for the experience and not for the price alone.

The so-called nature lover will take longer trips and spend more money per day than a traveler with less interest in nature, spending an average of any where from $225 to $500 per day, depending on the destination and tour components. This is a substantial increase from the client who suggests that nature was not important to his or her choice of destination and scheduled activities.

What types of tours interest the eco-tourist? He or she could be just anyone with a respect for nature, running the gamut from those who partake of nature incidentally and those who always seek out the unusual.

To lure an eco-tourist, it is recommended to have made an inventory of your "environmental riches" such as:

- Rain forest
- Offshore cays and coral reefs

- Mountains
- Glaciers
- Wildlife
- Kayaking
- Bird Watching

Adding Eco-Tours to Your Portfolio

You can offer experiences that enable visitors to discover natural areas while preserving their integrity, and to understand, through interpretation and education, the natural and cultural sense of place. It fosters respect towards the environment, reflects sustainable business practices, creates socio-economic benefits for communities/regions, and recognizes and respects local and indigenous cultures, traditions and values.

Case Study-Africa

Question: How much is a herd of elephant's worth to a tourist?

Answer: $610,000 per year

(*Source—Kenya's Amebas Eli National Park*)

Expected net returns from park tourism are $40 per hectare (less than half an acre) versus $0.80 per hectare for agricultural use.

Tourism now accounts for more foreign exchange revenue than any other economic activity in Kenya. 25% of revenues are channeled back to local communities to maintain the parks.

New "Non-Traditional" Opportunities for the Tour Operator

Cultural/Culturally-based and heritage tourism

Learning and enrichment travel refers to vacations with authentic, hands-on or interactive learning experiences featuring themes such as adventure, agriculture, anthropology, archeology, arts, culture, cuisine, education, forestry, gardening, language, maritime, mining, nature, science, spirituality, sports, wine, and wildlife to name a few! These are the travel experiences that broaden the mind and enrich the soul.

Spa/Wellness tourism

This is the sum of all the relationships and phenomena resulting from a journey and residence by people whose main motivation is to preserve or promote their health. They stay in a specialized hotel which provides the appropriate professional know-how and individual care. They require a comprehensive service package comprising physical fitness/beauty care, healthy nutrition/diet, relaxation/meditation and mental activity/education.

Discover the "Back roads and Highways Getaways" for small tour groups

For small groups and (FITs) independent traveler, developing themes, forming partnerships between nearby industries, and emphasizing the natural strengths of highway trails, be the cultural, historic, scenic or all three. The Back roads and Highways program is a unique way of integrating both restaurateurs and local agricultural producers into the trail experience.

The trail could boast a number of fine-dining restaurants which use regional produce in their cuisine. In turn, the farmer who produces special ingredients like the vegetable featured in their dishes, offers guided tours providing visitors with an opportunity to learn more about from where their food comes from.

Other "Back Roads and Highway Getaways" titles:

- Romantic stays at elegant country inns, spas and B&B'
- Wine Tasting and gourmet dining
- Boutique/Art & Crafts shopping
- Soft adventure:
- Guided waling tour
- Biking Programs
- Paddling adventure
- Horseback riding
- Fishing Packages

Wine/Culinary tourism

This is tourism in which the opportunities for wine and/or culinary related experiences contribute significantly to the reason for travel to the destination or to itinerary planning while at the destination. A destination that boasts an official wine route and which directs individuals or groups to the region's wineries can offer low or shoulder season travel. Signs clearly marking the route can unite the region's B & Bs and small hotels and inns, annual festivals and other leisure activities, resulting in a fully integrated "highway" or "trail" product. Additional promotional strength can derive from: local history, cultures, nature and outdoor activities.

Gay and Lesbian (GLBT) Travelers

Gay and lesbian travelers are high-yield, with above-average disposable incomes and high propensity to travel. A remarkable 82% of GLBT travelers hold university degrees. According to recent research, the GLBT market in the US represents roughly 10% of the overall travel market, and hold passports in higher percentages than the nation average 84% vs. 29%.

Research confirms the GLBT spend 54, 1 billion annually. They are more affluent and a loyal affinity group and are among the most liberal in their spending: willing to spend a minimum of $5,000 USD a week per person. They have less "mouths to feed," no early school-mornings, no babysitter arrangements to make, more disposable income, and, therefore, more free time to travel.

Case Study: Agriculture Tourism

Farming communities are becoming a number one seller in many countries where rural tourism is becoming popular. It is becoming a new type of agricultural management for farmers. In view of the impact of farm income from international free trade, it is important to help farmers increase the profitability of their farms as well as to improve the quality of rural life.

Gerald Mitchell

Methodology in Developing Non-Traditional Tours

Objectives: Agri-Tourism goal is to link people with agricultural products, service and experiences. The visitor benefits by:

- Enjoying peace and tranquility
- Developing interest in a natural environment
- Avoiding overcrowded resorts and cities
- Having An inexpensive getaway
- Learning about the farming industry, lifestyle and traditions
- Having security

Visitors search for the following guarantees on an Agri-Tour:

- Location-easy to get to by air/coach/auto
- Meet & Greet – Bilingual host owners
- Private, Accommodations, w/ fireplace, B&B, Cottages, Rooms
- Exploring with local knowledgeable guide
- No hidden costs
- Safety
- No crowds

The farming community and farmer benefit, too:

- Increase earn income to the farmer
- Increase tourism revenues to the destination
- Serve as a sales outlet for both raw and value-added agricultural products.
- Enhance agriculture awareness
- Increase the community's economic potential
- Are encouraged to develop additional attractions, museums, festival and the sponsorship of special events

Sample Agri-Tourism tour offerings for one day visit

- Fee fishing
- Horseback riding
- Farm museums/Demonstrations
- Petting zoos
- Heritage Education
- Local Arts & Crafts
- Nature Trails

Tour titles for extended all inclusive tours

- Traditional Country Christmas
- Wine harvest and festival
- Flower Power
- Local Country Cooking
- Yoga-Pilates Retreat
- Wilderness Birding Expeditions
- Fly Fishing Workshops

- Coffee Plantation Tour
- Family reunions
- Tour Highlights to be included in a Agri- tour package
- Fresh farm organic meals
- Abundant vegetables and fruits
- Regional Wines
- Local Art & crafts workshops
- Classes on gardening
- Wildlife sightseeing
- Horseback Riding
- Local Music
- Fishing
- Historical attractions 10 minutes from the farm

Prerequisites to developing an Agri- tour program

- Farm, farming community-easily accessible
- Comfortable, private accommodations
- Menu based on good wholesome food
- Scenic vistas and link to other tourist attractions
- Attractive, clean free or odor
- Guest participation in special events and food/wine festivals,
- Celebration of different seasons
- Provide local educational lectures to better understand the food chain

The Farm Owner's Social Skills & Responsibilities

- Review the goals and philosophies of the whole farm family
- Identify primary manager to perform administrative duties
- Prepared to hire and train, supervise staff
- Ability to promote themselves and their farm
- Be flexible
- Excited to meet new people
- Share farm life
- Define the amount of time to market tours and improve quality of product
- Keep tourist/guest safe

Developing a Agri-Tourism – Business Plan

- Conduct thorough market research
- Have necessary resource to establish an Agri-tourism enterprise
- Attend ongoing Agri-Tourism Workshops
- Obtain necessary Insurance/Liability for guest/travel industry
- Obtain support of the local and national tourism boards

Where to find the clients?

- Identify number of tourist visit the region
- Review demographics; sex, age, marriage status,
- Mode of travel
- Activity participation

Gerald Mitchell

Marketing channels to promote Agri-Tours

- Niche markets; youth, universities, special interest groups
- Networking with community activities and other farms
- Co-op marketing with Travel Industry
- Internet
- Attend trade shows

On going Management Strategies

- Achieving a desired "experience" for tour groups
- Budget advertising cost by promoting repeat clients
- Keeping capital cost down with what is already in place
- Controlling operating costs-financial management
- Plan for additional rooms/new markets: retreats, families, weddings
- Create "Off Season" tour programs: workshops, seminars, outdoor activities, wedding, family reunions holidays

Additional Income-Promote Market Value-added products

- Herbal plants
- Coffee, Wine
- Breeding exotic animals
- Specialty meats, cheeses, flowers, pastries
- Direct Mail/catalog of product/events

What are the risk factors and disadvantages of an Agri-Tourism Program?

- A high workload -compete with main farm operations
- Loss of privacy
- Extra responsibilities
- Modest financial returns
- Liability risk
- Financial investment
- Government regulation
- Variable guest nights
- Significant time to develop a market presence
- Lack of advertising and promotional funds
- Not properly trained

Become a Niche –Tour Developer

What are your area of expertise?

Now try this assignment: Design an Eight Day Tour, including all the following:

- Title (Signature item)
- Number of days
- Tour features
- Tour highlights
- Tour itinerary (No. 1) For the promotional brochure
- Tour itinerary (No. 2) To include departure times & pick up locations

Plan a 1 to 8 day tour itinerary for your promotional brochure:

Day 1 _____   Day 5 _____
       _____   _____
       _____   _____
       _____   _____
       _____   _____

Day 2 _____   Day 6 _____
       _____   _____
       _____   _____
       _____   _____
       _____   _____

Day 3 _____   Day 7 _____
       _____   _____
       _____   _____
       _____   _____
       _____   _____

Day 4 _____   Day 8 _____
       _____   _____
       _____   _____
       _____   _____
       _____   _____

Gerald Mitchell

What time of year can you operate your tour?

In the remarks column, make note of any changes in pricing, clothing suggestions, or how the client will benefit traveling at that particular time period.

Season	No. Days	Name of Tour	Remarks
_____	_____	_____	_____
_____	_____	_____	_____
_____	_____	_____	_____
_____	_____	_____	_____
_____	_____	_____	_____
_____	_____	_____	_____
_____	_____	_____	_____
_____	_____	_____	_____
_____	_____	_____	_____
_____	_____	_____	_____
_____	_____	_____	_____
_____	_____	_____	_____

Back-up contingency plan: What if it rains?

Many tours run smoothly with never a setback. However, most tours do encounter some problems en route, and it is in these problem areas that true leadership and professionalism surfaces.

A contingency or back-up plan to keep your clients occupied and appeased is necessary. What would you do in the event of?

Bad weather _____
_____

Strike _____
_____

Hotel/Airline overbooking _____
_____

Client poorly matched with this tour _____
_____

Pricing Tours for Profit!

Saving time and money is important today. How is value measured today? It used to be measured by this formula:

Price x Quality = Value

Today the equation is different:

Price x Quality x Personalization *divided by* **Time + Energy = Value**

Consumers have no time. We live in a time-deprived society. Six in ten leisure travelers do not feel they have enough vacation time. The value of a travel agent is the agent's ability to provide a personalized travel experience at the right quality and price and most importantly, to time and energy for the customer.

Of course, the tourist can save money going online and spending hours to find the best deal in terms of price. But an ITD does the work and has the insight to match the right travel product at the right price with the traveler's appropriate needs. In fact, the value of an ITD/Tour Operator will become more enhanced in the future as the world continues to remain complicated, time deprived, and stressful. Consumers will turn to travel experts who will act as *travel concierges and consultants* – one more new role for you as an ITD!

Price is important; however, leisure travelers are looking to ITD's/Tour Operators for more. Being knowledgeable, saving time and energy, offering the best options, staying current with safety/security issues, and delivering the best value are attributes leisure travelers desire in travel agents. In fact, as a group, these qualities are much more important than price.

Increase your buying power! Network with Travel consortiums

Joining a consortium offers purchasing power, training, a help desk, high override commissions, airline ticketing, and marketing assistance.

www.uniglobe.com
www.Etravnet.com
www.wtpa.com Travel Partners Affiliates
www.iatan.org International airlines Travel Agent Network (IATAN)
www.nacta.com National Association of Commission Travel Agents (NACTA)

Resources:

U.S. Tour Operators Association- www.ustoa.com
National Tour Association   www.ntaonline.com
American Society of Travel Agents www.astanet.com

There are three important elements to pricing your tours -- questions you must ask yourself for success.

The Three "Can I" Questions

- Can I compete with established tours?
- Can I sell the tour at the price being considered?
- Can I make a reasonable profit on my investment at the price being considered?

If the answer to all three questions is positive, then you should proceed to plan your tour pricing. Of course, by this time you will have already conducted the research necessary to ensure a positive response to each *"Can I"* question and have researched your competitors' price for similar tours to tourist destinations.

We may feel that by adding distinctive elements to the proposed package (highlight tour features which are absent in the packages be offered by competitors) we can ask for a higher price by promoting this package as *"different"* from that of the competitor. However, before making this assumption, you must have tested the market to ensure sufficient numbers of people are willing to pay a little more than the going rate because of the signature items in the tour package.

Finally, if you are designing a tour for a tourism agency, you need to be aware of each tour company's policy with regard to profit margins or mark-ups. Most corporations normally set a minimum mark-up below which they may not sell a product. The profit margin on the package will be something the company should be prepared to estimate wisely. Consequently, the tour designer will have to bear in mind company policy on profit margins. A "reasonable profit" means at least the minimum margin prescribed by company policy. Of course, the higher the price of the package, the higher the profits for the tour company.

Pricing Your Tours

The challenge is to price your tours without crossing the "price breakpoint," where you price yourself out of the market. Pricing is critical to marketing strategy. Your clients (individuals, tour operators, convention planner) will consider your tour prices as the key factor in selecting your services. The difference in price must be substantial enough to capture the target market's attention and leave enough margins to make a profit. You should also figure in a certain percentage for "mistakes" and time of year; high-, shoulder-, and low-seasons should position your tour programs in relation to the "psychographic" characteristics and your competition.

Costs vs. Profits

What is your estimated annual operating cost? _____

How many tours do you need to operate to break even? _____

Number of clients needed to break even _____

Number of clients to show a profit? _____

Types of Tours You Plan to Operate

    Motor Coach $_____

    Student $_____

    Special Interest Tours (SITs) $_____

    Foreign Independent Tours (FITs) $_____

    Leisure $_____

    Commercial $_____

    Other $_____

                                      Total $_____

Don't forget to add your operating costs into your tour pricing! These include fixed costs such as rent, phones, FAX, salaries, advertising, brochures, and tour development.

Per Person Cost for Tour Features

    <u>Tour Features</u>   <u>per Person Cost</u>

1. Feature: _____   _____
   _____
   _____

2. Feature: _____ $_____
   _____
   _____

3. Feature: _____ $_____
   _____
   _____

4. Feature: _____ $_____
   _____
   _____

5. Feature: _____ $_____
   _____
   _____

6. Feature: _____ $_____
   _____
   _____

Gerald Mitchell

Group Tour Pricing & Foreign Independent (FITs)

You will need to estimate pricing according to the type of tour group you are planning:

- Couples; honeymoon
- Groups of 15 or more
- Family Plan; children
- Senior Citizens Plans
- Physically disabled
- Seasons, High, Mid, low

Services: (Priced per person double occupancy – based on 40 fully paying passengers

Instructions: Complete the costs in each category (A, B, C, etc), then add all totals.

☐ *"A" Transportation (Per Person Costs)*

	Net	Gross*	Variable
Motor coach, Limo, van:	_____	_____	_____
Cruise:	_____	_____	_____
Airline:	_____	_____	_____
Other:	_____	_____	_____
Total	_____	_____	_____

* Gross includes mark-up to cover commission for profit

☐ *"B" Accommodations*

	Net	Gross*	Variable
Hotel rooms:**	_____	_____	_____
Hotel tax:	_____	_____	_____
Vat:	_____	_____	_____
Gratuities:	_____	_____	_____
Baggage Handling in/out:	_____	_____	_____
Total	_____	_____	_____

* Gross includes mark-up to cover commission for profit
** Based on double occupancy per person per night

☐ *"C" Meals (Per Person Costs)*

	Net	Gross*	Variable
Welcome Reception:	_____	_____	_____
Farewell Reception:	_____	_____	_____
EP:	_____	_____	_____
CP:	_____	_____	_____
MAP:	_____	_____	_____
FAP:	_____	_____	_____
Tax:	_____	_____	_____
EP:	_____	_____	_____

Gratuities: _____ _____ _____
Wine & Cheese
Reception: _____ _____ _____
Lunches: _____ _____ _____
Other: _____ _____ _____
Tour features
& highlights: _____ _____ _____
    Total _____ _____ _____

Gross includes mark-up to cover commission for profit

☐   "D" Entertainment (Per Person Costs)

	Net	Gross*	Variable
Fashion Show:	_____	_____	_____
Guest Speakers:	_____	_____	_____
Night Club Show:	_____	_____	_____
Cocktail Party:	_____	_____	_____
Other:	_____	_____	_____
Total	_____	_____	_____

Gross includes mark-up to include commission for profit

☐   "E" Promotional Expenses

	Net	Gross*	Variable
Promotion:	_____	_____	_____
Postage & phone:	_____	_____	_____
Direct mail:	_____	_____	_____
Promotional Evening program:	_____	_____	_____
Advertising:	_____	_____	_____
Free trip for Organizer:	_____	_____	_____
Total	_____	_____	_____

Gross includes mark-up to cover commission for profit

Total Tour Costs: Multiply x 40 (passengers)

    Totals   A $_____
                 B $_____
                 C $_____
                 D $_____
                 E $_____

Total Net Cost per person $_____
Based on 40 full paying 40
Passengers with 1 escort $_____   *Optional expenses to be
                                                 Included in tour cost, if
<u>MARK UP 25% to 30%</u> $_____   not already figured into
                                                  Cost

Gerald Mitchell

Selling Gross Price

    (With Commissions) $_____

Single Supplement

For tourists traveling alone who have single room accommodations, you will need to perform a separate calculation.

    _____ Nights @ $ _____ per night $_____

                                                 Tax $_____

                                     Gratuities $_____

                  Total cost for single room: $_____

Minus half double rate shown in previous cost estimate   ($_____)

                                       Balance $_____

         Supplemental charge for single room $_____

                        Sell for an additional $_____

Agents/Tour Conductor Discounts

Why give the tour conductor a free or discounted trip?

The Tour Conductor, who will accompany the group from their home town, will stay with the group for the entire trip, and escort them home. Free trips for Tour Organizers are fixed costs. In many cases, the organizer will want one free trip for fifteen paid passengers. Free trips can be priced in simply by prorating them over the amount charged to the members of the group.

TIP: Cruise companies normally provide one free fare per 15 full-paying passengers. Tour companies' pricing may range from one free fare per 6 full-paying passengers to one free fare per 25 full-paying passengers.

Tour Organizer Incentives: Free or Discounted Tours

There's an old saying: "There's no such thing as a free lunch" -- and in this case, there's no such thing as a free tour. Tour organizers are expected to participate actively in exchange for their free fare. They should:

- Promotes the tour program
- Collects funds
- Manage and deliver the clients to your destination
- Act as a liaison between you and the members while on tour
- Work 24/7 to keep tour members happy
- Will continue to promote future tour programs you organize

How to Market Your Tour Programs

Four steps to promote your collateral materials include:

- *Step One* describe your trip using benefits rather than features. That is, don't just say what's included, but describe why that is a good thing for the travelers.
- *Step Two* promote mental imagery of the area to be visited. Paint pictures with words to put your prospects in the picture.
- *Step Three* is sure to hit the "hot buttons" of your travelers, depending on their travel style. For example, use words like "safe, secure and helpful" with "free time, activities" for Adventurers.
- *Step Four*, reinforce pre-existing positive images. That is, if you know your prospects associate a particular destination with fabulous scenery, make sure you play up this aspect in your collateral material.

Finding Clients

By the use of *"The Four P"* method, *prospecting, profiling, perseverance and payoff works!*

The sales department needs to find the right kind of customers or prospects -- whether it means going to their communities, church groups, or clubs, or getting lists from realtors. Then they do profiling to understand lifestyles, demographics, age groups, and income groups. By perseverance, they market with mailings, calls to action, and sales tools. Then they go back to the point of the marketing, making sure they promote the right kind of products, brands, styles and standards to the right audience. In order to promote your tours, you should:

- Have been in business for at least one year, with a proven track record of safe and professional operation;
- Provide contracted wholesale net rates to tour operators, travel wholesalers and retail travel agents. As a general guideline, requirements are 15% off retail for activities and transportation and 20-30% off retail for accommodation;
- Provide detailed pricing and program information to tour operators, travel wholesalers and retail travel agents at least one year in advance of selling season, e.g., May 2006 for the summer/fall 2007 season;
- Communicate and accept reservations by telephone, fax or email. Provide same-day confirmation of booking arrangements;
- Set up billing arrangements with the operator, agency or receptive tour operator. Accept client vouchers as confirmation of booking arrangements;
- Carry adequate business liability insurance;
- Provide support (free or at reduced rates) for international media and FAM tours; and
- Hold all appropriate operating licenses.

Promoting and advertising tours can be accomplished by using the following methods:

- Tour Brochures (mail out to groups and organizations, travel agents)
- Newspapers (Sunday Travel Section)
- Billboards (Busy traffic routes)
- Press releases (Guest speakers, new additions to the staff, new tour programs)
- Newsletters (Banks, corporations, organization newsletter-travel section)
- World Wide Web, e-commerce,
- Cruise Parties (guest speaker from the cruise lines which supply film and discount coupons and prizes)

- Travel Seminars (guest speakers on new destinations or cruises)
- Wine & Cheese receptions (to be included in all travel promotions programs)
- Post-Tour photo exchange parties (post-tour parties "Invite their friends")
- Wholesaling tours through the retail travel agents (Offer the Travel Agencies 10%/15% commission on scheduled tours)
- Promoting tours in nationwide print magazines i.e. A great publication for exciting unusual and adventure tour, such as Specialty Travel Index -- www.specialtytravel.com

Designing Your Promotional Brochure

Your tour brochure should literally "jump" from the agency's brochure rack into your prospective client's hands! There is a great deal of information you can include, but some items *must* be included to ensure that your clients' expectations match the tours you will provide.

General Information & Terms and Conditions

Suppliers and operators dealing with the traveling public must provide clear and concise information on all conditions affecting the provision of their product. These should be communicated in written form and provide the following information:

- A thorough description of what is included in the program
- All features and highlights should be listed and it should be noted whether or not they are included in the price quoted
- An indication of what periods the prices are quoted
- A clear description of payment procedures for deposit requirements, final payments, and cancellation procedures and charges.
- The pricing, such as single room charges or others should be spelled out
- Waivers—any conditions outlining responsibility must be clearly expressed in exact terms
- Insurance—any specific insurance requirements must be detailed exactly

Layout of a Tour Brochure

Page One

- Front cover with company logo
- Signature item
- Name of destination
- Sponsoring organization
- Tour date (optional)

Pages Two and Three

- Tour highlights
- Tour features
- Map
- General information about the destination
- Information about the company (optional)

Page Four

- Sample day by day itinerary
- Tour itinerary

Page Five

- Tour dates and cost
- Responsibility clause
- Tour conditions
- General tour information, terms and conditions

Brochure Supplement: Tour information form

Format

The brochure cover is your billboard to invite curiosity and invite your clients to look at the following pages.

Pages Two and Three set the tone. They contain an overview of the Tour Highlights and Tour Features. The tour brochure acts as your silent salesman, intriguing the prospective client with product benefits before spelling out the cost.

Page Four should contain a sample itinerary, meal plan, qualifications, and specialty of your tour escort. This should emphasize the delights of the package tour before going onto

Page Five should outline the tour conditions, price, visa, or passport requirements.

Page Six or a supplement to the tour brochure is a means of "closing" the sale. A coupon, return envelope or application should be attached.

Don't forget to print in bold:

- For additional information or reservations, contact: (Your name)
- Collect calls or toll free
- web site, email address
- Who to make the check out to
- Deposit and/or final payment schedule

Remember, once you have decided what to say and to whom you wish to say it, you must know how to present the information in an interesting and compelling manner. Here is where the creativity is a must. By "spotlighting the unique differences" such as attractive graphics, maps, and local artwork you can enhance a plain brochure into one that is successful and eye catching.

Prospective clients want the necessary facts rather then generalities. People want to know what they are getting for their money. Be direct, simple, yet appealing.

Your tour brochure design is a choice you and your staff must make. Decisions should be based on your markets, destinations, and your budget.

Gerald Mitchell

Tour Operator's Company Logo

"Your logo can help your company gain instant recognition!"

This is your signature, company logo, or emblem. It may merely be your company name in distinctive type or it could be a piece of art which includes the company designation. Whatever you choose should be pertinent, attractive, readable and flexible. Consider how it will look in an ad, on letterhead, on your window, or luggage or on brochures. Try to be original and distinctive.

Sample logo for your company

What is the name of your company?
_____

What does the name represent?
_____

"Sketch out some ideas for your company logo"

Global Tours

Leader in Global Journeys

Name your tours with your "signature"

What "Brand/Signature" names can you come up with for your tour packages?

Samples:

- *Winter Wilderness Vacation*
- *Arctic Safari*
- *Arctic Escape*
- *Husky Expedition*
- *Cultural Crossroads*
- *Cross-Country Trekking*
- *Home of the Fascinating Discoveries and Cultures*
- *Unique Activities in the Last Frontier*
- *Cultural Connection*
- *There is a Land of Mystery--Indonesia*
- *Treasures and Adventures of the Caribbean*
- *Safari for all Seasons and Reasons*

Name and brand your tours and services:

_____   _____
_____   _____
_____   _____
_____   _____
_____   _____
_____   _____

The Tour Designer Signature

The genuine tour designer is a true renaissance individual, much more than someone who merely throws together a basic tour together with transportation and accommodations or offers their clients a pre-packaged tour from the agency's rack. The tour designer includes interesting themes and psychological needs of the client.

By understanding the clientele for which he or she is designing, the tour designer is able to convey the proper ingredients into a rich, vibrant, exciting tour.

"Sample tour highlights"

Cruise the Spice Islands via private yacht   *Wine Your Way through France*
Skiing expedition through Finland   Costa Rica—Unspoiled Adventure
Dive Paradise! The Caribbean   California—Behind the Scenes

"Sample Tour Features"

All meals included in tour   *Hotel and Tent accommodations*
Fully escorted   *licensed tour guide*
Transportation via private coach   *Meet and Greet Service*

_____   _____
_____   _____
_____   _____
_____   _____
_____   _____
_____   _____

Here are two examples of contracts between the Tour Operator and the Client that should be present in all promotional materials and at time of reservations.

Special note: Be sure the ITD carries copies in their "trip kits" at all times.

_____*Exhibit "A" Sample Terms and Conditions*_____

Prices

These are quoted in dollars (US/Canadian) and are based on the cost per person sharing twin accommodations. Single accommodations can be provided at an additional charge of $60 per person per night. Pricing will remain unchanged during the validity shown except for any element of air transportation, which may be affected by later uncontrollable fuel price escalation.

Included in the Tour Price

All prices include roundtrip airfare from the cities listed, airport transfers, accommodations and three meals per day, and all items listed on the trip's itinerary.

Not included in Tour Price

- Items of personal nature
- Optional excursions not specified in the itinerary
- Seasons
- (List dates you operate tours)
- Departures
- (List from what city/community your tours depart)
- Returns
  "The company will not accept responsibility should flights be missed."

- Baggage
  "25 lb. (12 kilograms), plus photographic equipment within reason, is the maximum allowable baggage, and gear should be packed in one soft luggage bag of your choice. Tour Operators will not be responsible for the carriage of baggage exceeding this limitation nor for storage in the event of offloading. Arrangements for onward forwarding or storage of additional baggage must be made through your travel agent, airline or hotel of last departure."

- Deposits
  "A 20% non-refundable deposit is required to book. Final payment is due thirty-five days prior to departure."

- Groups
  "There is a special tariff for groups of 10 or more passengers."

- Clothing and accessories

Recommendations

List recommended photography suggestions as to equipment, film speed and pictures to be taken.

Cancellations Policy

If a booking is cancelled, the company reserves the right to retain the full deposit of 20%. If a booking is cancelled less than 21 days before departure, the Company retains the full deposit and in addition a cancellation fee will be charged as follows:

- Under 21 to 15 days notice: 45% of the total fare
- Under 15 to 7 days notice: 60% of the total fare
- Under 7 days notice: 80% of the total fare

Passports and Visas

It is the responsibility of the client or the travel agent to ensure that passports and visas are valid for the countries visited.

Curio Shops

In most communities, a limited range of more popular film is stocked along with safari accessories, wildlife books, locally manufactured artifacts and handicrafts.

Acceptance of Credit Cards

Major credit cards are accepted

Airline Clause

The carriers concerned are not to be held responsible for any act, omission or event during the time passengers are not aboard the aircraft or conveyance. The passenger ticket to use by the airline concerned when issued shall constitute the sole contract between the airline concerned and the purchase of these tours and/or the passenger.

Responsibility Clause

(Name of tour operator), your travel agent, operators of the tours and /or suppliers of services acting only as agents for the supplier advise you to be aware that during your participation in a tour, certain risks and dangers may arise including, but not limited to, the hazards of traveling in either the country of origin, destination or through passage, in undeveloped areas, travel by boat, aircraft or other means of conveyance, the forces of nature, political unrest or other military action and accident or illness in remote regions without means of rapid evacuation or medical facilities. Also be aware and clearly understand that (Name of tour operator) will not have liability regarding provision of medical care or the adequacy of any care that may be rendered and cannot accept any responsibilities for losses or additional expenses due to delay or changes in air schedules or other causes. All such losses or expenses will be the responsibility of the member of the tour, as the rates provided re for the arrangement only at the time stated. It is understood that (Name of tour operator) will use their best efforts to ensure that all adequate measures are taken to avoid such occurrences. The right is reserved to make minor adjustments to the itinerary and the right is reserved to cancel any tour prior to departure. (Name of tour operator) may not be held responsible for any loss or damage to luggage, before, during or after the tour program. The acceptance of final vouchers or tickets shall be deemed to be consent to the above conditions. Passengers will voluntarily participate in these activities with the knowledge of the dangers involved and therefore agree to accept any risks.

The Company may, at its discretion, and without liability or cost to itself at any time, cancel or terminate the passengers booking, and particular without limiting the generality of the foregoing, it shall be entitled to do so in the event of the illness or the illegal or incompatible behavior of the passenger, who shall in such circumstances not be entitled to any refund.

Exhibit "B" Sample Terms & Conditions-Effective January 2006

This sample shows the terms the GEM Group uses for tours.

Itinerary: The itinerary is the written travel schedule prepared by The GEM Group, Ltd., listing the scheduled daily activities and itemizing the travel services purchased, including, but not limited to, hotel accommodations, prepaid meals, and prepaid transportation, including self-driven vehicles and vehicles with a driver, sightseeing tours, and prepaid entertainment. In the event of a difference between the information contained in the brochure and that contained in the itinerary prepared for and delivered to the Purchaser, the language of the itinerary shall control.

Tour Voucher: Coupons delivered to Purchaser with the itinerary as part of the tour package constitute evidence of prepayment by Purchaser for various travel services. These vouchers may be exchanged on arrival for payment vouchers, representing the same services. The GEM Group, Ltd. is bound by only the terms, conditions, and representations, if any, which are contained on the vouchers it delivers to the Purchaser.

Tour Package Price: The price of the tour package includes all of the prepaid travel services represented by the vouchers provided to the Purchaser, together with the charges by The GEM Group, Ltd. for services in preparing the itinerary.

Until payment in full is received from the Purchaser, the cost represented by the vouchers are subject to change, without advance notice, due to fluctuations in the tariff, exchange rates, and other charges beyond The GEM Group, Ltd. Control and may result in a change of price to the Purchaser.

Price does not include charges for passports, visa, inoculations, laundry, liquor, soft drinks and beverages, cover charges, excess baggage charges, travel cancellation or interruption, accident, and baggage insurance, expenses for guides or transportation not included in the itinerary, optional tours, any items of a personal nature, any items not specifically listed as included, all international departure taxes, and International fares.

The GEM Group, Ltd. accepts personal checks, Visa, and MasterCard.

Cancellation by Traveler or Tour Participants: After the deposit has been received and the reservation is confirmed, cancellation by Purchaser of the entire tour package is subject to a basic cancellation charge of $200.00 per traveler or tour participant.

Cancellation within forty-five (45) days of the scheduled departure date is subject to a charge of $200.00 per person in addition to a basic cancellation charge stated above.

Any charges levied by any of the providers of travel services as cancellation charges will be added to the cancellation charges made by The GEM Group, Ltd.

Purchaser's failure to appear at the time of departure without prior written notice will result in a cancellation charge equal to 100% of the tour price.

For cancellation charges levied by airlines, refer to airfare fuels or contact your airline.

Refunds: In the absence of exceptional circumstances, no refunds are given for any unused prepaid services included the tour package or any changes made in the itinerary while en route, including, without exception, changes in hotel accommodations, sightseeing excursions, and transportation services. Charges included for services provided by The GEM Group, LTD or Agents or Travel Suppliers are not subject to refund.

A request for refund must be accompanied by a statement settings forth the claimed exceptional circumstance, the reason for the change in the itinerary, the change made in the itinerary, the reason for the failure to utilize the service provided, the item for which a refund is provided, the item for which a refund is requested, the unused vouchers, and receipts for the alternative services utilized, if any.

Changes In Itinerary By The Gem Group, Ltd.: A GEM Group Tour reserves the right to make changes in the suppliers of services included on the itinerary, including changing carriers and substituting similar hotel accommodations for those designated in the itinerary, where such are made necessary by circumstances beyond the control of The GEM Group, Ltd.

Custom Tour Packages: The custom itinerary is to be reviewed by Purchaser upon receipt for compliance with Purchaser's requests and exceptions and to inform The GEM Group of any changes deemed necessary. Purchaser's failure to request changes from The GEM Group, Ltd. in writing, constitutes Purchaser's representation to The GEM Group, Ltd. that the itinerary meets the Purchaser's expectations and requests.

Payment by Purchaser constitutes absolute confirmation that the itinerary meets traveler's requests and expectations.

Changes in the itinerary by Purchaser, after confirmation of reservation to Purchaser or payment in full has been received by The GEM Group, Ltd., will result in a service charge of $50.00 for each change requested and may result in a change in the tour price.

Release: Group organizer, travelers, and tour participants, individually and jointly, release The GEM Group, Ltd. from any and all liability and responsibility, known or unknown, present or future, for any and all loss, injury to person, damage to property, or accident, or which may be the result of any delay or change of itinerary, or irregularity connected with the tour package purchased, which is beyond its control, including but not limited to, acts of God, transportation problems, fire, machinery or equipment malfunction or failure, government actions, wars, civil disturbance, labor disputes, riots, thefts, sickness, or weather, and which includes all expenses or damages, direct or consequential, claimed or sustained by group organizers, tour participants, or travelers, who waive their individual rights and waive all claims against The GEM Group, Ltd. based on any claim of negligence by any of the suppliers of services included in the tour package. This release is binding upon group organizers, tour participants, travelers, their representatives, heirs, and assigns.

Travel Documents: Questions concerning detail of visa requirements and formalities of obtaining passports and supporting documents are the responsibility of the traveler.

Deposits and Final Payments: A deposit of $100.00 per person is required at the time travel arrangements are requested. The GEM Group, Ltd. must receive final payment of the total price of the tour package. No later than 45 days prior to departure.

Acceptance of and Fees for late Reservations: Provided that The GEM Group, Ltd. has received full payment for all included services, reservations for travel arrangements will be accepted up to seven days before departure. Fees for late reservations for travel arrangements are not assessed; however, extraordinary expenses incurred in processing such late billing will be charged to Purchaser.

Important Notice: The GEM Group, Ltd. reserves the right to cancel a tour prior to its start, in which case, its liability shall be limited to the refund of all monies paid by purchaser.

Gerald Mitchell

The GEM Group Ltd.
PO Box 21199
Charleston, South Carolina, USA
www.thegemgroup.org
gerry@shelovestotravel.com

Insurance Coverage

Don't forget to offer insurance coverage on all tours and cruises- Have the clients sign a form acknowledging they were offered the option to take the insurance and provide a copy to the ITD who will be escorting the tour/cruise.

In the interest of preventive legal planning, the Destination Management Firm or Tour Company should consult with their attorney to discuss contracts and review the necessary insurance coverage and the preparation of a responsibility clause for any tour brochures that are scheduled for distribution. The firm should be aware of the importance of liability protection, errors and omissions coverage, and the way to lessen risk against such things as travel suppliers' (airlines, hotels, tour companies) defaults, employees' illness or accident on tour, and the travel suppliers who do not live up to their contracts and commitments.

Liability Insurance

Liability insurance protects the firm in the event a tour member hurts him/herself and claims negligence, or if the transportation company carrying the group is involved in an accident or death. It is recommended that the tour group be named as a rider to the insurance policy for the duration of a specific trip.

Errors and Omissions Insurance

Errors and omissions insurance, or "E & 0" as it is often called in the travel industry, is equivalent to malpractice insurance. It protects the firm in the event staff or an outside contractor makes an error causing a client hardship and expense. There will be occasions where the tour did not live up to the client's expectations, and they will bring suit against the firm for the selection of a hotel or for having used poor judgment. Even if the destination travel firm is in the right, the cost of legal defense can be extremely high. Having the errors and omissions insurance company attorney work to settle such problems can prove invaluable.

Additional List of Services to Include in your Promotional Brochure

- Area served: Region or state
- Climate: Weather conditions for destination sites
- Equipment: Auto, motor coaches, boats, other
- Specialty: Nature based tours, historical tours, etc.
- Driver Guides: Services which are performed in English or language of their choice, licensed driver/guides
- Interpreters: French, German, Hebrew, Dutch, Spanish, and Japanese. List languages and rates (minimum of four hours). Meet and Greet service available in same languages.

In separate cover letter for travel agents or tour organizers, list the following:

- Commission to Travel Agent: (Do you pay standard 10%/12%/15% commission to Travel Agents?)
- Complimentary tours (1 free per 15 fully paying clients)

List group rates:

Number of passengers: 1-55 $_____

Number of passengers: 16-20 $_____

Season rates: All destinations have Low, Shoulder, High and Black out periods and should quote rates accordingly.

Special Note: You can design tours with the "no season ever the same" concept by creating unique experiences, opportunities that encourage the visitor to make reservations with your firm year round.

Chapter 10
Sample Tour Programs

Charleston-Awards & Honors

- Charleston, SC was ranked the number one safest and culturally most fascinating city in the US by *TravelSmart*.
- Among the "World's Best Unspoiled Destinations" -- *National Geographic Traveler*
- Charleston, South Carolina, named America's "most mannerly city" for 10th consecutive year -- Etiquette expert Mirabelle Young Stewart
- *Travel+Leisure* ranked Charleston the 8th "Top City in the United States & Canada"
- Charleston, SC area named a "Top 10 Art Destination in the USA " -- *American Style* magazine
- "Charleston is still an uncrowned city of human scale, where church steeples remain the highest points. As Emily Whaley says of her garden, this is a place to let your soul catch up with you." -- *Conde Nast Traveler*
- "The soul of horse drawn carriages. Mansions dressed up and looking almost bejeweled with their wrought iron terraces and gates. Secret alleys lit by flickering lamps. Charleston may well be the most romantic of cities." -- *National Geographic*
- "In my opinion there is nowhere in America which expresses the European appeal as much as Charleston, South Carolina. From the English to the Spanish influence it gives the city the most unique feeling in America."

Charleston's Spa, Culture, and Gourmet Tour

She Loves to Travel © . . . and shop, explore, dine & dance

Your personal four day (Thursday-Sunday, Monday-Thursday) Charleston, SC itinerary

Day One

- Arrival Meet & Greet at airport
- Managers cocktail party

- *Sunset evening tour* by horse-drawn carriage-Your guide will introduce you to Charleston's rich-history, from plantation culture, architecture, infused with European and Afro-Caribbean influences.
- *Welcome dinner reception* at High cotton, Maverick bar & Grill. A first class, high-spirited, living large atmosphere. Mahogany woodwork, old brick walls, evokes feeling of warmth and well-being. The food is hearty and robust featuring meat, game and fresh fish from the Low country.

Day Two

Breakfast with Storyteller Tim Lowry: "Priceless". "Authentically Southern!" This is what people are saying about storyteller Tim Lowry's interactive one-man show featuring ghost stories, Civil War tales, Low-country legends, and Gullah tales.

After breakfast we'll take a walking culinary Tour of Charleston:

Nationally recognized food expert, Amanda Dew Manning, shares her knowledge of the historical and cultural perspectives of her home state's distinctive cuisine. "Amanda tells rich, wonderful food stories about the South. I have had listeners tell me that they could almost smell the cornbread or taste the relish as Amanda describes it-that's a real accomplishment for radio," says Libby Hoyle, Clemson University professor and host of a weekday south Carolina public radio show. The culinary tour features chefs who take pride in the state's culinary history. The tour makes tasting stops at local restaurants, specialty shops, artisan bakeries, and chocolatiers. Amanda Dew Manning, a nationally known nutritionist has served on the National Board of the American Institute of Wine and Food, serves as your guide.

Optional tours

- Tour the harbor, cruise by sailboat
- French Quarter Art Tour
- Plantation tours
- Religious Tour
- Canoe & Kayak Tour
- Fishing charters

<u>Evening</u> Hotel Manager's cocktail party – then explore Charleston on your own. Your private guide will advise you of the "best places" to dine.

Day Three

Breakfast: Morning Introduction to the NIA Program: "Promoting holistic wellness. A non-impact aerobic form of systemic exercise. It provides an effective cardiovascular workout that is soothing and strengthening to muscles and joints while enhancing balance. Based on a variety of movement forms: Tai Chi, Yoga, Tae Kwon Do, Aikido, modern, ethnic, jazz and Duncan dance. www.nia-nia.com

Afternoon: After lunch, meet with your private tour guide for a special tour of the antique and French quarters of Charleston

Evening: Manager Cocktails

Dinner: Farewell Low Country Dinner at **Charleston Cooks!** Here's a chance to watch and learn …and, of course eat! Famous chefs demonstrate a variety of cuisines and recipes from the Low

Country. "Uptown/Downtown south' cuisine, Magnolia's combines old world charm with contemporary excitement,

Day Four: Hotel breakfast. Transfer to the airport via private limo service departure for home

She Loves to Travel ©

To Charleston

Tour Features & Highlights

What is included in your four-day tour:

Services
- Meet & Greet at airport
- Airport transfers-private limo service

Hotel Accommodations
- First Class (based on double or single rates)
  - Baggage handling
  - Hotels taxes, tips

Meals
- Breakfast each morning
- Two dinner receptions
- Hotel Managers cocktail party

Fully escorted touring
- Carriage tour
- Antique shopping Tour
- Southern Hospitality Culinary Tour

Guest speakers & Guides
- NIA-Instructor
- Tim Lowry, Low Country -Story Teller
- Fully escorted by GEM Tour Guides

"Free Time" in Charleston

Shopping

One of the things that make the Charleston area a veritable shopper's paradise is the variety of shops and vendors. Of course, when there is diversity in the kind of places that you can shop, there is diversity in the kind of things you can buy. Classic Georgian furniture, Victorian jewelry, and antebellum maps are just a few of the things that are waiting to be discovered in the area's antique shops. For the art lover, there are watercolors depicting low country scenes.

Gerald Mitchell

<u>Fine Arts</u>

American Style named Charleston one of the top 10 art destinations in the United States. A variety of art galleries surround the museums in the historic district.

Plantations and Gardens

Columned plantations houses, oak line lanes, splendid gardens and remnants of tidal rice impoundments are just some of the offerings of the region's numerous plantations and gardens that are open regularly for tours. Each property offers a different perspective and interpretation of the area's antebellum culture.

Fine Dining

"I can sit in my house and see a dozen chefs go by in their whites" Ms. Dupree, who is a best-selling cookbook author and the founder of southern Cooking movement, feels the "Southern city for food."

Possibly one of the first American cities to enjoy a distinctive regional cuisine, Charleston has many influences. On menus around town, guests will notice French, Mediterranean, Vietnamese and other international tastes. Charleston has long enjoyed scrumptious local vegetables, Carolina gold rice and just about any fresh catch in the sea. Such local ingredients are transformed into dishes with tastes all their own. Chefs are dressing up grits, putting a new spin on green tomatoes and serving up seafood with a twist. . Charleston claims many delicacies of its own and area restaurants have been using these delicacies to dazzle in the new Southern way.

Charleston Nightlife

For a laugh-out-loud evening, locals crowd Theatre 99 to see The Have Nots! a high-energy improvisational comedy troupe. The venue stages plays and musical acts throughout the year. Charleston's nightlife also includes a range of bars, microbreweries and eateries including several cocktail spots that feature live music six nights a week. If you see fliers around town announcing *shag* contests, stop in to watch loose limbed locals perform the official state dance

Terms and conditions:

Deluxe accommodations: $859.00 per person, based on double occupancy
Single rate upon request
Minimum number of clients: 15
Maximum: 20 + 1 escort
Tour Dates:

Global Tours

Classic Spanish La Rioja & Ribera del Duero Wine Journey

Tour Highlights and Tour Features Include:

- All Transportation and Transfers for 8 full days (unless otherwise indicated): For 12 People, by Mercedes Coach.
- Bilingual English-Spanish Guide, specialized in food and wine

- Accommodation for 7 nights in charming, very luxurious 4 & 5 star hotels, and a castle in wine country, double occupancy with private bath
- Minimum 7 VIP Winery Visits with Exclusive Cellar visits and Premium Wine Tasting of best wines
- Champagne Aperitif in VIP Area at 5* Star Hotels
- 5 Lunches with Wine (Tapas and formal sit down venues)
- 4 Gastronomic Dinners with Wine
- 7 Full breakfasts
- Bottled water, juice, soft drinks and snacks throughout the journey
- Keepsake Bound Itinerary with Wine Maps, City Profiles, Shopping Tips, etc of the destinations on your tour
- Keepsake menus, signed by the chefs
- Gourmet Gift on arrival in your room
- Various Wine Gifts
- All Activities Described in Itinerary (visit to the wine museums, castles, etc)s
- All Local Taxes

Introduction to the La Rioja and Ribera del Duero region

The Spanish wine regions of La Rioja and Ribera del Duero are two of the most famous and prestigious wine producing areas in the world. Wine Tours of these two regions can easily be combined with a fabulous city break to the buzzing Spanish capital of Madrid. This unique wine tasting journey takes in VIP private winery visits to such renowned estates as Pesquera and Marques de Riscal, not to mention a host of other smaller, interesting boutique wine producers such as Remirez de Ganuza. Apart from wine tasting, you'll enjoy delicious regional cuisine in charming, cozy restaurants; you'll sleep in luxurious inns and wine hotels and visit breathtaking monuments such as a 13th century Gothic Cathedral and an amazing crusader castle, perfectly shaped like a battleship and now home to a wine museum.

This Luxury Spanish Wine Tour begins in Madrid, Europe's best-kept secret. While Barcelona attracts a horde of tourists, Madrid is thankfully free of crowds. The Bourbon barrio, reminiscent of Paris architecturally, is gorgeous and you will enjoy a gastronomic walking tour of Madrid's most beautiful sights, sipping wine and munching on tapas on the way. After a few days of culture and shopping in Madrid, you'll begin your wine journey through the castle-studded region of Castile and the lovely vine-covered region of La Rioja. Highlights include: sipping wine in 15th century caves, sleeping in a castle, vineyard walks, private visits with winemakers (depending on time of year, you can participate in the harvest, pruning or other vineyard tasks) and above all the memorable meals of slow cooked roast lamb and peppers paired with magical wines, in delightful wine country restaurants. If you love Spanish wine and want a unique luxury holiday, this is it!

Day One

- Arrive Madrid, transfer by luxury Mercedes/ coach from the airport to your centrally located hotel, a converted palace dating back to the 1800's.
- Free afternoon in Madrid to catch up on your sleep, go shopping, have lunch, etc.
- Early evening Walking Tour of Madrid's historic Bourbon and Hapsburg quarters, to take in: The Royal Palace, Opera House, The Puerta del Sol, the Gran Via, Cibeles and Correos, Neptune's fountain, etc.
- The gastronomic walking tour will include: Champagne aperitifs, and various wines and tapas dishes such as smoked cod, spicy peppers, Bellota (acorn fed) ham, Spanish omelet, octopus, calamari and even paella. Wines by the glass from Rueda, Toro, Penedes and Jerez.

Late evening on your own to enjoy Madrid's nightlife, flamenco shows, etc

Gerald Mitchell

Day Two:

- Full Breakfast at Hotel in pretty room overlooking Opera House
- Free day on your own to enjoy the Prado Museum (classic painters such as Velazquez, Goya, El Greco Tiziano, Zurbaran, Murrillo, etc) and the Reina Sofia (Modern painters such as Picasso, Dali and Miro), etc
- In Madrid, there is also excellent shopping for top quality shoes, clothes, leather, perfumes, artisan ceramics and glassware, olive wood, and the best gourmet products Spain has to offer (virgin olive oils, wine vinegars, saffron, smoked paprika, etc)
- Tonight, dinner will be a night to remember: a Gourmet six course feat with wine matching at new avante garde restaurant in Madrid's charming Malasaña barrio

Day Three:

- Full breakfast Full Breakfast at Hotel in pretty room overlooking Opera House
- From Madrid, we will make our way north to the luscious red wine region of Ribera del Duero, where we will spend two wonderful nights at a hotel amid the vines, and take in various VIP winery visits to such famed cellars as Ismael Arroyo (with its 15th century wine caves), La Pesquera, Condado de Haza and Alion (owned by Vega Sicilia).
- First Winery visit, followed by typical Castilian lunch at a beautiful restaurant overlooking the Duero river, Second VIP winery visit and afternoon to relax at our 5* Wine Hotel (where we will have the option to enjoy vineyard walks before dinner).
- Dinner on your own at the highly esteemed restaurant at the wine hotel, Ribera del Duero.

Day Four:

- Full Breakfast at Hotel
- From Ribera del Duero - we'll visit a famed cellar such as Abadia Retuerta for a private tour and wine tasting. Before lunch, we'll visit the Ribera del Duero wine museum, located in a stunning castle in the vast plains of Castilla y Leon. The sommelier will lead us through a tasting of various local wines and we'll have free time to enjoy the museum and the views form the castle's ramparts.
- Lunch will be waiting for us in a medieval village below, in a typical "Asador", with a lunch to include roast lamb, slow cooked in ancient wood-fired ovens, unforgettable!
- The late afternoon will include an excursion to a pretty village nearby and we can even visit an excavated site of Roman mosaics.
- Dinner on your own at the hotel or taxi to a tavern in the village

Day Five:

- Full buffet breakfast in the castle
- From Ribera del Duero, we'll head northeast to the hillier, lovely wine region of La Rioja. We will enjoy a first visit to a historic winery, to see where Rioja's quality wine history began. This cellar dates back to the 1860's, and is French in style (the French lent much influence to Rioja during this period). A private visit followed by wine tasting and tapas (light lunch) will be on today's menu.
- After the visit, we'll carry on to the medieval hill top wine town of Laguardia. Check in to our wine hotel, with views of the vines. Afternoon on your own to relax and discover this pretty village, full of wine shops, mansions, and gorgeous views of the Cantabrian mountains and vineyard covered valley.
- Dinner will be exceptionally atmospheric gourmet dinner in an art nouveau castle, a gourmet Riojano feast. Overnight in the castle!

Day Six:

- Full buffet breakfast in the castle
- Today is a major wine tasting day, with VIP visits to 2 famous estates- one historic, one modern
- The first special winery visit is to Marques de Murrieta (beautiful, historic estate complete with castle). VIP winery visit and tasting of all wines on the market, along with special old vintages. The next winery visit is planned for the lovely modern cellars of Finca Valpiedra.
- Gourmet lunch in pretty, historic restaurant nearby in Rioja wine country, with vino, of course!
- Late afternoon and dinner on your own in the atmospheric medieval village, where a multitude of gourmet restaurants abound.
- Extras: Wine Gift at each winery, personalized tasting sheets

Day Seven:

- Full buffet breakfast in the castle
- The futuristic winery of Ysios, designed by Santiago Calatrava is the first visit today. The winery is tiny and the visit will be short, but you will marvel at his architectural genius and enjoy the views looking back up at Laguardia across the vines.
- From La Rioja, our wine journey continues on to Navarre, the beautiful aristocratic region just east of la Rioja, which borders France. We will visit the pretty village of Olite, a town famous for its fairy tale castle and its wine. We'll climb the ramparts and turrets of the castle, enjoy an aperitif in a 14th century converted monastery and then sit down to a gourmet feast paired with excellent wines from Navarra. Reservation only, lunch not included in price
- The drive back to La Rioja will take in ancient pilgrim roads, and we might even see some pilgrims with their scallop-shelled staffs, making their way for Santiago de Compostela on the route known as "Saint James Way".
- Our farewell dinner tonight will be marvelous, in a 16th century nobleman's mansion, now a gourmet restaurant. Day Eight: Full buffet breakfast in the castle

Day Eight:

- Today, we make our way back to Madrid, but first we'll stop in historic Burgos, with its 13th century Gothic Cathedral, for lunch. Lunch will be a rustic affair in a beautiful old restaurant with wood burning ovens.
- We'll visit the lovely "Casco Viejo" of this ancient village, the old stomping grounds for the Knights of the Templar, before driving south to Madrid. If time permits, we'll enjoy a coffee in the historic village of Lerma, near Burgos.
- Our wine journey ends in Madrid and we will drop you off at the airport or your next port of call.

End of services

Reservations

Tour Date(s): September 15th/2006
Limited to 20 passengers
Price per person (double occupancy) $1,800.00
Please note: airfare not included
Reservations: contact Global Tours-1-905-749-8305
You're personal Tour Director: Rose Watkins

Gerald Mitchell

"Eco-Tour"/High Adventure in Canadian Rockies

Canadian Rockies, Cariboo Helicopter Tour

Experience our most comprehensive journey through the Canadian Rocky Mountains! Spend two nights each at two legendary Rockies resorts, The Fairmont Banff Springs and The Fairmont Jasper Park Lodge, followed by an adventure into the alpine wonderland "at the top of the world," where you discover the secret pleasures of summer in the Rockies!

Arrive Calgary / Banff

Tour departs: Calgary Airport at 3:00 PM. Your Tour Director will be at the airport from 2:00 PM. If you arrive the day before, you may join the tour at the Delta Bow Valley at approximately 1:00 PM. Cross the last few miles of prairie and head into some of the most beautiful mountains in North America, the Canadian Rockies, arriving in Banff National Park at your magnificent resort set in the heart of the park. We invite you to join us tonight for a casual welcome dinner. Meals D

Banff National Park

Banff is a storybook village surrounded by magnificent alpine scenery! Start the day with a raft trip on the Bow River; see Bow Falls, Tunnel Mountain and Surprise Corner. The rest of the day is free for you to enjoy Banff's optional activities; take advantage of the resort's many facilities. Tackle one of the hotel's fine golf courses, pamper yourself in its world-renowned spa, or perhaps explore the charming town. Meals B,D

Lake Louise / Ice fields Parkway

Take a beautiful drive to see Lake Louise, traveling between towering peaks, over silver streams and past glacial gorges. Travel the Ice fields Parkway, one of the most awe-inspiring roads in North America; view the soft blue waters of Peyto Lake, named after one of the early mountain pioneers. Literally every bend of this road unfolds a panorama of snow-domed peaks, lakes and waterfalls! It is hard to imagine the forces of nature that created this scenery; you may see moose, elk, deer, bighorn sheep and black bears. View Athabasca Glacier, which feeds the water system for one quarter of North America. Your home for the next two nights is The Fairmont Jasper Park Lodge, one of Canada's most popular resorts, set right in the heart of the national park. Meals BLD

Jasper National Park

Today is at your leisure to spend in this lovely lakeside setting, with an opportunity to enjoy many optional activities. You might choose to hike, bike ride, swim, or just enjoy the scenic grandeur of the mountains and lakes surrounding your resort. Try a championship golf course, guided walks, tennis - or maybe even whitewater rafting! Meals BD

Helicopter to Cariboos

You are about to experience the thrill of heli-exploring! Travel through Yellowhead Pass to the helicopter staging area. From here each heli-group of 8 – 11 persons will shuttle into the Cariboo Mountains and the Cariboo Lodge. Meet your hiking guides and assemble on the pad to "lift off" into a wonderland of soaring peaks and emerald valleys. During the afternoon, your helicopter will transport you to several breathtaking alpine locations. The guided hikes are designed to accommodate everyone, with hikes suited for every generation of the family and every ability. Hiking elevations will vary in the Cariboo Mountains according to locations selected, but most will range in altitudes from 3,600 ft. to 9,900 ft. Your first taste of this adventure will energize you as you marvel at the endless vistas! Return to the lodge, located at a comfortable altitude of 3,600 ft., to enjoy the amenities and share tales! Meals BLD

Heli-Hike the Cariboos

After breakfast, begin a full day of heli-hiking. "Take-offs" and "landings" will position you for hikes in high alpine meadows watered by melting snow and dotted with bluebells, mountain alder and Indian paintbrush. Other flights will bring you to ridges surrounded by waterfalls, or you may be taken to the surface of a glacier; guides describe the geology and incredible sights around you. Back at the lodge, relax and reflect – the diversity of landscapes within the Cariboos also harbors diversity of wildlife habitats. Meals BLD

Cariboos to Calgary

Travel from the extraordinary alpine world of the Cariboos back to Calgary. View the rugged mountain scenery of the Canadian Rockies as you travel the Ice fields Parkway again; it will have new meaning after your days in Jasper and the Cariboos. Join us for a farewell toast this evening to celebrate this memorable adventure through the Canadian Rockies and the mountains beyond. Meals BLD

Journey Home

Tour ends: Delta Bow Valley, Calgary. Fly home anytime; airport transfers are not included. Allow a minimum of two hours for flight check-in - flights direct to the United States clear U.S. customs in Calgary. Meals B

Sample Study Tour to India

Sample cover letter to promote a tour to India:

The program offers a multitude of choices for travel to the subcontinent: traditional escorted journeys, tours accompanied by a guest lecturer and suggested itineraries for the independent traveler. India has many wonders to be seen besides the Taj Mahal, that glorious monument to undying love.

A great escorted journey for the first-time traveler to India is the "Classical Journey." This visits the Himalayan Kingdom of Nepal, where medieval coexists with modern; the sacred city of Benares, "resplendent with divine light," on the holy River Ganges; Delhi, Jaipur and Agra, and the Golden Triangle of the sub-continent; as well as Khajuraho, Udaipur, Aurangabad and Bombay. The very names evoke the multifarious strands of India's 4000 years of history: the Moghul Emperors with their forts and palaces, the British Raj, the Hindu and Muslim kingdoms.

Princely India can be relived in "Forts and Palaces of Rajputana," staying in the romantic royal residences that have been sympathetically restored and translated into luxurious hotels. A highlight of this tour is a stay in the world-famous Lake Palace Hotel, a precious pearl and haven of tranquility, shimmering in the water opposite Udaopur's City Palace.

A summer holiday can be spent on the beautifully appointed, carved wooden houseboats on the peaceful lakes of Kashmir, nestling under the grandeur of the mighty Himalayan peaks. Here all your needs are attended by a staff of servants, including a chauffeur-driven gondola! We suggest that this sybaritic delight be combined with a visit to the mountain fastnesses of Ladakh, the living repository of Tibetan Buddhist culture, often called the "Last Shangri-La."

Another world altogether can be experienced on the "Southern Trader" tour. The Dravidian South, is almost a different continent from the Gangetic plains and Himalayan ranges of the Hindi-speaking North, and has a magic all its own. Walk on the fabulous beaches of golden Goa, with its charming Portuguese flavor, the heritage of 450 years of empire. Ride across the still, sparkling lagoons of lush, tropical Karalla, delightfully verdant. Observe the activities of thousands of energetic pilgrims at the fantastically carved stone temple of Meenakshi in the colorful city of Madurai. Be intoxicated by the scent of sandalwood in Mysore, and sense the Imperial vision of Clive of India in Madras.

For the experienced traveler, the subcontinent can be explored in many different ways. With 23 years of service, <insert Tour Company Name> is proud of its ability to fashion "couture" itineraries for the individual or group. We enjoy working with our clients to match their desires with the serried marvels of India: thus we provide the precise and perfect journey for their ultimate enjoyment.

Sample Itinerary for India

Our jungle odyssey begins in the Vindhya Mountains in Bandhavgarh, central India. We travel on elephant-back, searching for tiger and its elusive prey. In Rajasthan, we visit Rathambore Tiger Reserve, the erstwhile hunting preserve of former maharajahs of Jaipur. Here we travel by jeep and look for tiger within the ruins of once-great forts. Nearby is the Bharatpur Bird Sanctuary, a haven for more than 350 species and winter home of the Siberian Crane. We also visit the semi-desert and thornscrub habitats of western India to see the rare wild ass and desert birds such as sand grouse and bustards.

Program:

Day 1: Fly to Delhi

Day 2: Arrive Delhi and stay at the Taj Palace Hotel. In the afternoon visit the legendary monuments of Old Delhi.

Day 3: Flight to Khajuraho, home to the 1,000-year-old temples of the Chandela kings.

Day 4: To Bandhavgarh National Park. Arrive at the park after a fascinating drive through the hills of Madhya Pradesh state.

Day 5: Game viewing in Bandhavgarh, famous for its tiger population. Other animals found here include the elusive leopard, jungle cat, gaur, deer, monkey and a wide variety of birds.

Day 6: Today you can search for tiger on elephant-back over otherwise impassable terrain.

Day 7: Return to Khajuraho to fly to Agra. Stay at the Taj View Hotel.

Day 8: Morning visit to the Taj Mahal. Afternoon visit to the nearby deserted city of Fatehpur Sikri, built by Akbar the Great. Continue to Bharatpur Bird Sanctuary and the Bharatpur Forest Lodge.

Day 9: Morning at Bharatpur Bird Sanctuary, home to more than 350 species. At midday relax in the gardens of your lodge before going back to the park in the afternoon to see more birds.

Day 10: To Pathambore National Park. Today we will drive into the heavily forested hills surrounding the ghostly remains of Rathambore Fort. Stay at the Adventure Camp.

Day 11: Explore for tigers in Rathambore. Other predators in the park include leopard, marsh crocodile, jungle cat and hyena. In the afternoon, visit the ruins of the fort, the abandoned and overgrown wells, battlements and mosques.

Day 12: Travel to Jaipur to stay at the most magnificent of all palace hotels, the Rambagh Palace. In the afternoon wander through the "pink city" and see the City Palace and astronomical observatory.

Day 13: Outside Jaipur is the Fort and the Palace of Amber. We climb up to the palace on elephant-back. Afternoon flight to Ahmedabad and stay at the Cama Hotel.

Day 14: Kutch and Zainabad. Morning drive to Kutch, stopping at Lake Nalsarover. Take the boat across to the island for bird watching. After a picnic lunch at Modhera, drive to Zainabad and stay at the Desert Courses Camp for 2 nights.

Day 15: Zainabad. Morning and afternoon wildlife viewing by jeep.

Day 16: Morning drive to Jasdan for a stay of 2 nights at the Jasdan Palace. Afternoon at leisure.

Day 17: Jasdan. Full day's wildlife viewing with a chance to see the vast flocks of common and demoiselle cranes, together with pelicans, storks, avocets and black-winged stilts on the nearby lakes. In the thornscrub, the now rare blackbuck are found in abundance.

Day 18: To Bombay. Overnight at the Searock Hotel.

Day 19: In Bombay. Day at leisure.

Day 20: Early morning flight home.

Sample Tour of Nova Scotia

NOVA SCOTIA............ *Welcomes you*

10 Days Deluxe Canadian "Atlantic Maritimes" Tour

There are (literally thousands of enchanting destinations in this world... lush islands. the sun.. . . lively cities. . . spectacular mountain retreats connoisseurs 'hideaways . . . secluded resorts with dramatic seascapes. where colorful culture are reminiscent of bygone years. You will discover all of these vacation themes are awaiting you. . . experience Atlantic Canada.

- Round-trip airfare from home town.
- Deluxe first-class hotel accommodations.
- Touring via "Private" air-conditioned motor coach.
- 3 Breakfasts -2 Dinners - plus Farewell Dinner.
- Admission to all attractions.
- All baggage handling.
- AU hotel taxes and tips for meals.
- Fully escorted.

Gerald Mitchell

- *Anne of Green Gables* Musical.

TOUR DATES: September 25 to October 4, 2006

TOUR PRICE: $1,250.00 per person (Double Occupancy)

$ 125.00 per person (Single Supplement)

$250.00 Deposit required with registration

$500.00 First payment due July 9, 2006

$500.00 Final payment due August 11, 2006

TOUR HIGHLIGHTS

- Halifax
- Nova Scotia
- Canada
- Peggy's Cove
- Annapolis Valley
- Champlain's Habitation
- Saint John
- Fundy National Park
- Prince Edward Island
- Green Gables
- Cape Breton Island
- Alexander Graham Bell's Summer Home
- Plus Much More!

Tour departs Olathe Public Library - Fully escorted from Olathe.

Sample Itinerary

DAY 1 Arrive in Halifax and check in at the Citadel Inn for a two night stay.

DAY 2 Enjoy a city tour this morning and the afternoon is free to further explore this harbor city.

DAY 3 Discover the rustic charm of Peggy's Cove. Travel to Grand Pre where the story of the expulsion of the Acadians is revealed. After lunch, motor through the lush Annapolis Valley to Champlain's Habitation, Canada's oldest permanent settlement. Soon you arrive in Digby for overnight at the Pines Hotel and Cottages — a delightful 300-acre resort.

DAY 4 The morning is at leisure. Board the Princess of Acadia for a two and one- half hour sail across the famous Bay of Fundy to New Brunswick. Soon you arrive in "the Loyalist City" — Saint John, where you visit Reversing Falls Rapids and see a few of the historical points of interest before checking in at the luxurious Deleta Brunswick Inn — downtown near award-winning Market Square.

DAY 5 Your guided tour continues through Fundy National Park to Hopewell Cape where fantastic forms have been carved by the action of the Fundy tides. Then it's all aboard the Salem & Hillsborough Railroad for a nine-mile steam train ride over trestle, marshlands and scenic countryside. Overnight is at the CN Hotel Beaujour in Moncton.

DAY 6 Ferry to Prince Edward Island. Visit the fabled home of "Green Gables," then enter P.E.I. National Park. This area has fine sand beaches and awesome red sandstone cliffs. Tour Charlottetown with its tree-lined avenues, flower gardens and historic buildings. The Charlottetown Hotel is home for the night. This evening enjoy a delicious lobster dinner.

DAY 7 From Wood Island, sail to Caribou, Nova Scotia. Then you'll proceed to Cape Breton Island — "The Scotland of America." Soon you find out why Alexander Graham Bell thought that the beautiful village of Baddeck would provide an appropriate setting for his summer home; visit the kite-shaped museum which exists to remind us of the many accomplishments of this genius. Spend the next two nights at the charming Inverary Inn.

DAY 8 Don't forget your camera! The scenery of Cape Breton Highlands National Park is yours today as you wind along the famous Cabot Trail. Frequent stops are made for pictures, handicrafts and exploring. Return to "the Inverary" late this afternoon. Tonight it's a special "Farewell to Nova Scotia" get together before dinner

DAY 9 Louisbourg National Historic Park, the Williamsburg of Canada awaits you. See the reconstruction of one-fifth of the town of 1744 — then the mightiest fortress in an eroding empire of France. Roam the streets talking with the costumed guides who remain in character, or sample the sustenance of an era. Your tour continues along the shores of *Bras d'Or* to the mainland. Early this evening, arrive in Halifax for a final night at the Citadel Inn.

DAY 10 Time to bid farewell to the Maritimes and depart for home. Transfers to the airport will be provided by our tour company.

TOUR DESIGNED BY: Rose Watkins, ITD-The GEM Group

TOUR DATES: August 15 24, 2006 10 Days

- Price per person double occupancy: $1800.00
- Single rate additional: $225.00
- Deposit of $200 no later than April 29, 2005
- Full Payment due July 8, 2006
- Included: Roundtrip limo service from your home to the airport.

Reservation: <Name of your company>

Montreal Spa and Shopping Tour

Day One (Thursday)

Welcome to the Paris of the North. Montreal

- Arrive Montreal
- Private transfers to your hotel
- Private welcome cocktail reception at the Ritz Carlton Hotel

Afternoon: Free

Evening: Welcome cocktail reception with your tour host and members of the She Loves To Travel staff.

Gerald Mitchell

Day Two (Friday)

Private sessions for complete makeover at Holt Renfrew. Includes shopping the latest in styles, one on one with international makeup artists and skin specialists.

For the next 5 hours you will introduce to North America's latest trends, your own personal shopping guide, Make-up class, private showing of the latest styles in clothing and furs. Once you have completed your shopping all items to be gift wrapped and delivered to your room at the Ritz Carlton.

About Holt Renfrew:

Founded in 1837 in Quebec City as a hat and fur shop, Holt Renfrew received five generations of royal warrants and secured the oldest existing contract with Christian Dior for the exclusive representation of its haute courtier furs. From there, the company grew quickly adding international designs fashions and securing additional locations in six cities across Canada.

Today, Holt Renfrew is a national specialty store of international renown and the headquarters for such prestigious names as Christian Dior, Donna Karan, Gucci, Chanal and Burberry. For additional information go to www.holtrenfrew.com

Enjoy a complete Makeover - Develop a unique style

Montreal is seen as the North America bridge to European fashion flair. The certain *je ne sais quoi* discreet charm of the *Québecoise* is ubiquitous, and likely to be spotted everywhere.

First, get a full one-on-one makeover from French Canadian Image Consultants Experts. They will help you through a complete transformation that includes hair, make-up and wardrobe with a talented team of stylists, hair and makeup artists. Then enjoy touring Holt Renfrew with your private shopping guide followed up with a skin specialist.

Followed by a delicious champagne lunch catered by the Ritz Carlton Hotel at this world-renowned venue - Holt Renfrew.

Friday Mid-afternoon

Historical Old Montreal Tour

We'll introduce you to Montreal via private coach and guide. Excellent opportunity to search out a place to dine tonight.

Tour Old Montreal takes you back 350 years in time. In this historic part of the city, Ville Marie was built in 1642. With a professional guide, discover our colorful past! A stroll through a maze of narrow lanes and old buildings provides a perfect opportunity to discover Old Montreal's history and charm. With their exuberant display of architecture, the streets and buildings testify to Montreal's rich heritage and illustrate a period of its history. The tour features a number of remarkable restorations that have breathed new life into the Old City: City Hall, Bonsecours Market, Place Royale, the World Trade Centre, Jacques Cartier Square , the Royal Bank, the Bank of Montreal and majestic Notre-Dame Basilica.

Evening Free: We have made a selection of several restaurants recommended by your tour designer, Gerald Mitchell some of his favorite spots. Please have your hotel make reservations. Sample list of She Loves to Travel recommendations'

Day Three Saturday morning - International discount shopping tour

Private escorted tour where you will be introduce to She Loves to Travel © latest shopping secret. Chabanel Discount garment District Montreal's bargain hunter's paradise! The buildings on this block run from eight to sixteen stories and are chock full of manufacturers, importers, agents, buyers and deals.

The district is very much open to the public on Saturday mornings from around 9 a.m. to 1 p.m., though there are a few floors in a few buildings that are open during the week. In the 99 Chabanel building it's the fourth floor, the 111 Chabanel building it's the seventh floor and in the 333 Chabanel building it's the third floor.

I n terms of price and style, a loose rule of thumb is that the higher the address number of the building the more expensive the garment and the more of a fashion statement it makes. So the 555 Chabanel building on the far end of the street near Meilleur Street would house the importers from France, and also sports a beautiful mall-like mezzanine concourse for those of you who do not enjoy perusing warehouses and racks.

Afternoon Time to take in a spa-optional tour-or continue to discover shops and points of interest in Old Montreal

Evening: Meet in the lobby at the Ritz for private transfers to your Farewell dinner in Old Montreal.

Day Four: Sunday

Private Transfer to the airport for return flight home.

User Reservations

Schedule Montreal , Canada Tour Dates:

Departures:

Twice a month, every Thursday through Sunday. Optional to extend you stay an additional night to visit Quebec City.

<u>Pricing Information-2006</u>

Low Season: $1,075.00 per person (air not included)

February 12 -15

March 18-21

December 16-20 - Extra night Additional $175.00 Christmas program

December 30 - New Years program

Gerald Mitchell

CROATIA – A HIDDEN GEM

Impress your palate, revive your senses, enrich your knowledge, walk off the Beaten paths

Day 1 – Zagreb, the capital of Croatia

Arrival to Zagreb airport. Meet & greet by an English speaking guide. Transfer to hotel. . Welcome dinner in a local restaurant.

Overnight in hotel (bed & breakfast)

Day 2 – National Park "Plitvice lakes" – UNESCO world heritage site

After breakfast, transfer to Plitvice lakes (UNESCO world natural heritage site). On the way, make a stop in a nice village Rastoke, with old watermills. There, on a local propriety, it is possible to have a short 30-45 min visit with a guide, presenting village life, its history, etc., and after to taste traditional bread, pie, sour milk, cheese, etc. Arrival to Plitvice, rest of the day free for exploring the wondrous Plitvice lakes national park, with 16 beautiful lakes culminating in 78 m high „Big waterfall" – the highest waterfall in Croatia. Lunch in a local restaurant, tasting trout or other river fish, for which the area is widely known.

Overnight in the hotel (half board).

Day 3 – Zadar – stone architecture, Roman foundations, Venetian imprint

After breakfast, transfer to the town of Zadar, prehistorique settlement visit a beautiful old town made of stone, with many churches, palaces and temples. Zadar is a historical centre of North Dalmatia, and as such has had a rich history, from the times of Rome onwards. Guided visit of the town. Lunch in a local restaurant. Free afternoon for a walk through the streets of old town or enjoying the sound of one of the first sea-organs in the world, situated on the

Towns "korzo" (promenade along the sea). Don't forget to wait for the sunset on the very same "korzo" – back in the early '70s, famous director Alfred Hitchcock, after returning from a search for film locations, said to his American colleagues "In Zadar, you will see the most beautiful sunset in the world!".

Dinner and overnight in the hotel (half board).

Day 4 – National Park "Krka", Ethno village Dalmati, town of Sibenik – UNESCO world heritage site

After breakfast, excursion to the national park Krka, with its beautiful waterfalls and magnificent views. The area of Krka River was firstly discovered and put under special care by the Austro-Hungarian emperor Franz Joseph I. After the visit of the park, transfer to a nearby ethno village „ETNOLAND Dalmati", with a very nice presentation of the village life in the innerlands of Dalmatia, with an English speaking guide dressed in local clothes. Tasting of "rakija" (traditional brandy in Croatia) and original Dalmatian prosciutto – Krka area offers some of the best prosciutto in Croatia, due to good wind conditions (used for drying). After that, wash the salty taste of prosciutto with a glass of good home made wine in a typical Dalmatian cellar. Finalize the visit by having a traditional village lunch accompanied by sounds of live traditional music (guitar and mandolin)!

After lunch, transfer to town of Sibenik, and guided visit of the old town with many monasteries, churches, medieval palaces and St. Jacob's catedral – UNESCO cultural heritage site – as the highlight of the visit. In the late afternoon-evening, return to Zadar. Dinner and overnight in the hotel (half board).

Day 5 – Island of Pag – exquisite lamb and sheep cheese, mystery of Pag triangle

In the morning, after breakfast, bus excursion to Island of Pag. Pag is famous for:

- first class Pag sheep cheese and Pag lamb (Paska janjetina) – both of these specialties are famous for its intensive salty taste, coming from the sea salt brought onto the herbs on the island, by the strong „bura" wind
- famous lace work – „Paska čipka", or lace from Pag, where every lace item presents a unique work
- salt pools used to manufacture salt
- a series of beautiful beaches and „Moon-like" rocks, in the Pag bay

In the morning, on the way to town of Pag, make a short stop at „Fortica", the remains of an old fortress that was controlling the traffic of the ships in the area (thus, the site offers a very nice panorama). After, visit the town of Pag and its surroundings (old town of Pag).

Possibility of climbing the highest peak of the island, St. Vid (342 m), with a mangificient view of the Pag bay. Also, possibility of visiting Pag triangle, a phenomenon which attracts the attention of believers, alternative researchers of history and the UFO investigators.

During the day, lunch in one of the local restaurants, with a tasting of the rich flavoured sheep cheese and lamb for the main course. In the late afternoon, transfer to the island and the town of Rab. Dinner and overnight in the hotel (halfboard).

Day 6 – Rab, beautiful island town; Opatija – the Adriatic gem

After breakfast, morning visit of Rab, a beautiful medieval town and the centre of the island of Rab. After, transfer to Opatija, the Adriatic gem on the coast of the Gulf of Kvarner in North Adriatic. Opatija is the first tourist resort in Croatia, with more than a 100 year old tourism tradition, dating from the end of the 19th century and the times when Hapsburg imeprial family built their villas in Opatija (many of whom are now hotels).

Accommodation in hotel and lunch in a local restaurant. We suggest trying the scampi „nabuzaru" (scampi cooked in their own juice, with an exquisite mixture of Mediterranean herbes and spices, white wine, garlic and olive oil).

Afternoon free for swimming or a walk along the beautiful promenade of the

Austrian emperor Franz Joseph I, following the coastal line several kilometres, going all the way to the neighbouring towns Icici and Ika.

Possibility of organizing an afternoon visit of the nearby Ucka mountain, the highest mountain of the Istrian peninsula, overlooking the Gulf of Kvarner – a combination of bus ride and short walks, offering magnificient views of North Adriatic.

In the evening, try out some of the excellent wellness offered in hotels, enjoy the vivid nightlife or just relax on the balcony late at night, with a glass of wine and the beautiful view withthe moon glowing over the sea.

Dinner and overnight in the hotel in Opatija (halfboard).

Day 7 – island of Cres – Roman town of Beli, Eco-center and endangered Eurasian griffons, Tramontana family pension specialties, marine town of Cres.

After breakfast, transfer by bus and ferry to the nearby island of Cres. Visit the ancient town of Beli, on the north-east coast of Cres. Beli is a very beautiful little town, built in Roman times. Beli „sits" on high cliffs, as a forteress overlooking the chanell between 2 biggest Croatian islands, Cres and Krk. In Beli, visit the world-known Eco Center, famous for taking care of one of the last stable population of Eurasian griffons (endangered in Europe). The center is supported by volunteers and donators from all over the world and has a permanent exhibition on the topic of life of griffons. After the visit, just a few metres away from the centre, on the terrace of the family pension Tramontana, a tasting of homemade products: - includes: prosciutto, home made sheep cheese, salted sardins (or enchovies) in olive oil, olives and a Mediterannean spread from tomato with home made bread,accompanied with a glass of honey brandy and a glass of wine. After the tasting, lunch on the terrace. For this lunch, there is also a possibility to prepare the lamb „under peka" (meat put under an iron pot, with potatotes and vegetables, and cooked in its own juice, with the pot put in the middle of the fire). Cres is also very known for it's good quality lamb (similar to Pag lamb, but a little less salty), with gentle meat and refreshing taste of fresh cheese). After lunch, transfer to the town of Cres, a medieval marine town and a center of the island. After the visit, return to the hotel in Opatija. Dinner and overnight in the hotel (halfboard).

Day 8 – Eno-gastronomic adventure in Istria (wine roads, olive oil farms, Guiness record white truffles) + town of Porec (UNESCO world heritage site)

Full day visit of Istria with the following highlights:

- - wine tasting in different wine cellars, on the "Istrian wine road"
- - extraordinary olives and olive oil, famous for its intensive taste and honourable tradition, dating from Roman times - visit of several little "acropola" towns in the innerlands of Istria, with very nice medieval architecture and beautiful views on the green Istrian innerlands; lunch in one of the traditional restaurants on the wine road;

Trufflehunting (depending on the season)

- visit of the town of Porec, on the west coast of Istria, with the 6th century Basilica of Eufrasius – UNESCO world cultural heritage site – as the highlight of the visit Possibility of organizing lunch or dinner in the restaurant „Zigante Tartufi" – a Truffle heaven famous for holding a Guiness record for the biggest white truffle ever found – the truffle was found by the owner of the restaurant, Giancarlo Zigante and his truffle hunting dog Diana, and has weighed 2.89 pounds! Enjoy some of the best Istrian traditional cooking in the hilly surroundings of vineyards, olive farms and medieval towns built in the Venetian times. We suggest trying the Istrian Smoked Ham and Cheese with Truffles to start with and Baby Beef Tagliata or Fish Capriccio with Truffles for the main course. To finish, try some of the deserts mixed with, of course, Truffles! After dinner, enjoy the warm ambience of the old stone fireplace or a vivid conversation with Istrian local people, accompanied by Istrian „Supa" – a concoction of red wine, olive oil, sugar, pepper and roasted bread – served in terracotta pitchers.

Day 9 – Wildlife of Gorski kotar, return to Zagreb

After breakfast, leaving from the hotel in Opatija and heading towards Zagreb. Between Opatija and Zagreb, there is a beautiful wildlife area of Gorski kotar, offering many nice walks – possible visit to

National Park „Risnjak". Lunch in some of the local restaurants, with simple and very tasty moutain food presenting the moutain life, which was never luxurious and pompous, but was always full of healthy and good food.

Arrival to Zagreb in the late afternoon or evening. According to the time of arrival, possibility of organizing a farewell dinner, to mark the end of the programe. Overnight in the hotel (bed & breakfast + dinner outside the hotel).

Day 10 – Zagreb surroundings, flight home

In the morning, according to the time of the airplane departure, possibility to visit the town some more or have a half-day excursion in the surroundings of Zagreb, if time allows. Zagreb is surrounded by several beautiful medieval castles, built as summer residences of Croatian and Austrian noblemen. Also, possibility to visit the nearby archeological park „Scitarjevo", built on the place of an old Roman settlement. Transfer to the airport. Flight home.

HIGHLIGHTS OF YOUR CROATIAN PROGRAMME:

Cultural visits:

- Town of Zagreb – capital of Croatia, with a beautiful old town, good night life and interesting restaurants offering cuisine under influence of the Austro-Hungarian gastrotradition. Zagreb offers the possibility of visiting the surrounding medieval castles or the nearby Roman site – archeological park Scitarjevo.
- Town of Zadar – ancient Roman town, center of North Dalmatia, beautiful stone architecture
- Town of Sibenik – beautiful Dalmatian town, stone architecture and UNESCO cultural heritage site (St. Jacob's cathedral)
- Old island towns of Pag and Rab
- Eco-center in Beli, famous for the work on helping to preserve one of the last European population of the endangered species of vultures
- Many nice little towns and villages on the coast (Cres, Beli) and in innerlands (Rastoke– near Plitvice, „acropola towns" in the inner Istria, Ethno village Dalmati), showing the old ways of life
- Town of Porec – UNESCO cultural heritage site (Basilica of Eufrasius) constructed at the beginning of the Middle Ages (6th century), with the basilica's Apse Mosaics that offer a powerful and rich cultural experience

Nature:

- National park Plitvice lakes – UNESCO world natural heritage site
- National park of Krka – a complexed web of lakes and waterfalls, „sitting" between the Krka canyon rocks
- Pag triangle – an unusual geological site, attracting the attention of UFO investigators, believers, etc. plus, additional numerous sites with magnificent views and unordinary sceneries

Gastronomy:

- Cuisine of North Croatia (Zagreb and its' surroundings), with a very noticable Austro-Hungarian cuisine influence
- Meat – extraordinary lamb „under peka" in Pag and Cres; good meat in mountains
- Fish and sea food – extraordinary river fish in Plitvice area (trouts), and very good seafish and sea food in Dalmatia, as a part of a Mediterranean cuisine area;
- · Istrian cuisine with truffles as a highlight
- · Traditional home made products: prosciutto, sheep cheese, olive oil and olives, sage and honey

Chapter 11

How to Conduct On-Site Inspection Tours

The most powerful thing for an ITD/Tour Operator/Tour Designer is to experience the product -- to understand, for example, the value of good Inbound Destination Tour Management companies, Interpretive Tour Guides, hotels, and restaurants, different modes of transportation, and tourism sites and attractions. Travel literature often overlooks the shortcomings of the country or city it is promoting. It is your task to objectively review the destination and be able to advertise your office staff and clients. As an interpretive tour guide, you are the evaluator of your travel product.

There will be many aspects of your destination to take into account. Observe the political/crime climate; grade hotels, restaurants, and tour sites; rate the acceptance of the local community to tourism and your services. Aside from the basic transportation services, you must also consider weather conditions, attractions, nightlife and food, new tour developments.

Ask questions. Will your clients be able to walk the streets or visit the countryside without fear of being molested or approached by solicitors? Will it be necessary to stay confined to the hotel and surrounding area? Should that be the case, what tour packages can you, as an interpretive tour guide, offer?

Benefits of Experiencing the Product

Conducting an on-site inspection is essential for the ITD/Tour Operator and it is recommended that it be done twice a year -- at the beginning of your season and at the end of your season. Your job will be to look at ways to improve your existing tour package and seek new programs for your clients.

To assist you with the task of your valuation, we have included the following forms:

- Visitor's Bureau/Government Tourist Office
- Tour Guide Evaluation Form: Information Updates & Destination Highlights
- Motor Coach Inspection Form
- Restaurant Selection
- Hotel Inspection
- Sample Tour Evaluation Sheet for the interpretive guide for the training of staff and video taping their presentations.

Gerald Mitchell

Visitor's Bureau

Tourist Board/Chamber of Commerce

Date:_____ Inspector: _____

Name of Tourism Office: _____

Phone Information

Business: _____ Fax: _____

Web Site_ _____ E-mail:_____

Name & Address of contacts:

_____
_____
_____

List of wholesalers representing the Destination:

_____
_____
_____
_____

Sales – Service – Promotional Assistance

Films	Y____ N____		Guest Speakers	Y____ N____
Slides	Y____ N____		Maps	Y____ N____
Shells	Y____ N____		Guide Books	Y____ N____
Photographs	Y____ N____		Hotel Lists	Y____ N____
Posters	Y____ N____		Restaurant Lists	Y____ N____

Other: _____

Local Tour Operator/Guide Service Listings   Y____ N____

Schedules of Celebrations, Festivals & Events   Y____ N____

Remarks_____

_____
_____
_____
_____
_____

Information Updates

Date of Entry _____

Changes _____
_____
_____
_____

Signature _____

Date of Entry _____

Changes _____
_____
_____
_____

Signature _____

Date of Entry _____

Changes _____
_____
_____

Signature _____

Destination Highlights Selection

National Holidays and Festivals (List dates and special events):

Conventions and Trade Fairs _____

Cultural Activities: _____

Other: _____

FOOD:

Type of Local Foods: _____

Specialties: _____

Local Wines and Liquors: _____

List of Recommended Restaurants:

    Name/Location   Cost   Hours   Dress   Entertainment

Gerald Mitchell

_____ $_____   _____   _____   _____
_____ $_____   _____   _____   _____
_____ $_____   _____   _____   _____
_____ $_____   _____   _____   _____
_____ $_____   _____   _____   _____

NIGHTLIFE:

List type of entertainment, charges, location, local or international cast, dress, etc.:

_____
_____
_____
_____
_____

Nightclubs: _____

Theatre: _____

Opera: _____

Ballet: _____

Folkloric Plays: _____

Dances: _____

Casinos (public or private): _____

Remarks: _____
_____
_____

SHOPPING:

Duty Free Shops (locations and hours): _____
_____

Recommended Stores: _____
_____

Best Buys: _____

Local Crafts: _____

Open Markets: _____

Food Items: _____

Comments: _____

_____

_____

SIGHT-SEEING:

Public Transportation (taxi, bus, other and costs): _____

_____

Local Attractions: _____

Historic/Famous Buildings/Landmarks (admission costs): _____

_____

Guide Services (names, Phone and fees): _____

_____

Special Interest Tours: _____

Recommended Tours: _____

RECREATIONAL ACTIVITIES:

Special Sporting Events (dates and costs): _____

_____

High Adventure Trips: _____

Sporting Activities Available (costs, hours and location): _____

Golf $_____ Y_____ N_____   Tennis $_____ Y_____ N_____

Skiing $_____ Y_____ N_____   Fishing $_____ Y_____ N_____

Other: _____

National Holidays and Festivals (List dates and special events):

_____

_____

_____

_____

Conventions and Trade Fairs:_____

_____

_____

_____

Cultural Activities: _____

_____

Other: _____

Comments: _____

Motor Coach Selection / Inspection

One of the most important decisions to be made is the selection of the motor coach and driver. When it comes to selecting a coach, go for the best and most reliable equipment. You will have less chance of breakdown, air conditioning units that fail, a public address system that does not work, or a driver who is rude and unfamiliar with the tour route.

The following pages give you a complete inspection report form. This should be fully completed and updated semi-annually. Also, make note of important items such as:

1. Necessary licenses, both local and interstate.
2. Check the carrier's insurance that he or she has airport rights for pick up and drop off at departure gates.
3. In the event of a breakdown, verify how many pieces of equipment are in his or her inventory for back up.
4. Check to verify if the coach company is charging "deadhead miles." If this is the case, the Destination Manager might consider other alternatives to keep the costs down.
5. Confirm with the client how many seats aboard the motor coach will be available for sale. The front two seats are normally set aside for the tour director, tour escort, and tour guide. It is advisable not to fill a motor coach to full capacity on a one day or extended tour.

Motor Coach Inspection Form

Date: _____

Name of Motor Coach Firm and Address: _____

Emergency Contact: _____

Phone: _____

Fax: _____   Country: _____

Sales and Operation Office: _____

Office Manager: _____

Fax: _____   email: _____

Labor Force:

Union_____   Non-Union_____

Permits for city touring: Yes: _____ No:_____

Cost of permits: $_____

Personnel: _____
_____
_____

Preferred Drivers Name(s) _____

First Impression:

Authority to Service Particular Areas (State, Countries): _____
_____
_____

Number of vehicles Owned by Company:

Motor Coaches	Y_____	N_____
Vans	Y_____	N_____
Mini-coaches	Y_____	N_____
Other	Y_____	N_____
New	Y_____	N_____
Used	Y_____	N_____
Back-up Equipment	Y_____	N_____

Amenities: _____
_____
_____

Lavatories	Y_____	N_____
Air Conditioning	Y_____	N_____
P.A. Systems	Y_____	N_____
Card Tables	Y_____	N_____
Kitchen	Y_____	N_____
Bars	Y_____	N_____
VCR	Y_____	N_____
Other	Y_____	N_____

Gerald Mitchell

Motor Coach Seats and Numbers

    Reclining_____ Non-Reclining_____

    Smoking_____ Non-Smoking_____

Specialties of Company

    FITs   Y_____   N_____

    VIP Service   Y_____   N_____

    Conventions   Y_____   N_____

    Students   Y_____   N_____

    Retirees   Y_____   N_____

    Special Interest   Y_____   N_____

    Groups   Y_____   N_____

    High Adventure   Y_____   N_____

    In house Packages   Y_____   N_____

    Other   Y_____   N_____

    Clean, well maintained

    1_____   2_____   3_____   4_____

    Seats comfortable

    1_____   2_____   3_____   4_____

    Visibility for Viewing

    1_____   2_____   3_____   4_____

    Food and Beverage Service

    1_____   2_____   3_____   4_____

Motor Coach Selection / Inspection

Group Net _____ (Non-commissionable)

Gross Prices _____ (Commissionable)

Daily Charges

$_____

Overnight Charges

$_____

Commission Structure: _____

Touring (Driver/Guide Service): _____

In-house Tour Programs: _____

Extra Charges: _____

Comments: _____

_____
_____
_____
_____
_____

Restaurant Selection / Inspection

It is often overlooked that a typical tour group will spend more money each day for meals than any other tour component, including lodging, sightseeing, and guide service. Breakfasts are generally provided at the overnight accommodation. However, most group tours will use restaurants for lunches and dinners. If table service is requested, the Destination Manager may schedule the meal stops around the restaurants off peak hours to ensure quality service. In many cases, the tour price will not include meals. If so, the restaurant selected should have a diverse selection and a wide price range.

Below is a list of important items a restaurant should consider when marketing to and servicing the group travel market:

- *Group menus:* If a special menu is offered to a tour group, it should have a diverse selection including both light meals and full meals.
- *Flexibility:* Some group members may be on restricted diets. Restaurants should be flexible. If a buffet is served, group members should be able to order from the menu as well.
- *Service:* Restaurant service should be fast, friendly, and efficient. Tour groups should receive the same service as all other patrons. Destination Managers should look for restaurants that can serve the entire tour group within 60-90 minutes.
- *Tip and Tax:* Many tour operators prefer restaurants to include tip and tax on the bill. Whatever the agreement is made should be agreeable to both parties.
- *Attractiveness:* Destination Managers often select restaurants that offer individual character. Restaurants that have a special ambience characteristic to the area make the tour destination more memorable.
- *Group size:* Minimum and maximum number of clients they can accommodate
- *Individual:* Will discounts or commissions be offered for a number of clients refereed to the restaurant during any one calendar year?
- *Escorts/Tour Guides/Tour Directors:* Are they given complimentary meals while escorting a group?
- *Bus Driver:* Complimentary meals? Area to wait and relax during the group's function?
- *Prices:* Cost per person, taxes and gratuities
- Seating arrangements for groups: Close to entertainment, stairs, handicap accessibility
- *Dining:* Buffet or sit down, menu choices
- *Entertainment:* Type, time (weekdays or weekends)
- *Parking for motor coach:* Can the motor coaches get to the front door in case of bad weather?
- *Method of payment:* Company check, credit card, partial payment, final payment

- *Welcome signs for groups:* Make them feel welcome
- *Special themes/Food preparation:* Birthdays, special events
- *Contact person:* Who signs the contract and will be there during your function
- *Reservation and Cancellation policies:* Amount of money to secure the reservation, cost per person with tax and gratuity (other fees)

Notes: _____
_____
_____

Restaurant Inspection Form

Food (types) _____
_____
_____
_____

Specialties

Dinners: _____
_____
_____

Local Wines and Liquors: _____
_____
_____

Signature Items:
_____
_____
_____
_____
_____

List of Recommended Restaurants

Name/Location	Cost	Hours	Dress	Entertainment

Gerald Mitchell

Hotel Inspection

This is an intricate part of your clients' travel plans, whether it is for business or a leisure trip. A sense of security and relaxation is necessary while residing in an unfamiliar environment. A tour or business function can turn sour when a client experiences a hotel that is overbooked, rooms not up to the client's standards, poor hotel services, or an undesirable location. These will all have repercussions for the booking agency.

- A good tour guide must keep abreast of the continuous changes in the hotel industry. There are older properties that never change, but remain stable and consistent in the services they provide. On the other hand, new hotels, acquisitions, renovations, and changes in management are just some of the reasons most of your recommended accommodations to clients should be inspected. It is up to you to make note of these changes.
- With respect to tour groups, the on-site inspection is necessary not only to inspect the hotel property, but also to meet with the hotel staff and develop a working relationship as well as a solid understanding of the nature of group functions. The hotel and staff will become an extension of your firm.
- The GEM Institute of Travel Career Development has compiled *The Travel Consultant's On-Site Inspection Journal* especially for this purpose. Please contact our office for information regarding purchase.

Special Note: After an independent assessment of the hotel and facilities, the Tour Guide/Destination Manager can often design a tour package which will include the hotel recreational facilities, night clubs, and restaurants. Many resort hotels have full-time staff preparing and organizing activities (spas, yoga, wine tasting) to keep the client occupied when not out in the local community.

Primary Hotel Inspection Form

Date:_____ Inspector:_____

Name of Hotel and Address:

_____

_____

Country:_____

Owned and operated by:_____

Type of Property:_____

Commerical:_____

Resort:_____

All-inclusive:_____ Yes:_____No:_____

Location of hotel: City____Beach_____Mountain_____other_____

HoelManager:_____

City:_____

Phone:_____Emial:_____

Web Site:_____Fax:_____

FirstImpression:_____

   Hotel Proximity Information (Record distance to):_____

   NearestAirport:_____

   Hotel to airport limousine service: Y_____ N_____

ConventionSite:_____

   Embassy or Consulate:_____

Shopping:_____

   CulturalAttractions:_____

   Hospital:_____

   Hospital Address and Phone number:_____

Type of clientele you would recommend for this destination:

_____

_____

Information Updates

   Date of Entry: _____ Changes: _____

_____

_____

   Signature: _____

   Date of Entry: _____ Changes:_____

_____

_____

   Signature: _____

Gerald Mitchell

FAMs: Familiarization / Study Tours

For each of the ten cultural aspects noted below, identify which are available in the community and region.

1. ❏ Native Foods
2. ❏ Ethnic Diversity
3. ❏ Languages
4. ❏ Traditions
5. ❏ Arts and Crafts
6. ❏ Festivals
7. ❏ High Adventure
8. ❏ Soft Adventure
9. ❏ Trekking
10. ❏ Other

Provide details

Local Food

_____
_____
_____

Ethnic Diversity

_____
_____
_____

Languages _____
_____

Local Traditions & Arts and Crafts

_____
_____

Festivals & Special Events

_____
_____
_____

Tours/Special Events/Other possibilities:

_____
_____
_____

Soft Adventure

_____
_____
_____

Trekking

_____
_____
_____

Other activities and potential tour programs

_____
_____
_____
_____
_____

Types of Tour Packages You Plan to Offer

_____	_____	_____
Senior Groups	Students	Deluxe Tours
_____	_____	_____
Motor Coach	Soft Adventure	High Adventure
_____	_____	_____
Cruise	Special Interest	FITs
_____		
Other		

Remarks

_____
_____
_____
_____
_____
_____
_____
_____
_____

Appendix

- **Sample Forms**
- **Glossary of Terms**
- **US & International Tourism Offices**
- **GEM Consulting Services**

CHECK LIST FOR *ALL* TOURS

Group: _____ # Pass: _____

Tour: _____ Date: _____

Trip Escorts: _____

Check When Complete: Date _____

- ☐ Trip Kits to tour participants (baggage tags, etc.)
- ☐ Tour Voucher (See Page 41)
- ☐ Trip instructions to tour members, copies to hotels
- ☐ Money to escorts: Amount _____
  Check # Payee: _____

- ☐ Rooming list to hotels, bell captains, tour operators, cruise lines (with tour group's itinerary)
- ☐ Payment to hotels: Deposit ___Final Billing: $_____
- ☐ Instructions to transportation companies:
  - ❧ Air: _____
  - ❧ Flight #'s, V.I.P. Lounge, seat assignments, smoking/non-smoking
- ☐ Bus Company: _____
  - ❧ (Name of driver, pick-up locations)
- ☐ Cruise Ship: _____
  - ❧ Berth, transfers, seating assignments, dining room
  - ❧ Transfer Service: _____ (airport, hotel, cruise ship)
  - ❧ Destination Management Firm:_____
- ☐ Payment to transportation companies:
  - ❧ Air: _____ Amount of deposit: _____
  - ❧ Bus Company: _____ Amount of deposit: _____
  - ❧ Cruise Ship: _____ Amount of deposit: _____
  - ❧ Transfer Company: _____ Amount of deposit: _____
  - ❧ Tour Operator: _____ Amount of deposit: _____
- ☐ Meals: Letter of Instructions to all restaurants - Final counts of tour members with payment, special diets, special occasions
- ☐ Tour Guide Services: Send Instructions along with payment (copy of final tour itinerary)
- ☐ Copy of tour itinerary to all transfer companies, bell captains, travel suppliers
- ☐ Collect monies due
- ☐ Arrange seating on bus/airline
- ☐ Name tags
- ☐ Copy of trip insurance file (See Chapter Seven)
- ☐ First-aid kit
- ☐ Drink tickets (for airlines)
- ☐ Passports/Visas
- ☐ Emergency phone numbers
- ☐ Other: _____

Note: Have in your possession at all times your contacts/office/emergency phone numbers and addresses. If possible, include home phone numbers.

Gerald Mitchell

Pre-Departure Briefing Check List

Tour Designer: _____
Briefing Location: _____
Account Name: _____
Date: _____ Destination: _____
Attendance: _____
Dates of Travel: _____
No. of People: _____
Passports/Visas: (what is required): _____
Do all Participants have Necessary Documents? _____

Air Transportation

Airline: _____ Gateway: _____
Seats Pre-Assigned? _____ Smoking/Non-Smoking? _____
Special Meals? _____
Schedule - Any Problems? Tickets? Routings? _____
_____
Any Deviation in Accounting Procedures? _____
Registration Cards? _____

Hospitality Desk

Material to be Distributed at Desk? _____
Any Material Shipped? _____ How? _____ Receipts? _____
Activity Cards for Sports/Sight-Seeing? _____
Lists? _____ Departure Notices? _____
Balance Pre-Trip Materials? _____

Restaurants, Nightclubs, etc.

Which Restaurants? _____
Contact(s)? _____
Menus_____
What are Billing Instructions? _____
Have Times Been Verified? _____
Transfers? _____

Sight-Seeing, Sports

Fishing? Boats? _____
Golf? _____ Tee-Off Time for Golf? _____
Rental Equipment for Golf? _____

Travel

Extended Connecting Times at Airports? _____
Overnights: _____ Where? _____
Who will Cover? _____
Departure City Assistance? _____
Touch-Down Pool? _____

Airport Arrangements

Check-In Counter/Sign: _____ Coffee; Drinks to be Served? _____
(V.I.P. Room) _____
Flight Bags? When given out? _____
Photographs? _____ Gifts? _____
VIPs: _____ Early Arrivals? _____

Hotels

Rooms Booked and Verified? _____
Any Suites? _____
Special Arrangements? _____ Liquor? _____ Flowers? _____
Fruit? _____ Information, Client Profiles? _____

Baggage Handling

Tipping? _____ How Much? _____ When? _____ Which? _____

Tours

Air-Conditioned Busses for Tours? _____
Lunch Arrangements During Full-Day Tour? _____
_____

Cruise

With or Without Lunch? _____ Refreshments? _____
Music? _____ Other: _____

General Items

Does a Holiday Occur During the Trip? _____
What Arrangements Are Made For It? _____
Any Audience Participation Events? _____
Birthdays/Anniversaries? _____

Costs

Any Extra Billing Items (i.e., Tips, Gifts, Admissions Fees): _____

Tour Director

All necessary info? _____ Pre-trip packet to each Trip Director? _____
Tickets? Flights? _____
Money - Additional Necessitated? _____
Hotel Advised of Tour Director's arrival? _____ Time expected? _____
Customs? _____
Coded Bag Tags? _____
Forwarded to Ground Operator and Bell Captain _____

Gerald Mitchell

Transfers

Transfer Agent?_____
Contact(s)? Times, Pick-Up Points, Etc.: _____
Equipment? _____
Times Established? _____
How Far From Hotel to Airport? _____ Hotel: _____
Names of Hotels? _____

Contacts

General Manager_____ Mgr., Food & Beverage_____
Sales _____ Controller_____
Adequate Rooms? _____Check-Out Time? _____
Comp. for Tour Director? _____
Special Requests for Flowers, Liquor, etc., In Rooms? _____
Functions in Hotel Set Up? _____
Names of Rooms? _____Time of Activity? _____
Special Menus for (Luncheons) Dinners? _____
 Any expected problems or complications: _____
Meeting Comments: _____
NOTE: Copies of contracts to be carried by Tour Director at all times.
Coordinator_____ Date _____
Tour Director-in-Charge _____ Date _____
 Notes: _____

ITD's TRIP KIT CHECK LIST

Review this list with your clients are the pre-tour orientation meeting.

- ☐ Final itinerary
- ☐ Name tags
- ☐ Baggage tags
- ☐ List of hotels with phone numbers and addresses
- ☐ Tour Guide's name
- ☐ Insurance and health information
- ☐ Clothing list
- ☐ Do's and don't's of the country they will be visiting
- ☐ Rooming list
- ☐ Temperatures
- ☐ Food advice
- ☐ Money exchange
- ☐ Emergency phone number
- ☐ Extra itineraries for tour members to leave at home with next of kin
- ☐ Airline tickets/cruise tickets (who is responsible for them?)
- ☐ Pick-up points
- ☐ Luggage limitation (do not pack medicines and money)
- ☐ Map of city showing the hotel location
- ☐ General information on destination
- ☐ List of tour participants
- ☐ Clothing checklist
- ☐ Passports

Gerald Mitchell

Trip Kit Mailing Verification List

Tour group name:_____

Departure date:_____

File number:_____

Voucher number:_____

Name of agent preparing trip kits:_____

Date vouchers mailed out:_____

Mailed by: (UPS, FEDEXP, Regular, other:_____

Agent's Initials_____

    ☐ Hotel Voucher: ____
    ☐ Airline/cruise Tickets: ____
    ☐ Transfer Voucher _____
    ☐ Outfitter's Vouchers:____
    ☐ Guide's Service Voucher:_____
    ☐ Meal Vouchers:____
    ☐ Baggage Tags:_____
    ☐ Trip Insurance:_____
    ☐ Information regarding tour guides/trip director:_____
    ☐ Contact for next of kin/family members:_____

Additional Notes:_____

_____

_____

_____

_____

Interpretive Tour Guide Evaluation Form

Part One: The Attraction/Tourist site

Evaluated by:_____ Date:_____

Tour Program:_____

Physical Resources	Excellent	Good	Fair	Poor
The Meeting Area	4	3	2	1
Pleasant Surroundings	4	3	2	1
Parking Area	4	3	2	1
Rest Rooms	4	3	2	1
Covered waiting area/seating	4	3	2	1
Signs with times of tours, cost, length, etc	4	3	2	1
Literature available	4	3	2	1
Landscaping/beautification	4	3	2	1

Comments: _____
_____
_____
_____

Theme of the Tour	Excellent	Good	Fair	Poor
A theme or story has been developed for the attraction	4	3	2	1
The theme is in keeping with the basic resources	4	3	2	1

Resources	Excellent	Good	Fair	Poor
The attraction is historically or ecologically significant	4	3	2	1
The area has been well developed	4	3	2	1
The area is well maintained	4	3	2	1
There are sufficient resources to support the theme or story	4	3	2	1
The activity is not overly strenuous for most visitors	4	3	2	1

Comments: _____
_____
_____
_____

Transportation	Excellent	Good	Fair	Poor
Well maintained	4	3	2	1
Good safety features	4	3	2	1
Appropriate for the attraction	4	3	2	1

Comments: _____
_____
_____

The Tour Arrangements	Excellent	Good	Fair	Poor
The interpreter arrived early at the meeting site	4	3	2	1
The interpreter mixed with visitors	4	3	2	1
The interpreter did not congregate with other tour guides	4	3	2	1
Any special equipment required for-the tour was on hand	4	3	2	1

Orientation Presentation	Excellent	Good	Fair	Poor
The interpreter took charge of the group	4	3	2	1
An introduction was given to identify the guide and his or her organization	4	3	2	1
Drinking water, rest rooms etc. were pointed out	4	3	2	1
The interpreter gave the tour/activity by name	4	3	2	1
Any special touring conditions (i.e., steep terrain, etc.) were stated	4	3	2	1
Participants were informed of any of any special gear or clothing required	4	3	2	1
The highlights of the tour/activity were covered	4	3	2	1
The group was encouraged to ask questions and become involved	4	3	2	1
Rules and safety precautions were clearly stated	4	3	2	1

Part Two: Tour Presentations

Quality of the Tour Presentation	Excellent	Good	Fair	Poor
The interpreter set a good pace for the participants	4	3	2	1
The interpreter stayed in the lead (for -walks)	4	3	2	1
The interpreter collected the group before starting to talk	4	3	2	1
Good use was made of questions to stimulate visitor involvement	4	3	2	1
The presentation was concise and clear	4	3	2	1
The interpreter responded well to visitor questions	4	3	2	1
Technical terminology, jargon and slang were avoided	4	3	2	1
The presentation seemed interesting to the visitors and appeared-to hold their attention	4	3	2	1
The interpreter positioned him/herself at stops so that all visitors could see and hear	4	3	2	1
The interpreter maintained control of the group	4	3	2	1
The interpreter made good use of illustrations and demonstrations	4	3	2	1
The interpreter avoided the use of pure facts in the presentation	4	3	2	1
The interpreter actively involved the participants in the activity whenever possible	4	3	2	1
The interpreter related the subjects being discussed back to common things	4	3	2	1
Announcements were made at the end and the tour was declared terminated	4	3	2	1
The tour/activity was not too long (Distance) nor did it consume to much time at each stop	4	3	2	1

The Interpreter's Delivery	Excellent	Good	Fair	Poor
Loudness	4	3	2	1
Rate of speech	4	3	2	1
Clarity	4	3	2	1
Pronunciation	4	3	2	1
Grammar	4	3	2	1
Conversational style	4	3	2	1
Eye contact	4	3	2	1
Enthusiasm	4	3	2	1

Comments: _____

_____

International Tour Director's Evaluation Form

Copy to: **Tour Operator/Tour Designers/Sales/Operations**

1. Did the tour meet your expectations?   ___Yes ___No ___Not sure

2. What was your opinion about the pacing of the tour?

   A) ___Too rushed   ___Too slow   ___Just right

   B) ___Not enough free time   ___Too much free time

How did you feel about the balance of activities on tour? (Sightseeing, museum visits, shopping, cultural events, etc.?)

   There was a good balance of activities.   ___Yes   ___No

   Too many of the same types of activities   ___Yes   ___No

   Too many different types of activities   ___Yes   ___No

4. Which parts of the tour did you like best?_____

5. Which parts of the tour did you like least? _____

6. What changes, in your opinion, would have made this a better tour?

_____

_____

Tour features/highlights to leave out: _____

_____

_____

Keep same hotels or change to a different location: _____

_____

_____

Recommendations (hotels): _____

_____

_____

Improve activities: _____

_____

_____

Delete activities: _____

_____

_____

New programs that are available that should be included in future tours:_____
_____
_____

7. What was your opinion about the meals provided on tour?

   (A) ___Too many meals packaged into the tour

   ___ Not enough meals packaged into the tour

   (B) ___Not enough variety in the cuisine

   ___Too many strange native foods

   ___Too much standard American fare

How was the staff? _____
_____
_____

8. How would you rate the price and value of this tour?

   ___Too expensive ___Just right ___A bargain

Recommendations for other dinning establishments:
_____
_____

Contacts:

9. What was your opinion of the hotels you stayed in?

   ___Good ___ Bad ___Average

   Comments: _____

Recommendations for other hotels within the vicinity:
_____
_____

Contacts: _____

10. What was your opinion of the airlines (domestic, international, or both) you flew?
_____
_____

11. Please rate the performance of the tour guides (step-on guides) who met the group

   Local Guides: (fill in name or city)

   _____Yes No Why: _____

_____Yes No Why: _____

_____Yes No Why: _____

12.   How would you evaluate the service you received from the In-Bound Destination Management Company?   ___Good ___Bad ___Average

Contacts: _____

Comments: _____

_____

_____

_____

_____

13.   How did the clients learn about this tour? (Circle all that apply)

-From the sponsoring organization

-From other tour members: __

-Travel agent: __

-Tour flyer Advertisement: __

-Direct mail:__

14.   When is the best time of year to run this type of tour? Yes_____No:_____

15.   What length of time would your recommend for this tour?

___5 days ___7 days___10 days ___2 weeks ___3 weeks ___1 month

Would you manage this group again? Yes:_____ No:_____

ADDITIONAL COMMENTS: _____

_____

_____

_____

_____

_____

ITD Name:_____Date:_____

Name of Group_____ Group Leader: _____

Contact: Phone:_____email: _____

Address:_____

Gerald Mitchell

Confirmation –Pre-Departure Check List for Trip Kits/Suppliers

Group: _____ # Pass: _____

Tour: _____ Date: _____

ITD in charge of the group:: _____

Check When Complete: Date

- ☐ 1. Trip Kits to tour participants (baggage tags, etc.)
- ☐ 2. Tour Voucher (See appendix)
- ☐ 3. Trip instructions to tour members, copies to hotels
- ☐ 4. Money to escorts: Amount _____
- ☐   Check # Payee: _____
- ☐ 5. Rooming list to hotels, bell captains, tour operators, cruise lines (with your itinerary)

- ☐ 6. Payment to hotels: Deposit ___Final Billing: $_____
- ☐ 7. Instructions to transportation companies:
  Air: _____

  Flight #'s, V.I.P. Lounge, seat assignments, smoking/non-smoking

  Bus Company: _____

  (Name of driver, pick-up locations)

  Cruise Ship: _____

  Berth, transfers, seating assignments, dining room

  Transfer Service: _____ (airport, hotel, cruise ship)

  Destination Management Firm:_____

- ☐ 8. Payment to transportation companies:
  Air: _____ Amount of deposit: _____

  Bus Company: _____ Amount of deposit: _____

  Cruise Ship: _____ Amount of deposit: _____

  Transfer Company: _____ Amount of deposit: _____

  Tour Operator: _____ Amount of deposit: _____

- ☐ 9. Meals: Letter of Instructions to all restaurants - Final counts of tour members with payment, special diets, special occasions
- ☐ 10. Tour Guide Services: Send Instructions along with payment (copy of final tour itinerary)
- ☐ 11. Copy of tour itinerary to all transfer companies, bell captains, travel suppliers
- ☐ 12. Collect monies due
- ☐ 13. Arrange seating on bus/airline
- ☐ 14. Name tags

- ☐ 15. Copy of trip insurance file (See Chapter Seven)
- ☐ 16. First-aid kit
- ☐ 17. Drink tickets (for airlines)
- ☐ 18. Passports/Visas
- ☐ 19. Emergency phone numbers
- ☐ 20. Other: _____

Note: Have in your possession at all times your contacts/office/emergency phone numbers and addresses. If possible, include home phone numbers.

ITD's Pre-Departure Briefing Check

page -1/4

_____

Briefing Location:_____

Account Name: _____

Date:_____ Destination: _____

Attendance:_____

Dates of Travel: _____

No. of People: _____

Passports/Visas: (what is required):_____

Do all Participants have Necessary Documents? _____

Air Transportation

Airline:_____ Gateway:_____

Seats Pre-Assigned?_____ Smoking/Non-Smoking? _____

Special Meals?_____

Schedule - Any Problems? Tickets? Routings?_____

_____

Any Deviation in Accounting Procedures?_____

Registration Cards?_____

Travel

Extended Connecting Times at Airports? _____

Overnight?: _____ Where? _____

Who will cover? _____

Departure City Assistance?_____

Touch-Down Pool?_____

Airport Arrangements

Check-In Counter/Sign: _____Coffee; Drinks to be Served? _____

(V.I.P. Room) _____

Flight Bags? When given out? _____

Photographs?_____ Gifts?_____

VIPs: _____Early Arrivals?_____

Hotels

Rooms Booked and Verified?_____

Any Suites? _____

Special Arrangements?_____ Liquor?_____ Flowers?_____

Fruit? _____ Information, Client Profiles? _____

Baggage Handling

Tipping?_____ How Much?_____ When?_____ Which? _____

Continued on next page

_____
_____

Tours

Air-Conditioned Buses for Tours? _____

Lunch Arrangements for Full-Day Tour? _____

Day Cruises

With or Without Lunch? _____Refreshments? _____

Music? _____ Other: _____

General Items

Does a Holiday Occur During the Trip? _____

What Arrangements Are Made For It? _____

Any Audience Participation Events? _____

Birthdays/Anniversaries? _____

Costs

Any Extra Billing Items (i.e., Tips, Gifts, Admissions Fees): _____

Tour leaders Kit

All necessary info? _____Pre-trip packet to each Trip Director? _____

Tickets? Flights? _____

Money Additional Necessitated? _____

Hotel Advised of Tour Director's arrival?_____ Time expected? _____

Customs? _____

Page 4

Coded Bag Tags? _____

Forwarded to Ground Operator and Bell Captain _____

Transfers

Transfer Agent?_____

Contact(s)? Times, Pick-Up Points, Etc.: _____

Equipment? _____

Times Established? _____

How Far From Hotel to Airport? _____ Hotel: _____

Names of Hotels? _____

Contacts

General Manager_____ Mgr., Food & Beverage_____

Sales _____ Controller_____

Adequate Rooms? _____ Check-Out Time? _____

Comp. for Tour Director? _____

Special Requests for Flowers, Liquor, etc., In Rooms? _____

Functions in Hotel Set Up? _____

Meeting Comments:

_____
_____
_____
_____
_____

Trip Kit Checklist for Mailing	
Preparer is to check off each item and insert initials & date in right-hand column	

FILE VOUCHER #_____ CLIENT'S NAME:_____	
Total items in Kit: ____	Initials & Date
Preparer Mailed Kit On: _____	

TRIP INFORMATION	
1. Hotel Voucher	
2. Airline Tickets	
3. Transfer Voucher	
4. Outfitter's Voucher	
5. Guide's Service Voucher	
6. Restaurant Voucher	
7. Baggage Tags	
Remarks:_____ _____ _____ ___ Notes:	

How to Travel Free as an International Tour Director

SAMPLE COVER LETTER FOR TRIP KIT

Date: _____

Dear _____

This trip information is extremely important and we urge you to read it carefully and take it with you on your trip. (Name of Tour Director) cannot be responsible for services you may miss if you fail to read this information. This cover letter is accompanied by the final trip information on the following:

- Necessary clothing
- Sample menu
- Any changes in tour itinerary
- Weather conditions
- Name of tour guide who will meet them at the airport
- Reminder to attach enclosed baggage tag to their luggage
- Do's and Don't's of the community/country
- Shopping

Ensure that the client has proper walking shoes and clothing for inclement weather. Prepare the client for the level of activity which he will encounter, whether it be:

- Soft adventure
- Medium adventure
- High-risk adventure

Following is a sample of the information to be included in the client's trip kits mailed to them.

Don't forget to do the following:

- Check to see that your passport is valid
- Attach baggage tags to your luggage
- Check with doctor about malaria prevention and other health concerns
- Don't forget your airline tickets

Essential personal items to take on the trip.

- Sunglasses
- Sunscreen
- Camera, film, batteries, zip-lock bags
- Copy of any prescription and amply supply of prescription medications
- Flashlight, batteries
- Insect repellent
- Field glasses
- Lightweight poncho
- Hat with brim for sun protection
- Lip balm
- First-aid kit
- Swiss army knife
- Water bottle
- *Clothing Suggestions:*
- To protect yourself in case of rain and from the sun, both short- and long-sleeved cotton shirts

163

- Jeans and hiking pants
- Light-weight jacket or wind-breaker, and cotton sweater
- Walking and tennis shoes
- Swimming attire
- Snorkeling and diving equipment

Luggage

- Medium-sized suitcase or duffle bag
- Waterproof cover or bag

Documents and Accessories

- Copy of travel insurance and number in case of an accident
- Travel documents
- Inoculations and medication
- Money
- Water
- Routing
- Tipping instructions
- Airport "Meet and Greet" service
- Final instuctions.
- What not to take
- "Do's and Don'ts" while on tour

Tour Vouchers & Client Instructions

Arrival / Transfers

All tour participants will be met upon arrival at the Airport. Please hand the enclosed Arrival Transfer Voucher to your driver when you arrive.

Tour Guide Services Voucher

Enclosed is a voucher for the: Client Name:_____

Date:_____

Tour(s) & Services_____Value:$ _____

Welcome and Farewell Dinner Voucher

Our welcome and farewell dinners will be held on the following dates:

Welcome Dinner Day/Date: _____Location: _____

Farewell Dinner Day/Date: _____Location: _____

Value: $____ Included/Not includes(list)

Hotel Voucher

Date:_____Dear:_____

A voucher covering your hotel reservation is enclosed. Please have this voucher with you when you check into the _____ Hotel(s)_____

Hotel voucher indicates, on the upper left-side of the page, the amount you have prepaid to us for your hotel accommodations. When you check out of the hotel, you will be responsible for paying for any other charges you may have incurred such as laundry, phone calls, etc. The hotel will accept cash, travelers' checks, and major credit cards. They will not accept either a personal or business check unless you have made prior arrangements with the hotel manager or Tour Director.

Sample Hotel Voucher

Hotel Voucher

Voucher No. _____ *Present This Coupon For Reservations Specified.*

VALUE $_____ Number in party: _____

To: <u>(Name of Hotel)</u> _____

For: <u>(Client)</u> _____

Street Address _____

City, State, Zip _____

Provide: 3 Double rooms + Tax _____

Special Request: Rooms to be adjoining _____

Arrival Date: _____ Departure Date:_____

Value stated includes reservation only as specified. Other charges should be paid directly to hotel or party supplying additional services.

Tour Director (Signature)_____

<u>Distribution</u>:Original - Client /1st Copy – Hotel/2nd Copy - Travel Agency (Tour Wholesaler)

3rd Copy - Tour Director/Client's file

Work list of Travel Partners

Phone_____ email:_____ web site:_____

(Res.)_____ Cell phone:_____

References:

Specialties

Remarks:

Signature ITD_____ Copy to:

Date:_____

Sample Baggage Claim Form

Date:_____

Full Name:

Address: _____

City:_____ _____Zip:_____

(Please complete the following):

Date and time of loss or damage: _____

How and where did loss or damage occur? Give full details: _____
_____

Did this occur while your property was In custody of hotel, airline, steamship line or railroad? If so, give name and number of transport: _____

Identify particular trip by name: _____

Has a final claim been made against hotel/carrier? Yes_____ No_____

If yes, date made:_____

If theft or loss, has report been made to police?

Where? When?_____

Have you collected part or all of this claim from any carrier/insurance company? ____

Name of carrier or Insurance company: _____

How many pieces of luggage accompanied you during entire trip? _____

Value of luggage, excluding contents: _____

Value of contents:_____

Value of all jewelry worn or carried in luggage: _____

Medicines in luggage: _____

Baggage claim check #'s: _____

Hotel room number:_____

How to Travel Free as an International Tour Director

Sample Baggage Claim Form

Covering: Loss ☐   Damage ☐   Delayed ☐

*Airlin(s)e:*_____/_____

Routing: _____
_____
_____

*Flight numbers:*_____/_____/_____

Use a separate sheet, if needed (claims must be supported by invoices or bills of sale).

In consideration of the payment to be made hereunder, I hereby subrogate to the company all rights, title, and interest in and to the property for which claim is being made. I also agree that in the event of this property being recovered at any time, to refund to the company, in full, any amount that it may have advanced to me on account of said loss; it being understood that the company is to pay the cost of restoring it to sound condition, if recovered in a damaged condition.

It is expressly understood and agreed that the furnishing of this form to the insured or the assistance of any adjuster or agent of the company in the making of this proof is an act of courtesy, and is not a waiver of any of the rights of the company; and other Information and documents required by the company will be furnished.

Witness Hand by This _____ day of 20_____

Insured _____

Description of Article	Where Purchased	Date of Purchase	Cost	*Depreciation	Amount Claimed
list below					

_____
_____
_____
_____
_____
_____

ITD Name_____Date: _____

***A proper depreciation allowance must be shown, or it is understood
that Insured agrees to accept company's valuation.**

Sight-Seeing Booking Form

NAME	Room Number	Name of tour	$
1.			
2.			
3.			
4.			
5.			
6.			
7.			
8.			
9.			
10.			

Airline Change Request Form

Name of tour group: _____

Client's name(s): _____

Hotel: Room no.:_____

Date of departure: _____ 2nd choice: _____

Airline: Contact:_____

Date Confirmed: _____ Class: F____ Bus.____ Coach____

Standby: Yes____ No ____

Fare Structure: Additional amount of $_____

Issuing agency: _____

Remarks: _____

Flight connection:_____

Confined: _____ By:_____

Date: _____ Standby: Yes____ No____

Routing information:_____

Remarks: _____

Special requests: Smoking: Yes_ No_ VIP Lounge: Yes_ No_

Wheel chair:_____ Special Meals: _____Other:_____

Tour Director in charge: _____

Client's Tour Evaluation Form

Dear _____ Date:_____

Tour: _____

Name of ITD:_____

Date of tour: _____ Destination/Cruise:_____

To help us serve you better in the future, we ask you to take a few moments to complete this tour evaluation form. A postage- paid return envelope is enclosed.

We thank you, and look forward to seeing you on another tour.

1. Did the tour meet your expectations? ___Yes ___No ___Not sure

2. What was your opinion about the pacing of the tour?

   A) ___Too rushed ___Too slow ___Just right

   B) ___Not enough free time ___Too much free time

3. How did you feel about the balance of activities on tour? (Sightseeing, museum visits, shopping, cultural events, etc.?)

   There was a good balance of activities. ___Yes ___No

   Too many of the same types of activities ___Yes ___No

   Too many different types of activities ___Yes ___No

4. Which parts of the tour did you like best?_____

5. Which parts of the tour did you like least? _____

6. What changes, in your opinion, would have made this a better tour?

(Things to Include, things to leave out, different hotels, different activities, etc.) _____
_____
_____
_____
_____

_____

7. What was your opinion about the meals provided on tour?

   (A) ___Too many meals packaged into the tour

   ___ Not enough meals packaged into the tour

   (B) ___Not enough variety in the cuisine

   ___Too many strange native foods

   ___Too much standard American fare

Gerald Mitchell

8. How would you rate the price and value of this tour?

___Too expensive   ___Just right   ___A bargain

9. What was your opinion of the hotels you stayed in?

___Good   ___ Bad ___Average

Comments: _____
_____
_____

10. What was your opinion of the airlines (domestic, international, or both) you flew?

_____
_____
_____

11. Please rate the performance of the tour staff who accompanied you on   tour. Would you like to travel with this person again?

Tour Manager:___ Yes ...___No Why: _____

Group Leader:___ Yes ...___No Why: _____

Local Guides: (fill in name or city)

_____Yes No Why: _____

_____Yes No Why: _____

_____Yes No Why: _____

12. How would you evaluate the service you received from (Name of Tour Company) before, during and after the tour?

___Good   ___Bad   ___Average

Comments: _____
_____
_____

How did you learn about this tour? (Circle all that apply)

From the organization from other tour members

Trade show Meeting from the travel agent

Tour flyer Advertisement Direct mail

14. When is the best time of year for you to travel?_____

15. What length of tour do you prefer?

___5 days   ___7 days ___10 days   ___2 weeks   ___3 weeks   ___1 month

16.   I would like to received information on (Name of Tour Company) next   tour.

___Yes   ___No

If you have any friends who might enjoy learning about our upcoming tours, please provide their names and addresses and we will add them to our mailing list. (Please print or type.)

Name/Address   _____

Name/Address   _____

Name/Address   _____

ADDITIONAL COMMENTS: _____

_____

_____

_____

_____

_____

_____

Date: _____

Glossary Of Travel Terms

Accommodations: rooms in hotel, motel B&B.

Adjoining rooms: Two rooms located next to each other, usually with no door connecting them.

Adventure tour: A tour designed around an adventurous activity such as rafting, hiking, or mountain climbing.

Affinity group: A group of people that share a common hobby, interest, or activity, or that are united through regular participation in shared outings. Also see preformed group

After-departure charge: Charges that do not appear on the guest's bill at check out such as telephone or dining charges.

Agent: One who has the power to act at the representative of another. Most frequently in travel, a specific kind of agent such as a travel agent.

AIO variables: Activities, interests, and opinions-used to measure and categorize customer lifestyles.

Air sea: A cruises or travel package in which one or more transportation elements are provided by air and one or more by sea. The package is usually combined with local lodging.

Airline fare: Price charged for an airline ticket. Several types of fares exist and can change with market conditions.

Airlines Reporting Corporation (ARC): An organization that provides a method of approving authorized agency locations for the sale of transportation and cost-effective procedures for processing records and funds of such sales to carrier customers.

All-inclusive package: A tour package in which most travel elements are purchased for set price. Also called an all-expense package.

Alumni tour: A tour created for customers who have previously traveled with a tour operator. Also called a reunion tour.

Amenity package: A cluster of special features, such as complimentary shore excursions, bar or boutique credit, or wine at dinner offered to clients on a given tour or cruise, usually as a bonus or extra feature. Usually used to induce clients to book through a particular travel agency or organization.

Attractions: An item or specific interest to travelers, such as natural wonders, manmade facilities and structures, entertainment, and activities.

Average room rate: The total guest room revenue for a given period divided by the number of rooms occupied for the same period.

Back to back: A term used to describe tours operating on a consistent, continuing basis. For instance, a motor coach arriving in a city from a cross-country tour may conclude the first tour upon arrival, and then transport a second group back along the same route to the origination city of the first tour.

Baggage handler: See porter

Baggage master: The person who controls baggage handling on a ship.

Bed and breakfast (B&B): Overnight accommodations usually in a private home or boarding house, often with a full American-style or Continental breakfast included in one rate.

Bell captain: The person in charge of luggage at a hotel.

Block: A number of rooms, seats, or space reserved in advance, usually by wholesalers, tour operators, or receptive operators who intend to sell them as components of tour packages.

Boarding pass: The document that allows a traveler to pass through the gate area and onto a plane or ship.

Booking form: A document which purchasers of tours must complete to give the operator full particulars about who is buying the tour. It states exactly what is being purchased (including options) and must be signed as acknowledgment that the liability clause has been read and understood.

Breakage: Expenses budgeted for a tour but not used or expended, thus resulting in additional profit to the tour operator. Examples include meals budgeted but not consumed, currency fluctuations in favor of the tour operator, or the tour selling too much larger numbers of passengers than expected.

Break-even point (BEP): The point at which revenues and expenses are the same. For example, the BEP is the number of products (or seats, cabins, tickets, etc.) that must be sold for a company to break even. The BEP is calculated as fixed costs divided by the selling price less variable costs. See reasonable number

Break-even pricing: Pricing a product based on a forecast of the break-even point and the cost of achieving the break-even point.

Budgeted balance sheet: A budget that measures total assets and liabilities.

Budgeted income statement: A budget that tracks revenues and expenses. Also called the profit and loss statement.

Cabin: A sleeping room on a ship.

Carrier: A company that provides transportation services, such as motor coach companies, airlines, cruise lines, and rental car agencies.

Cash flow: Monies available to meet a company's daily operating expenses, as opposed to equity, accounts receivable, or other credits not immediately accessible.

Cash budget: A budget that monitors cash flow and funds available to meet current expenses.

Casual research: A form of marketing research that is used to test cause-and-effect relationships between a marketing program and customers.

Certified Tour Professional (CTP): A designation conferred upon tour professionals who have completed a prescribed course of academic study, professional service, tour employment, and evaluation requirements. The CTP program is administered by the National Tour Association (Lexington, KY) and is open to individuals employed in any segment of the tourism industry.

Certified Travel Counselor (CTC): A designation attesting to professional competence as a travel agent. It is conferred upon travel professionals with five or more years of industry experience who compete a two-year graduate-level travel management program administered by the Institute of Certified Travel Agents (Wellesley, MA).

Certified Travel Industry Specialist (CTIS): A designation conferred upon American Bus Association member company employees who successfully complete five correspondence courses (three) required and two electives and written evaluation of eight marketplace seminars.

Chain-ratio method: A method for forecasting market demand by multiplying a base market figure by a series of consumption constraints.

Chamber of Commerce: A DMO that operates at the local level and is comprised of businesses that are not necessarily associated with the tourism industry.

Charter: To hire the exclusive use of any aircraft, motor coach, or other vehicle.

Charter service: The transportation of preformed groups (organized by someone other than the carrier), which have the exclusive use of the vehicle.

Circle itinerary: A travel routing design that overnights in different locations and returns to the point of departure without retracing the travel route.

City guide: A tour guide who points out and comments on the highlights of a city, usually from a motor coach or van.

City tour: A sightseeing trip through a city, usually lasting a half-day or a full day, during which a guide points out the city's highlights.

Client list: A printout of the names of all tour participants.

Client mix: Objectives set by companies to achieve percentages of customers from different market segments.

Closed-end question: A question for which the answers are provided for the respondent, who chooses only from those answers.

Closeout: Finalization of a tour, cruise, or similar group travel project after which time no further clients are accepted. Any unsold air or hotel space is released, and final lists and payments are sent to all suppliers.

Commission: A percentage of a travel product's price that is returned to the distributor when the product is sold.

Commissionable tour: A tour available through retail and wholesale travel agencies, which provides for a payment of an agreed-upon sales commission to the retailer or wholesale seller.

Common carrier: Any person or organization that offers transportation for a fee.

Comp policy: Arrangements for free tickets, rooms, meals, etc.

Complimentary (comps): Items provided free of charge, such as rooms, meals, tickets, airfare, gifts, souvenirs, etc.

Computerized reservation system (CRS): An automated system used by travel agents that contains pricing, availability and product descriptions for hotels, car rentals, cruises, and air transportation.

Conditions: The section or clause of a transportation or tour contract that specifies what is not offered and that may spell out the circumstances under which the contract may be invalidated (in whole or in part).

Configuration: The interior arrangement of a vehicle, particularly an airplane. The same airplane, for example, may be configured for 190 coach-class passengers, or it may hold 12 first-class passengers and 170 coach passengers, or any other combination within its capacity.

Confirmed reservation: An oral or written statement by a supplier that he has received and will honor a reservation. Oral confirmations have virtually no legal weight. Even written or faxed confirmations have specified or implied limitations. For example, a hotel is usually not obliged to honor a reservation if a guest arrives after 6 p.m., unless late arrival has been guaranteed.

Connecting flight: A flight that requires a passenger to change planes as part of the itinerary.

Connecting room: Two rooms that are connected to each other by a door.

Consolidator: A person or company that forms groups to travel on air charters at group rates on scheduled flights to increase sales, earn override commissions, or reduce the possibility of tour cancellations.

Consolidation: Cancellation by a charter tour operator of one more flights associated with a specific charter departure or departure period, with the transfer of passengers to another charter flight or flights to depart on or near the same day. Also, selling the same tour with identical departure dates through a number of wholesalers, cooperatives, or other outlets in order to increase sales and reduce the possibility of tour cancellations.

Consortium: A collection of organizations made up of independently owned and managed agencies that band together to increase their buying power.

Consumer protection plan: A plan offered by a company and/or association that protects the customer's deposits and payments from loss in the event of company bankruptcy.

Consumer: The actual user of a product or service. See also customer

Consumption constraints: Issues that limit the number of people in a market who will purchase a product.

Continental breakfast: At a minimum, a beverage (coffee, tea, or milk) and rolls and toast, with fruit juice sometimes included.

Contract: A legally enforceable agreement between two or more parties.

Convenience sample: A collection of research subjects who are the easiest for the researcher to select.

Convention and Visitors Bureau (CVB): A nonprofit DMO that operates at the county and city level. A CVB typically encourages groups to hold meetings, conventions, and trade shows in its city.

Cooperative (co-op) advertising: An agreement between two parties to share the cost of placing an advertisement.

Co-op tour: Selling a tour through a number of wholesalers, cooperatives, or other outlets in order to increase sales and reduce the possibility of tour cancellations.

Costing: The process of itemizing and calculating all the costs the tour operator will pay on a given tour.

Cost-plus pricing: See markup pricing

Coupon: See voucher

Custom tour: A travel package created specifically for a preformed group or niche market.

Customer: The buyer of a product or service. See consumer

Customs: The common term for U.S. Customs Service, the federal agency charged with collecting duty on specified items imported into the country. The agency also restricts the entry of forbidden items.

Database: A computerized, organized collection of individual customer information.

Day rate: Also called a day room. A reduced rate granted for the use of a guest room during the daytime, not overnight occupancy. Usually provided on a tour when a very late-night departure is scheduled.

Day tour: An escorted or unescorted tour that lasts less than 24 hours and usually departs and returns on the same day. See sightseeing tour

Deadheading: Making a trip or a segment of a trip without passengers, such as driving an empty motor coach somewhere.

Demand generators: Strategies and programs developed by DMOs and suppliers to generate destination demand. Examples include festivals, events, cultural tours, and consumer promotion.

Demands: A consumer's wants backed by the ability to purchase.

Demographics: Population measures, such as age, gender, income, education, race/ethnicity, religion, marital status, household size, and occupation.

Departure point: The location or destination from which a tour officially begins.

Departure tax: Fee collected from a traveler by the host country at the time of departure.

Deposit: An advance payment required to obtain and confirm space.

Deposit policy: A specified amount or a percentage of the total bill due on a specified date prior to arrival.

Descriptive research: a form of marketing research that is used to provide detailed answers about customer markets.

Destination: The geographic place to which a traveler is going.

Destination alliance: A DMO that operates as a for-profit association of select suppliers who form a paid-membership network to promote their services to travelers.

Destination management company (DMC): A for-profit company that operates similar to a CVB by providing planning and execution services for the convention and meeting market.

Destination marketing organization (DMO): An organization that promotes a location (city, region, state province, country) as a travel destination.

Direct flight: A flight that stops one or more times on the way to a destination, but does not require travelers to change planes.

Direct marketing: Sales and marketing communication that feature direct interaction between a company and its customers without any distribution intermediaries.

Double double: A room with two double beds.

Double-occupancy rate: The price per person for a room to be shared with another person; the rate most frequently quoted in tour brochures.

Double-room rate: The full price of a room for two people (twice the double-occupancy rate.)

Docent: A tour guide who works free of charge at a museum.

Downgrade: To move to a lesser level of accommodations or a lower class of service.

Driver-guide: A tour guide who does double duty by driving a vehicle while narrating.

Duty-free imports: Item amounts and categories specified by a government that are fee of tax or duty charges when brought into the country.

Economic impact study: Research into the dollars generated by an industry and how these dollars impact the economy through direct spending and the indirect impact of additional job creation and the generation of income and tax revenue.

Eco-tour: A tour designed to focus on preserving the environment, or a tour traveling to environmentally sensitive areas.

Educational tour: A tour designed around an educational activity, such as studying art.

Environmental scanning: The process of monitoring important forces in the business environment for trends and changes that may impact a company.

Errors and Omissions Insurance: Insurance coverage equivalent to malpractice insurance, protecting an agent or operator's staff if an act of negligence, an error, or an omission occurs that causes a client great hardship or expense.

Escort: See tour director

Escorted group tour: A group tour that features a tour director who travels with the group throughout the trip to provide sightseeing commentary and coordinate all group movement and activities.

Escrow accounts: Funds placed in the custody of licensed financial institutions for safekeeping. Many contracts in travel require that agents and tour operators maintain customers' deposits and prepayments in escrow accounts.

Exchange order: See voucher

Exploratory research: A form of marketing research that's used to obtain preliminary information and clues. It is most often used when the marketing problem is ambiguous.

Extension: A fully arranged sub-tour offered optionally at extra cost to buyers of a tour or cruise. Extensions may occur before, during, or after the basic travel program.

FAM (familiarization) tour: A free or reduced-rate trip offered to travel professionals to acquaint them with what a destination, attraction, or supplier has to offer.

Fixed costs: Costs that don't change with sales or production levels.

Fly/drive tour: An F.I.T. package that always includes air travel and a rental car and sometimes other travel components.

Folio: An itemized record of a guest's charges and credits, which is maintained in the front office until departure. Also referred to as a guest bill or guest statement.

Frequent Independent travel (F.I.T.): A custom-designed, prepaid travel package with many individualized arrangements. F.I.T. are unescorted and usually has no formal itinerary.

Full house: A hotel with all guest rooms occupied.

Function room: A special room that is used primarily for private parties, banquets, and meetings. Also called banquet rooms.

Gateway: City, airport, or area from which a flight or tour departs.

Gateway city: City with an international airport.

Ground operator: See receptive operator

Group leader: An individual who has been given the responsibility of coordinating tour and travel arrangements for a group. The group leader may act as a liaison to a tour operator or may develop a tour independently (and sometimes serve as the tour director).

Group rate: A special discounted rate charged by suppliers to groups. Also called tour rate.

Group tour: A travel package for an assembly of travelers that has a common itinerary, travel date, and transportation. Group tours are usually prearranged, prepaid, and include transportation, lodging, dining, and attraction admissions. See also escorted group tour

Guaranteed tour: A tour guaranteed to operate unless canceled before an established cutoff date (usually 60 days prior to departure).

Guest account: See folio

Guide or guide service: A person or company qualified to conduct tours of specific localities or attractions.

Guided tour: A local sightseeing trip conducted by a guide.

Head tax: Fee charged for arriving and departing passengers in some foreign countries.

High season: See peak season

Hosted group tour: A group tour that features a representative (the host) of the tour operator, destination, or other tour provider, who interacts with the group only for a few hours a day to provide information and arrange for transportation. The host usually does not accompany the group as it travels.

House: A synonym used for hotel.

Hub-and-spoke itinerary: A travel routing design that uses a central destination as the departure and return point for day trips to outlying destinations and attractions.

Inbound operator: A receptive operator that usually serves groups arriving from another country.

Inbound tour: A tour for groups of travelers whose trip originates in another location, usually another country.

Incentive or incentive commission: See override

Incentive tour: A trip offered as a prize, particularly to stimulate the productivity of employees or sales agents.

Incidentals: Charges incurred by the participants of a tour, but which are not included in the tour price.

Inclusive tour: See all-inclusive package

Independent tour: A travel package in which a tour operator is involved only with the planning, marketing, and selling of the package, but is not involved with the passengers while the tour is in progress. See also frequent independent travel (F.I.T.)

Interlobular tour: A tour that uses several forms of transportation, such as a plane, motor coach, cruise ship, and train.

Involvement device: An element of direct mail that gets the reader involved in the process of evaluating and/or responding to the solicitation.

Itinerary: A list of a tour's schedule and major travel elements.

Judgment sample: A sample based on the researcher's choice of subjects for a study.

Land operator: See receptive operator

Leg: Portion of a journey between two scheduled stops.

Letter of agreement: A letter from the buyer to the supplier accepting the terms of the proposal. This may also be the supplier's first proposal that has been initialed by the buyer.

List broker: A seller of mail lists for direct marketing.

Load factor: The number of passengers traveling on a vehicle, vessel, or aircraft compared to the number of available seats or cabins.

Locator map: A map of an area or a city, showing locations of attractions and hotels.

Lodging: Any establishment that provides shelter and overnight accommodations to travelers.

Logistics: Management of the details of an operation.

Low season: See off peak

Microenvironment: The broad forces in society and the business world that impact most companies.

Management Company: a firm that owns several lodging properties.

Manifest: Final official listing of all passengers and/or cargo aboard a transportation vehicle or vessel.

Market demand: The amount of a specific product or service that may be purchased during a certain period of time in a particular geographic area.

Market forecast: The realistic demand within a given time period for the products produced by all companies within a certain industry or product category.

Market segmentation: The process of dividing a broad market into smaller, specific markets based on customer characteristics, buying power, and other variables.

Market share: The measure of company sales versus total sales for a specific product category or industry.

Market: All existing and potential customers for a product or service.

Marketing mix: The 4 Ps of marketing: product, price, promotion, place (distribution).

Marketing plan: A written report that details marketing objectives for a product or service, and recommends strategies for achieving these objectives.

Marketing research: The function that links the consumer, customer, and public to the marketer through the systematic gathering and analyzing of information.

Markup pricing: Pricing a product by adding a standard markup to costs. Also called cost-plus pricing

Markup: A percentage added to the cost of a product to achieve a selling price.

Master account: The guest account for a particular group or function that will be paid by the sponsoring organization. See folio

Media: Communications channel such as broadcast (radio, TV), print (newspapers, magazines, direct mail), outdoor (billboards), and multimedia (Internet).

Meet-and-greet service: A pre-purchased service for meeting and greeting clients upon arrival in a city, usually at the airport, pier, or rail station, and assisting clients with entrance formalities, collecting baggage, and obtaining transportation.

Meeting/conference tour: A tour designed around a specific meeting or conference for the participants.

Microenvironment: Those forces close to a company that impact operations and marketing programs.

Mission statement: The concise description of what an organization is its purpose, and what it intends to accomplish.

Motor coach tour: A tour that features the motor coach the form of transportation to and from destinations.

Motor coach tour operators: Tour operators that own their own motor coaches.

Motor coach: A large, comfortable bus that can transport travelers and their luggage long distances.

Multi-day tour: A travel package of two or more days. Most multi-day tours are escorted, all-inclusive packages.

Murder-mystery tour: A tour that features a staged "murder" and involves travelers in solving the crime.

Mystery tour: A journey to unpublicized destinations in which tour takers aren't told where they will be going until en route or upon arrival.

National tourism organization (NTO): A federal-government-level DMO that promotes country as a travel destination.

Needs: Those aspects of the life a person can't do without.

Net wholesale rate: A rate usually slightly lower than the wholesale rate, applicable to groups of individuals when a hotel is specifically mentioned in a tour brochure. The rate is marked up by wholesale sellers of tours to cover distribution and promotion costs.

Niche market: A highly specialized segment of the travel market, such as an affinity group with a unique special interest.

No show: A guest with confirmed reservations who does not arrive and whose reservation was not canceled.

Objective and task method: A process for creating a promotion budget that sets objectives first, then defines the tasks needed to achieve those objectives, and then commits funds necessary to perform the tasks.

Occupancy: The percentage of available rooms occupied for a given period. It is computed by dividing the number of rooms occupied for a period by the number of rooms available for the same period.

Off peak: Slow booking periods for suppliers. Also called the low season.

On-site guide: A tour guide who conducts tours of one or several hours' duration at a specific building, attraction, or site.

Open-ended question: A question that allows the respondent to provide a free-response answer.

Open-jaw itinerary: A travel routing design that departs from one location and returns to another. For example, travelers may fly into one city and depart from another one. Or a traveler may purchase round-trip transportation from the point of origin to one destination, at which another form of transportation is used to reach a second destination, where the traveler resumes the initial form of transportation to return to the point of origin.

Operations: Performing the practical work of operating a tour or travel program.

Operator: See Tour Operator

Optionals: Optional tour features that are not included in the base tour price, such as sightseeing excursions or special activities.

Outbound operator: A company that takes groups from a given city or country to another city or country.

Outbound tour: A tour that takes travelers out of the area, usually from a domestic city to another country.

Overbook: Accepting reservations for more space than is available.

Overhead: Those fixed costs involved in regular operations, such as rent, insurance, management salaries, and utilities.

Override: A commission over and above the normal base commission percentage.

Packaged travel: A package in combination of two or more types of tour components into a product, which is produced, assembled, promoted and sold as a package by a tour operator for an all-inclusive price.

Passenger vessel: Ships, yachts, ferries, boats, etc.

Patronage Program: A program that rewards the customer for loyalty and repeat purchase, such as frequent-flyer programs.

Peak season: A destination's high season when demand is strong. Also called the high season.

Per capita costs: Per-person costs.

Per capita tour: See scheduled tour

Perceived value: The ratio of perceived benefits to perceived price.

Port of entry: Destination providing customs and immigration services.

Porter: A person who handles luggage at an airport, train station, etc.; also called skycap or baggage handler.

Positioning strategy: The development of a clear, unique, and attractive image for a company and/or product in the minds of target customers.

Pre-deduct commission: When a distributor such as a travel agent takes up front the commission on a sale and sends the supplier the balance of the sales price.

Preferred Supplier: The selection of specific supplier(s) for priority promotion to customers and/or integration in travel packages in exchange for reduced rates and/or higher commission.

Preformed group: A pre-existing collection of travelers, such as affinity groups and travel clubs, whose members share a common interest or organizational affiliation.

Pre- and post-trip tour: An optional extension or side trip package before and/or after a meeting, gathering, or convention.

Primary research: The collection of data specifically to solve the marketing problem at hand.

Profit margin: A dollar value that represents the markup of a product's price over its costs.

Promotion mix: Promotion tools including advertising, direct marketing, sales promotion, and public relations.

Promotional group tour: A travel package composed of tour elements that match the specific needs and wants of niche customers who aren't part of an organized or preformed group.

Promotional partnership: The combination of two or more companies to offer special incentives to customers.

Property: A specific lodging structure, such as a hotel, and the ground on which it is built.

Protection overbooking: The practice of blocking space that will likely be in excess of what will actually be needed.

Psychographics: Measures of a person's lifestyle. See also AIO variables.

Public relations (PR): A management function that determines the attitudes and opinions of an organization's publics, identifies its policies with the interests of its publics, and formulates and executes a program of action to earn public understanding and goodwill.

Public tours: See scheduled tour

Pull strategy: A marketing approach that creates demand at the customer level by generating awareness, interest, and desire so customers pull a product through a distribution channel by demanding it.

Push strategy: A marketing approach that creates demand at the distributor level by providing resellers with an incentive to push (sell) a product to end consumers.

Query: The process of sorting and retrieving information from a database.

Quota sample: A research sample that involves forming groups based on certain characteristics. A random sample can then be selected form the quota segments.

Rack rate: The published (brochure) rate for a travel component.

Reach: The measure of how many people in a market will be exposed to a certain advertisement via a specific medium.

Reasonable number: A forecast of the break-even point for a tour.

Receptive operator: A local tour company that specializes in services for incoming visitors, often for tour operator groups.

Relationship marketing: The process of building and nurturing ongoing, solid relationship with customers.

Research constraints: Those issues, such as cost and timing that will limit the scope of marketing research.

Reseller: See retailer and wholesaler

Reservation fee: A customer payment for a certain percentage of the travel package price that's made immediately after booking.

Retail price: The actual price a customer pays for a travel element or tour.

Retail tour: See scheduled tour

Retailer: A middleman, such as a travel agent, who sells directly to the customer.

Room rates: The various rates used by lodging properties to price rooms. These include: day rate (usually one half the regular rate for a room used by a guest during the day up to 5 p.m.-sometimes called a use rate), flat rate (a specific room rate for a group agreed upon by the hotel and group in advance), group rate (same as flat rate), net group rate (a wholesale rate for group business to which an operator may add a markup if desired), net wholesale rate (a rate usually lower than the group rate and applicable to groups or individuals when a hotel is specifically mentioned in a tour folder), and published rate (a full rate available to or advertised to the public-also called the rack rate.)

Rooming list: A printout of the names of all tour participants that also lists special lodging requests and provides a spot for the hotel or cruise ship to fill in the passenger's room number.

Run-of-the-house rate: A flat rate for which a lodging property agrees to offer any of its available rooms to a group. Final assignment of the rooms is at the discretion of lodging management.

Sales margin: A term used by resellers to describe profit as a percentage of sales revenue.

Sample: The portion of a population chosen to represent the population being studied for research.

Scandals tour: A light-hearted history tour that shows locations where interesting scandals took place.

Scheduled flights: Air flights that are publicly scheduled and promoted by major airlines.

Scheduled tour: A tour that's set in a tour operator's regular schedule of tour departures and that's often sold to the general public. Also called public tour or retail tour.

Secondary information: Research data that was collected by another company or person and usually for a purpose that's different than the research objectives and tasks at hand.

Shells: Preprinted brochures with photos, illustrations, and graphics but no text; also called slicks.

Shore excursion: A land tour, usually available at ports of call, sold by cruise lines or tour operators to cruise passengers.

Shoulder season: Those periods between the peak and off season when destination demand is moderate.

Sightseeing companies: Organizations that provide local guided tours

Sightseeing guide: See driver/guide

Sightseeing tour: Short excursions of usually a few hours that focus on sightseeing and/or attraction visits.

Simple random sample: A sample that draws a group of respondents randomly from all members of the population.

Special event tour: A travel package that features major happenings, such as concerts or sporting events, as the reason for the journey.

Split itinerary: An itinerary in which part of the group does one thing while the other part does something else.

Step-on guide: A tour guide who boards a motor coach to give detailed, expert commentary about the city or area being visited.

Strategic plan: A report that describes a company's mission statement, goals, objectives and strategic actions.

Subcontractor: A local operator who provides services for a wholesaler.

Supplier: The actual producer and seller of travel components.

SWOT analysis: A summary of a company's strengths and weaknesses, and the environmental opportunities and threats that will most influence it.

Target market: The group of customers who will be the focus of a company's marketing efforts.

Tariff: (1) Fare or rate from a supplier; (2) Class or type of a fare or rate; (3) Published list of fares or rates from a supplier; (4) Official publication compiling rates or fares and conditions of service.

Telemarketing: Direct marketing via the telephone.

Terminal: A building where clients report for trips via train, plane, etc.; also called a depot or a station.

Theme tour: A tour that's designed around a concept of specific interest to the tour takers, such as history or sports.

Tickler system: A method for monitoring reservations and payments that's arranged by date and points out late payments so customers can be contacted.

Tiered pricing: When suppliers offer different prices to receptive operators, tour operators, and group leaders, so each party can earn a profit by marking up the supplier's price while still offering a fair price to customers.

Tiered override plan: When commissions rise proportionately with a corresponding increase in sales.

Tour: A prearranged, prepaid journey to one or more destinations that generally returns to the point of origin, is usually arranged with an itinerary of leisure activities, and includes at least two travel elements.

Tour broker: See tour operator

Tour catalog: A publication by tour wholesalers listing their tour offerings. Catalogs are distributed to retail agents who make them available to their customers. Bookings by retail agents are commissionable.

Tour conductor: See tour director

Tour departure: The date of the start by any individual or group of a tour program or, by extension, the entire operation of that single tour.

Tour director: Also called tour manager, tour conductor, and tour escort. The person who is responsible for a group on tour and for most aspects of a tour's execution.

Tour escort: See tour director

Tour guide: A person qualified (and often certified) to conduct tours of specific locations or attractions. See also step-on guide, city guide, on-site guide, and docent.

Tour manager: See tour director

Tour manual: A compendium of facts about a destination, tour procedures, forms, and other information that a tour operator gives to its tour directors.

Tour menu: A menu that limits group clients to two or three choices.

Tour operator: A person or company that contracts with suppliers to create and/or market a tour and/or subcontract their performance.

Tour planner: A person who researches destinations and suppliers, negotiates contracts, and creates itineraries for travel packages.

Tour order: A voucher given to the purchaser of a tour package that identifies the tour, the seller, and the fact that the tour is prepaid. The purchaser then uses this form as proof of payment and receives vouchers for meals, porterage, transfers, entrance fees, and other expenses. See also voucher

Tour rate: See group rate

Tour series: Multiple departures to the same destination throughout the year.

Tourism: The business of providing marketing services and facilities for leisure travelers.

Tracking study: A survey of customers before and after implementing a promotion campaign to assess changes in consumer behavior.

Transfer: Local transportation and porterage from one carrier terminal to another, from a terminal to a hotel, or from a hotel to an attraction.

Transit visa: A visa allowing the holder to stop over in a country or make a travel connection or a brief visit.

Transportation: Any method of moving travelers from one point in a journey to another, such as air, ship, rail, and motor coach travel.

Travel agent: A person or firm qualified to arrange for lodging, meals, transportation, cruises, tours, and other travel elements

Travel component: Transportation, lodging, dining, attractions, entertainment, guide services, and other travel elements offered as part of a travel package.

Trip Cancellation Insurance: Sold through travel agencies, special insurance for travelers. Cover air, cruise or tour fares, as well as charter agreements, which carry high cancellation penalties. In case of cancellation due to illness or personal emergency, it covers your trip-related Moines.

Trip director: An escort for an incentive company. Larger companies reserve this title for the person who directs all personnel and activities for a particular incentive trip.

Turnaway: A potential reservation that couldn't be satisfied because the tour (or hotel, ship, etc.) was fully booked.

Upgrade: To move to a better accommodation or class of service.

Value season: See off season

Value: The relationship between the benefits associated with a product or service and the costs of obtaining the product or service. See also perceived value

Value-added tax (VAT): A type of tax system which adds a fixed percentage of taxation on products and services at each step of production or service delivery.

Value-based pricing: Pricing a product based on buyer perceptions of value rather than actual product costs.

Variable costs: Costs that change with sales or production levels.

Variance report: A summary of how much a company has gone above or below budget.

Visa: Stamp of approval recorded in a traveler's passport to enter a country for a specific purpose.

Volume incentive: See override

Volume purchase: The purchase of large quantities of a product or service.

Voucher: Documents that are exchanged for goods and service to substantiate payment that will be or already has been made.

Waitlist: A list of clients awaiting transportation or accommodations at times when they are not available. Waitlisted clients are confirmed as a result of subsequent cancellations.

Wants: Ways in which a person satisfies a basic need.

Wholesale: Sale of travel products through an intermediary in exchange for a commission or fee generally at reduced tariffs.

Word-of-mouth promotion: Personal communication about a product or service from one customer to another.

Yield management: Calculating and analyzing the profits earned per customer.

Vouchers: Tour Documents or coupons issued to clients by tour operators to be exchanged for services such as accommodations, meals, sightseeing, etc.

Travel and Tourism Resources

"Tools of the Trade"

While taking you behind the scenes of learning the inside facts of today's travel industry, I have some personal resources/tips to make your journey in learning more enjoyable.

How to Start an International Tour Director Company

Travel The World FREE!

If you wish to join the ranks of professional Tour Directors, then this is the manual for you. How to become a professional International Tour Director, by Gerald E. Mitchell, provides you with everything you ever wanted to know about this career, and should motivate and assist many who aspire to travel while earning a respectable income. Being an international Tour Director is one of the most attractive and sought after jobs in the travel industry. Drawing on past experiences, the author, Gerald E. Mitchell, challenges your assumptions and offers proven strategies for observing your clients' behavior, recognizing individual limitations, and auditing your own decision –making processes, to help you manage the best possible tour or cruise for your client. It is easy to see why a good Tour Director can Travel free…Earn High Income…Work full or Part-time. If you want to gain the confidence and tact of a diplomat, the deep knowledge of a scholar, the performance skills of an entertainer, and the organizational abilities of a management expert, aim your sights toward the world. Your career hobby will offer you the privilege to travel and mingle with people of all walks of LIFE.

The Official Airline Guide (North American and Worldwide Edition International) is the nonofficial "Bible" of the travel industry. Aside from offering a complete list of scheduled airline flights - direct and connecting, departure and arrival times, baggage allowance and rates, and city airport codes - it also contains a list of airlines, maps, airline mileage, minimum connect times, postal information (first-class rates), and transportation taxes.

> ***Tip*** When escorting a tour, carry the *OAG Pocket Flight Guide*. Aside from flight schedules, it contains a list of local reservation offices, which makes it a lot easier than looking up information at a public telephone booth.

The Official Airline Guide (OAG) Travel Planner: Holds a wealth of travel data. Besides hotel/motel information, there is an airline directory; airline routing maps; airport diagrams (important for the tour escort leading a group through an airport); banking, business and shopping hours for individual country listings; a calendar of events for many foreign countries; a car-rental directory; city-center maps for major international countries; a list of foreign clothing sizes; a list of consulate offices; listings of charter, rental, and tour operations; currency-conversion rates/customs; a list of U.S. documentary requirements; and information on how to obtain entry and driving permits.

Also, there is general travel information; information on airport facilities for the handicapped and elderly, liquor allowances, medical assistance, military installations within the U.S., how to obtain a passport information, and per-diem deductions for government employees; and an alphabetical listing of

Pacific-area rail companies including North American and Pacific office locations and reservation phone numbers. The OAG explains roadway signs, international telephone tips, telex area codes, tourist board office locations, and visa information. The OAG is printed in three editions: the North American, the European, and the Pacific area. These guides are unsurpassed for business or pleasure travel data.

The OAG Worldwide Cruise and Ship Line Guide is an encyclopedia of the cruise and ship line business which is updated every other month. It has cruise itineraries and prices, port-to-port and ferry schedules, ship profiles, maps of sea routes, and sales reservation office numbers.

To Order OAG Travel Manuals:

Official Airline Guides
2000 Clearwater Drive
Dept. J921
Oak Brook, IL 60521-9953
1-800-323-3537, Ext. J-921

Hotel and Travel Index is published quarterly. It lists major hotels/motels worldwide. A key code is next to each property, which lists agent's commission, number of rooms, rates, number of beds, meal plans available, rooms with bath, credit cards accepted, reservation and addresses of hotels, and telex data, plus 1,000 frequently booked properties are highlighted and there are over 130 city maps. You can quickly pinpoint a hotel's exact location and its accessibility to transportation, business and recreation centers, as well as major area attractions. Do not overlook the services of hotel representatives that are noted in the beginning of the hotel and travel index.

OHRG - Official Hotel Resort Guide is an excellent cross-reference guide when selecting hotels. It does not contain as many hotel/motel listings as the Hotel and Travel Index; however, it will give you a better description of the hotel/motel/resort property.

To order: Ziff-Davis Publishing Company
One Park Avenue
New York, NY 10016
Phone: (212) 503-5600

TIP These manuals are expensive. Try to obtain a used one by checking with your local travel agency for one of their used copies.

The Travel Agent: The travel industry's personnel directory never leaves the tour desk. In general, it lists airlines, cruise lines, automobile rental companies, motor coach sight-seeing/tour operators, government tourist offices, travel organizations, government agencies, and hotel representatives. This book gives you the name and title of persons connected to the business. It helps tremendously if you know *whom to address* your telephone call or correspondence to in order to get to the person in charge. To order:

The American Travel Division
Capital Cities Media, Inc.
2 West 46th Street
New York, NY 10036

Gray Line Official Sightseeing Sales & Tour Guide: No tour designer could operate without this book. Gray Line Sight-Seeing Company acts as host in any given city throughout the world. What you'll find in the Gray Line Sales and Tour Guide will be lists of half-day or multi-day package tours. There are multi-lingual guides, boat/cruise sightseeing, limousine services, airport transfer information and prepaid sightseeing tour order information. When your clients pre-pay for a tour, you collect the gross amount (retail price) and forward the net (your cost) to Gray Line. The difference is your profit! Agents, with their busy schedules, often overlook the "instant commission" they can make on these side excursions. Otherwise, your clients end up buying the tours through some local operator at the other end, who makes the commission from your efforts.

> *Tip:* Commencing in 1987, Gray Line Tour Guide has devised a shore-excursion program for ready sale to your cruise passengers, resulting in greater client satisfaction, and instant added commission. We lost a good number of commissions by letting our clients purchase their shore excursions aboard ship. No more!

Gray Line offers the tour designer an opportunity to compute net cost and length of tours, tour pacing, and a brief itinerary for groups or individuals. When we receive requests for a tour proposal (individual or group)-and the client is still unsure about contracting with our office, or may still be in the planning stages of an itinerary. ⊠We will present a brief tour program and an estimated price for the land portion from facts obtained in the *Gray Line Sight-Seeing Manual*. This saves time and money in long-distance phone calls, letters, telexes etc. Gray Line Tour Companies are located in most major cities around the world.

AAA - American Automobile Association: If you don't already belong, we recommend purchasing their membership. For the nominal fee, AAA offers an untold source of travel assistance. We often cross-reference our hotel selection with the AAA Tour Book. It offers an opportunity to re-affirm the hotel/motel rating, location, facilities and price. It also has listings on restaurants, historic sites, and major annual events. In planning a motor coach tour, travel time between two locations is crucial (taking into account rest stops, meals, attractions, and hotel check-in). One mistake in the timing will throw the entire tour out of synchronization. . Your AAA travel consultant will work with you and provide up-to-date information on the routing proposed for your clients.

To order: Contact your local AAA Club
Or Write: American Automobile Association
8111 Gatehouse Road
Falls Church, VA 22047

Travel – Tourism Periodicals

Find time to read them! Often agents put the travel periodicals aside or don't pass them around. It is imperative a professional Agent keep updated with current travel news that has taken place the past week.

Your resource manuals are helpful in designing your tour programs; however, nothing stays the same in this industry. A few of the items that you may read about in your travel magazines include a change in the political climate of a destination, currency exchange rates (which affect the cost of the tour), pending labor disputes that may be taking place within the hotel and transportation companies, and industry personnel changes. An agent must keep his finger on the pulse of the travel industry - or be left behind!

As you leaf through your travel magazines, make notes of the following: Travel shows, FAM tours (agent familiarization tours), education and training seminars, market guides (domestic-international), agency operations, business and employment opportunities, quizzes for travel agents, plus new ideas for your promotional brochures.

Fodor's Travel Guides: Fodor's offers useful general information designed to help plan and research a destination. Helpful hints include business hours, local holidays, time zones, and customs. There are essays to help you with insights and information about regional food and drink.

This travel guide offers a detailed breakdown of the geographical area. Each chapter begins with a description of the area; followed by practical information including addresses, directions, phone numbers, etc. It is a handy book for your clients to read prior to the trip.

Michelin Guides: These high-quality guides used by travelers since the early 1900s, highlight Europe, Canada, and the Eastern United States. They provide an excellent source of information pertaining to dining and hotel accommodations.

International Travel News: Edited for the high-frequency international traveler, it is intended to be a valuable news source and communication medium for business and pleasure travelers to overseas destinations.

> To order: ITN
> 1779 Tribute Road, Suite L
> Sacramento, CA. 95815
> Phone: (916) 457-3643

Jax Fax Travel Marketing Magazine: This magazine offers an update on current travel news and events, a list of FAM tours, workshops and seminars; a list of tour-operator servicing destinations throughout the world; and a directory of their reservation offices Published monthly by:

> Jet Air Transport Exchange, Inc. (JAX)
> 280 Tokeneke Rd.
> Darien, CT 06820-4899
> Phone: (203) 655-8746

Know Before You Go: A brochure on customs requirements issued by the U.S. Department of State, Washington, D.C, on the dos and don'ts of returning home with items from abroad.

Resource publications for the International Tour Director

Step in the Right Direction by Don Geary

> A basic map and compass book.
> Stackpole Books
> P. 0. Box 1831
> Harrisburg, PA, 17105.

Discovering Dixie....Along the Magnolia Trail by Richard Louis Polese

> The day-by-day travel guide to the best of the deep south.
> Ocean Tree Books
> P. 0. Box 1295
> Santa Fe, New Mexico, 87504

New England Walking Atlas by Gary Yanker and Carol Tarlow

> The walking atlas of America.
> McGraw-Hill Publishing Company

The American Walk Book by Jean Craighead

> George Major historic and natural walking trails from New England to the Pacific Coast.

Birdwatchers Guide to Wildlife Sanctuaries by Jessie Kitchiner

> Arco Publishing Company, Inc.
> New York.

Exxon Travel Club Travel Guide

> *Travel Vision Publications and Mobil Travel Guide,* Prentice Hall Travel
> Both guides contain:
> - Handicapped traveler information
> - Travel tips
> - Maps and map coordinates
> - What to see and do
> - Special travel features
> - Hotel/Motel toll-free "800" numbers

ECO & Cultural Resources Experiencing America's Past by Gerald and Patricia Guter

> A travel guide to museum villages.
> John Wiley and Sons, Inc.

Travel Books for Children

> *Great Vacations with Your Kids* by Dorothy Ann Jordon and Marjorie Adolf Cotter.
> The complete guide for family vacations in the U.S.A. from infants to teenagers.
> E . P. Dutton, New York.

Professional Organizations and Associations

www.Taedge.com: Travel-related associations, trade shows and publication. Up to the minute information on travel-related data, over 2,000 tour operators to promote your services and tours.

ABA (American Bus Association)

    1100 New York Ave.
    Suite 1050
    Washington, DC 20005-3934
    1-800-283-2877

NTA-National Tour Association

    546 E. Main St.
    PO Box 3071
    Lexington KY 40596-3071
    1-800-NTA-8886

Organizers of Group Tours Trade Shows and Conferences

Local Chamber of Commerce: Join your local chamber of commerce for a list of contacts and marketing opportunities for your tours and services.

US Chamber of Commerce: Worldchamberdirectory@compurserve.com: Will promote your services abroad.

United State Travel Council: Contact U.S. Department of Commerce, International Trade Administration, Trade Development, Tourism Industries, Washington, D.C. 20230; Phone; (202) 482-4029 for information on all of the information available from Tourism Industries, visit the web site at http://tinet.ita.doc.gov.

Greyline Sightseeing Tours: www.greylinetours.com: List rates and services for tours within the United States and around the world. Excellent source of tours and prices.

Leisure Group Travel: www.leisuregrouptravel.com excellent resource and opportunity to promote your tours and services.

International Association of Convention & Visitors Bureaus-IACVB

>2000 L St., NW
>Suite 702
>Washington, DC 20036-4990

United Bus Owners of America:

>1300 L Ave. NW
>Suite 1050
>Washington, DC 2000 4107
>1-800-424-8262

Government and State Tourism Offices

The importance of working with government and state tourist offices is being able to acqu information on a destination. Aside from the general information that is readily available, certa heads will offer advice on planning tour itineraries and recommend qualified land operator services, hotels and transportation companies. For planning a group function, the government or state tourist office will make available films and slides subject to their budget and the nature of the group function, and will sometimes offer a guest speaker knowledgeable on the destination being promoted.

Alaska
Alaska Travel Industry Association
2600 Cordova Street, Ste. 201
Anchorage, AK 99503
E-mail: info@alaskatia.org
Web site: http://www.travelalaska.com/

Arizona
1110 West Washington, Suite 155
Phoenix, AZ 85007
(602) 364-3700 or (866) 275-5816
Web site: http://www.arizonaguide.com

Arkansas
Arkansas Department of Parks & Tourism Office
1 Capitol Mall
Little Rock, AR 72201
(800) 628-8725 or (501) 682-7777
Web site: http://www.arkansas.com

California
California Office of Tourism
(800) 462-2543 or (800)TO-CALIFORNIA
Email: caltour@commerce.ca.gov
Web site: http://www.gocalif.ca.gov

Colorado
Colorado Tourism Office
1625 Broadway, Ste. 1700
Denver, CO 80202
(800) 265-6726
Web site: http://www.colorado.com

Connecticut
Connecticut Tourism
(800) 282-6863
Email: German.Rivera@po.state.ct.us
Web site: http://www.tourism.state.ct.us/

District of Columbia
Washington Convention and Visitors Association

Gerald Mitchell

901 7th Street NW, 4th Floor
Washington, DC 20001-3719
(202) 789-7000
Fax: (202) 789-7037
Web site: http://www.washington.org

Delaware
Delaware Tourism Office
99 Kings Highway, Box 1401
Dover, DE 19903
(866) 284-7483 or (302) 739-4271
Fax: (302) 739-5749
Web site: http://www.visitdelaware.com

Florida
Florida Division of Tourism
661 East Jefferson Street, Suite 300
Tallahassee, Florida 32301
(888) 735-2872
Web site: http://www.flausa.com/

Georgia
Georgia Department of Industry, Trade & Tourism
Tel: (800) 847-4842
Web site: http://www.georgia.org

Hawaii
Hawaii Visitors Bureau
Waikiki Business Plaza
2270 Kalakaua Ave #801
Honolulu, HI 96815
(800) 464-2924 or (808) 923-1811
Fax: (808) 922-8991
Email: info@hvcb.org
Web site: http://www.gohawaii.com

Idaho
Idaho Department of Commerce
Division of Tourism Development
700 West State Street
P.O. Box 83720
Boise, ID 83720-0093
(208) 334-2470
Fax: (208) 334-2631
Web site: http://www.visitid.org/

Illinois
Illinois Bureau of Tourism
100 West Randolph #3-400
Chicago, IL 60601

1-800-2CONNECT
Email: Tourism@illinoisbiz.biz
Web site: http://www.enjoyillinois.com

Indiana
Indiana Tourism Division
1 North Capitol Ave #700
Indianapolis, IN 46204
1-800-ENJOY-IN
Fax:317-233-6887
Email: webmaster@enjoyindiana.com
Web site: http://www.in.gov/enjoyindiana/

Iowa
Iowa Department of Tourism
200 East Grand Ave.
Des Moines, IA 50309
888-472-6035
Fax: 515-242-4718
Email: tourism@ided.state.ia.us.
Web site: httphttp://www.traveliowa.com/

Kansas
Kansas Travel and Tourism Division
1000 S.W. Jackson Street, Suite 100
Topeka, Kansas 66612-1354
1-800-2KANSAS
Fax: (913) 296-5055
Email: travtour@kansascommerce.com
Web site: http://www.travelks.com

Kentucky
Kentucky Department of Travel Development Visitors Information Service
500 Mero St
Frankfort, KY 40601
(800) 225-8747 or (502) 564-4930
Fax: (502) 564-5695
Web site: http://www.kytourism.com

Louisiana
Louisiana Office of Tourism
(800) 33-GUMBO or (225) 342-8100
Fax: (225) 342-8390
Email: free.info@crt.state.la.us
Web site: http://www.louisianatravel.com

Maine
Maine Office of Tourism
#59 State House Station
Augusta, ME 04333-0059

Gerald Mitchell

1-888-624-6345
Web site: http://www.visitmaine.com/

Maryland
Maryland Office of Tourism Development
217 East Redwood St, 9th Floor
Baltimore, MD 21202
(800) 634-7386
Web site: http://www.mdisfun.org

Massachusetts
Massachusetts Office of Travel and Tourism
10 Park Plaza, Suite 4510
Boston, MA 02116
(800) 227-MASS or (617) 973-8500
Email: VacationInfo@state.ma.us
Web site: http://www.mass-vacation.com/

Michigan
Michigan Travel Bureau
300 N. Washington Square, 2nd Floor
Lansing, Michigan 48913
(888) 78-GREAT or (517) 373-0670
Fax: (517) 373-0059
Web site: http://travel.michigan.org

Minnesota
Minnesota Office of Tourism
100 Metro Square, 121 7th Place E.
St. Paul, MN 55101
(800) 657-3700 or (612) 296-5029
Email: explore@state.mn.us
Web site: http://www.exploreminnesota.com

Mississippi
Mississippi Division of Tourism Development
Post Office Box 849
Jackson, MS 39205
(866) 733-6477 or (601) 359.3297
Fax: (601) 359-5757
Email: lturnage@mississippi.org
Web site: http://www.visitmississippi.net

Missouri
Missouri Division of Tourism
Post Office Box 1055
Jefferson City, MO 65102
(800) 810-5500 or (573) 751-4133
Fax: (573) 751-5160
Web site: http://www.missouritourism.org

Montana
Travel Montana
Post Office Box 200533
Helena, MT 59620
(800) 847-4868 or (406) 841-2870
Fax: (406) 841-2871
Web site: http://www.visitmt.com

Nebraska
Nebraska Division of Travel & Tourism
Post Office Box 98907
Lincoln, NE 68509
1-877-NEBRASKA
Email: tourism@visitnebraska.org
Web site: http://www.visitnebraska.org/

Nevada
Nevada Commission on Tourism
401 North Carson Street
Carson City, NV 89701
(800) 638-2328 or (775) 687-4322
Fax: (775) 687-6779
Email: ncot@travelnevada.com
Web site: http://www.travelnevada.com

New Hampshire
New Hampshire Office of Travel and Tourism
PO Box 1856
Concord NH 03302-1856
1-800-FUN-IN-NH or (603) 271-2665
Fax: (603) 271-6870
Email: travel@dred.st.nh.us
Web site: http://www.visitnh.gov/

New Jersey
New Jersey Commerce & Economic Growth Commission P.O. Box 820
Trenton, NJ 08625-0820
1-800-VISIT-NJ or (609) 777- 0885
Web site: http://www.state.nj.us/travel

New Mexico
New Mexico Department of Tourism
491 Old Santa Fe Trail
Santa Fe, NM 87503
(800) 733-6396 ext 0643
Fax: (505) 827-7402
Web site: http://www.newmexico.org/

New York

Gerald Mitchell

New York State Travel Info Center
1 Commerce Plaza
Albany, NY 12245
(800) 225-5697
Web site: http://www.iloveny.state.ny.us

North Carolina
North Carolina State Board of Tourism
301 North Wilmington St.
Raleigh, NC 27601
(800) VISIT NC or (919) 733-8372
Fax: (919) 715-3097
Web site: http://www.visitnc.com

North Dakota
North Dakota Tourism Division
Century Center
1600 E. Century Ave. Suite 2
PO Box 2057
Bismarck, N.D. 58503
(800) 435-5663 or (701) 328-2525
Fax: (701) 328-4878
Email: tourism@state.nd.us
Web site: http://www.ndtourism.com

Ohio
Ohio Division of Travel and Tourism
77 S. High St., 29th Floor
Columbus, OH 43215
(800) 282-5393
Web site: http://www.ohiotourism.com

Oklahoma
Oklahoma Tourism And Recreation Department
Travel & Tourism Division
15 N. Robinson, Suite 801
PO Box 52002
Oklahoma City, OK 73152-2002
(800) 652-6552 or (405)521-2406
Fax: (405)521-3992
Email: information@TravelOK.com
Web site: http://www.travelok.com

Oregon
Oregon Tourism Commission
775 Summer St NE
Salem, OR 97310
(800) 547-7842 or (503) 986-0000
Fax: (503) 986-0001
Email: info@traveloregon.com

Web site: http://www.traveloregon.com

Pennsylvania
Pennsylvania Department of Community and Economic Development
Office of Tourism, Film and Economic Development Marketing
4th Floor, Commonwealth Keystone Building
400 North Street
Harrisburg, PA 17120-0225 USA
(800) 237-4363 or (717) 787-5453
Fax: (717) 787-0687
Web site: http://www.experiencepa.com

Rhode Island
Rhode Island Tourism Division
1 West Exchange Street
Providence, RI 02903
800-556-2484
(401) 222-2601
Fax: (401) 273-8720
Email: visitrhodeisland@riedc.com
Web site: http://www.visitrhodeisland.com/

South Carolina
South Carolina Department of Parks, Recreation and Tourism
1205 Pendleton Street
Columbia, South Carolina 29201
(803) 734-1700
Fax: (803) 273-8270
Web site: http://www.discoversouthcarolina.com

South Dakota
South Dakota Department of Tourism
711 East Wells Ave
Pierre, SD 57501
(800) 732-5682 or (605) 773-3301
Fax: (605) 773-3256
E-mail: sdinfo@state.sd.us
Web site: http://www.travelsd.com

Tennessee
Tennessee Tourism Division
Wm. Snodgrass/Tennessee Tower
312 8th Avenue North, 25th Floor
Nashville, TN 37243
(800) 836-6200 or (615) 741-2159
Web site: http://www.tnvacation.com/

Texas
Texas Department of Tourism
Post Office Box 12728

Gerald Mitchell

Austin, TX 78711
(800) 888-8839 or (512) 462-9191
Web site: http://www.traveltex.com

Utah
Utah Travel Council
Council Hall
300 North State
Salt Lake City, UT 84114
1-800 UTAH-FUN, (800) 200-1160 or (801) 538-1030
Web site: http://www.utah.com

Vermont
Vermont Dept. of Tourism and Marketing
6 Baldwin St., Drawer 33
Montpelier, VT 05633-1301
(800) 837-6668 or (802) 828-3676
E-mail: info@VermontVacation.com
Web site: http://www.travel-vermont.com

Virginia
Virginia Tourism Corporation
901 E. Byrd Street
Richmond, VA 23219
(800) VISIT VA
Email:VAinfo@helloinc.com
Web site: http://www.virginia.org

Washington
Washington State Tourism (800) 544-1800
Web site: http://www.tourism.wa.gov

West Virginia
West Virginia Division of Tourism
90 MacCorkle Ave. SW
South Charleston WV 25303
(800) 225-5982 or (304) 558-2200
Web site: http://www.wva.state.wv.us/callwva/

Wisconsin
Wisconsin Department of Tourism
201 West Washington Avenue
PO Box 8690
Madison WI 53708-8690
(800) 432-8747 or (608) 266-2161
Email: tourinfo@travelwisconsin.com
Web site: http://www.travelwisconsin.com

Wyoming
Wyoming Division of Tourism

I-25 at College Dr
Cheyenne, WY 82002
(800) 225-5996 or (307) 777-7777
Fax: (307) 777-2877

Gerald Mitchell

International Tourism Offices

Web site: http://www.wyomingtourism.org
Anguilla
Anguilla Tourist Information
c/o Medhurst & Associates, Inc.
271 Main Street
Northport, NY 11768
(800) 553-4939
Web Site: http://net.ai/

Antigua
Antigua & Barbuda Department of Tourism & Trade
610 Fifth Avenue #311
New York, NY 10020
1-888-268-4227
FAX: (212) 757-1607
E-MAIL: info@antigua-barbuda.org
Web Site: http://www.antigua-barbuda.org/

Argentina
National Tourist Council
12 West 56th Street
New York, NY 10019
(212) 603-0443
FAX: (212) 315-5545
Web site: http://www.sectur.gov.ar

Aruba
Aruba Tourism Authority
1000 Harbor Blvd.
Weehawken, NJ 07087
(800) TO-ARUBA
(201) 330-0800, (212) 246-3030
FAX: (201) 330-8757
E-MAIL: atanjix@aruba.com
Web Site: http://www.olmco.com/aruba/

Australia
Australian Tourist Commission
1601 Massachusetts Ave NW
Washington, DC 20036
(202) 797-3000
FAX: (202) 797-3100
Web Site: www.australia.com

Australian Tourist Commission
Century Plaza Towers
2049 Century Plaza East

Los Angeles, CA 90067
(310) 229-4870
Web Site: www.australia.com

Austria
Austrian National Tourist Office
P.O. Box 1142- Times Square
New York, NY 10108-1142
(212) 944-6880
Web Site (North America): http://www.anto.com/
Web Site (International): http://austria-info.at/content.html

Bahamas
Bahamas Tourist Office
150 East 52nd Street
New York, NY 10022
(800) 422-4262
(212) 758-2777
FAX: (212) 753-6531

Bahamas Tourist Office
3450 Wilshire Blvd. #208
Los Angeles, CA 90010
(800) 439-6993
Web Site: http://www.interknowledge.com/bahamas/main.html

Barbados
Barbados Tourism Authority
800 Second Avenue
New York, NY 10017
(800) 221-9831, (212) 986-6516
FAX: (212) 573-9850
Web Site: http://www.barbados.org/

Belgium
Belgian Tourist Office
780 Third Avenue
New York, NY 10017
(212) 758-8130
FAX: (212) 355-7675
Email: info@visitbelgium.com
Website: edhttp://www.visitbelgium.com

Belize
Belize Tourism Board
New Central Bank Building, Level 2
Gabourel Lane
P.O. Box 325
Belize City, Belize
Tel: 011-501-2-31913 or

Gerald Mitchell

1-800-624-0686
Fax: 011-501-2-31943
Email: info@travelbelize.org
Websites: http://www.travelbelize.org and http://www.belizetourism.org

Bermuda
Bermuda Department of Tourism
310 Madison Avenue
New York, NY 10017
(800) 223-6106, (212) 818-9800
Web Site: http://www.bermudatourism.com/

Bonaire
Bonaire Tourist Board
10 Rockefeller Plaza
New York, NY 10020
(212) 956-5911
Web Site: http://www.infobonaire.com

British Virgin Islands
British Virgin Islands Tourist Board
370 Lexington Avenue
New York, NY 10017
(800) 835-8530, (212) 696-0400
FAX: (212) 949-8254

British Virgin Islands Tourist Board
1804 Union Street
San Francisco, CA 94123
(415) 775-0344
FAX: (415) 775-2554
Web Site: http://bviwelcome.com

Bulgaria
Bulgarian Tourist Information Center
1170 Broadway Room 611
New York, NY 10017
(212) 252-9277
e-mail: btc2000@earthlink.net
Web site info: www.btc2000.com

Caribbean
Caribbean Tourism Organization
80 Broad St. 32nd Floor
New York, NY 10017
(212) 635-9530

FAX: (212) 635-9511
Web Site: http://www.doitcaribbean.com

Cayman Islands
Cayman Islands Tourist Office
6100 Blue Lagoon
Miami, FL 33126
(800) 327-8777
FAX: (305) 267-2931
Web Site: http://www.caymans.com

Cayman Islands Tourist Office
3440 Wilshire Blvd. Ste. 1202
Los Angeles, CA 90010
(213) 738-1968
FAX: (213) 738-1829
Web Site: http://www.caymans.com

Chile
Chilean National Tourist Board
Sernatur
Avenue Providencia 1550
Santiago, Chile
(800) CHILE 66 (Automated)
Fax: 001-562-251-8469
Web Site: http://www.segegob.cl/sernatur/inicio.html

China
China National Tourist Office
350 Fifth Avenue Rm #6413
New York, NY 10018
(212) 760-1710 (Automated), 212-760-8218
FAX: 212-760 8809
www.cnta.com

China National Tourist Office
333 West Broadway #3201
Glendale, CA 91204
(818) 545-7505 (Automated), 818-545-7507
FAX: 818 -545 7506
www.cnta.com

Cook Islands
Cook Islands Tourist Authority
5757 Century Blvd. Suite #660
Los Angeles, CA 90045
(310)641-5621

Costa Rica
Costa Rica National Tourist Board

Gerald Mitchell
P. O. Box 12766-1000
San Jose, Costa Rica
(800) 343-6332, (506) 222-1090 or 223-1733, ext. 277
Fax: (506)257-6325-5452
Web Site: http://www.tourism-costarica.com

Cuba
Cubatur
Calle 23 #156
Vedado, Habana
Cuba

Curacao
Curacao Tourist Board
7951 SW 6th St., Ste. 216
Plantation, FL 33324
Toll Free: (800) 328-7222
Web Site: http://www.curacao-tourism.com

Cyprus
Cyprus Tourism
13 East 40th Street
New York, NY 10016
Tel: (212) 683-5280
Fax: (212) 683-5282
Email: gocyprus@aol.com
Web Site: http://www.cyprustourism.org

Czech & Slovak Republics
Czech & Slovak Service Center
1511 K Street NW, Suite 1030
Washington, DC 20005
(202) 638-5505
FAX: (202) 638-5308
Email: cztc@cztc.demon.co.uk
Web Site: http://www.czech-slovak-tourist.co.uk/index.html

Denmark
Scandinavian National Tourist Offices
655 Third Avenue
New York, NY 10017
(212) 885-9700
Web Site: http://www.goscandinavia.com

Dominica
Dominica Tourist Office
800 Second Ave
New York, New York 10017
(212) 599-8478
FAX (212) 808-4975

Email: dmaun@undp.org

Dominican Republic
Dominican Republic Tourist Office
2355 Falzedo St. Suite 307
Coral Gables, FLA
(888) 358-9594; (305) 444-4592
FAX: (305) 444-4845

Egypt
Egyptian Tourist Authority
630 Fifth Ave #1706
New York, NY 10111
(212) 332-2570
FAX: (212) 956-6439
Web Site: http://touregypt.net

Egyptian Tourist Authority
8383 Wilshire Blvd #215
Beverly Hills, CA 90211
(213) 653-8815
FAX: (213) 653-8961
Web Site: http://touregypt.net

England
(See Great Britain Tourist Authority)

Europe
European Travel Commission
1 Rockefeller Plaza, Room 214
New York, NY 10020
(212) 218-1200
FAX: (212) 218-1205
E-MAIL: DNMCO@aol.com
Web Site: http://www.visiteurope.com

Fiji
Fiji Visitors Bureau
5777 Century Blvd #220
Los Angeles, CA 90045
(800) 932-3454, (310) 568-1616
FAX: (310) 670-2318
E-MAIL: infodesk@bulafiji-americas.com
Web Site: http://www.fijifvb.gov.fj

Finland
Finnish Tourist Board
655 Third Avenue
New York, NY 10017
(800) 346-4636

Gerald Mitchell

(212) 949-2333
FAX: (212) 983-5260
Web Site: http://www.mek.fi/

France
French Government Tourist Office
444 Madison Ave
New York, NY 10022
212-838-7800
Email:info@frenchtourism.com
French Government Tourist Information Line
(900) 990-0040 ($.95/minute)
Web Site: http://www.francetourism.com/

French Government Tourist Office
9454 Wilshire Blvd. #715
Los Angeles, CA 90212
(310) 271-2358
Web Site: http://www.francetourism.com/

French Government Tourist Office
676 North Michigan Ave. Ste 3360
Chicago, IL 60611-2819
(312) 751-7800
FAX: (312) 337-6339
Web Site: http://www.francetourism.com/

French West Indies
(Guadeloupe, St. Barts, St. Martin)
(See French Government Tourist Office)

Germany
German National Tourist Office
122 E 42nd St. 52nd Floor
New York, NY 10168
(212) 661-7200
FAX: (212) 661-7174
E-MAIL: gntony@aol.com
Web site: http://www.germany-tourism.de/

Great Britain
(England, Scotland, Wales, Northern Ireland)
British Tourist Authority 551 5th Ave #701
New York, NY 10176
(800) 462-2748, (212) 986-2200
FAX: (212) 986-1188
Email: travelinfo@bta.org.uk
Web Site: http://www.visitbritain.com/

Greek National Tourist Office

645 Fifth Ave
New York, NY 10022
(212) 421-5777
FAX: (212) 826-6940

Grenada
Grenada Board of Tourism
800 Second Ave, Suite 400K
New York, NY 10017
(800) 927-9554, (212) 687-9554
FAX: (212) 573-9731
Web Site: http://www.grenada.org

Guam
Guam Visitors Bureau - North America
1336-C Park Street
Alameda, CA 94501
phone: 510.865.0366
toll free 1.800.873.4826
fax: 510.865.5165
e-mail: guam@avisoinc.com
Web Site: www.visitguam.org

Guatemala
Guatemalan Tourist Commission
299 Alhambra Circle #510
Miami, FL 33134
(305) 442-0651

Honduras
Honduras Tourist Office
P.O. Box 140458
Coral Gables, FL 33114
(800) 410-9608
FAX: (305)461-0602
E-MAIL: 104202.3433@compuserve.com
Web Site: http://www.hondurasinfo.hn

Hong Kong
Hong Kong Tourist Association
590 Fifth Ave
New York, NY 10036
(212) 869-5008
FAX: (212) 730-2605
E-MAIL: hktanyc@aol.com
Web Site: http://www.hkta.org

Hong Kong Tourist Association
10940 Wilshire Blvd #1220
Los Angeles, CA 90024

Gerald Mitchell

(310) 208-4582
FAX: (310) 208-1869
E-MAIL: hktalax@aol.com
Web Site: http://www.hkta.org

Hungary
Hungarian Tourist Board
150 East 58th Street
New York, NY 10510-0001
(212) 355-0240
Email: info@gotohungary.com
Web Site: http://www.hungary.com/

Iceland
Scandinavian National Tourist Offices
655 Third Ave
New York, NY 10017
(212) 885-9700
Web Site: http://www.goiceland.com

India
India Tourist Office
30 Rockefeller Plaza, North Mezzanine
New York, NY 10112
1-800-953-9399
FAX: (212) 582-3274
Web Site: http://www.tourindia.com

India Tourist Office
3550 Wilshire Blvd #204
Los Angeles, CA 90010
(213) 380-8855
FAX: (213) 380-6111
Web Site: http://www.tourindia.com

Indonesia
Indonesia Tourist Promotion Office
3457 Wilshire Blvd #104
Los Angeles, CA 90010
(213) 387-8309, (213) 387-2078
FAX: (213) 380-4876

Ireland
Irish Tourist Board
345 Park Ave
New York, NY 10154
(800) SHAMROCK, (800) 223-6470
(212) 418-0800
FAX: (212) 371-9052
Email: Contact through the Web site

Web Site: http://www.ireland.travel.ie/

Israel
Israel Government Tourist Info Center
800 Second Avenue
New York, NY 10017
(800) 596-1199, (212) 560-0650
FAX: (212) 499-5645
E-MAIL: hgolan@imot.org
Web Site: http://www.infotour.co.il

Israel Government Tourist Office
6380 Wilshire Blvd #1700
Los Angeles, CA 90048
(800) 596-1199, (213) 658-7462
FAX: (213) 658-6543
Web Site: http://www.infotour.co.il

Italy
Rockefeller Center
630 Fifth Ave
New York, NY 10111
212-245-4822 5618
FAX: (212) 586-9249
Web Site: http://www.italiantourism.com
500 North Michigan Ave
Chicago, IL 60611
(312) 644-0996
FAX: (312) 644-3019

Italian Government Tourist Board
12400 Wilshire Blvd #550
Los Angeles, CA 90025
(310) 820-1898
FAX: (310) 820-6537

Jamaica
Jamaica Tourist Board
3440 Wilshire Blvd, Suite 1207
Los Angeles, CA 90010
(800) 233-4582, (213) 384-1123
FAX: (213) 384-1780
Web Site: http://www.jamaicatravel.com/jtboffice.html

Japan
Japan National Tourist Organization
1 Rockefeller Plaza Ste. 1250
New York, NY 10020
(212) 757-5640
FAX: (212) 307-6754

Gerald Mitchell

E-MAIL: jntonyc@interport.net
Web Site: http://www.jnto.go.jp

Japan National Tourist Organization
360 Post Street Suite 601
San Francisco, CA 94108
(415) 989-7140
FAX: (415) 398-5461
E-MAIL: sfjnto@msn.com
Web Site: http://www.jnto.go.jp

Kenya
Kenya Consulate & Tourist Office
424 Madison Ave
New York, NY 10017
(212) 486-1300
FAX: (212) 688-0911
Email: kenya2day@aol.com
Web Site: http://www.embassyofkenya.com

Kenya Consulate & Tourist Office
9150 Wilshire Blvd #160
Beverly Hills, CA 90212
(310) 274-6635
FAX: (310) 859-7010
Web Site: http://www.embassyofkenya.com

Korea
Korea National Tourism Office
1 Executive Drive 7th Floor
Fort Lee, NJ 07024
(201)585-0909
FAX: (201) 585-9041
Web Site: http://www.knto.or.kr

Korea National Tourism Corporation
3435 Wilshire Blvd #350
Los Angeles, CA 90010
(213) 382-3435
FAX: (213) 480-0483
Web Site: http://www.knto.or.kr

Luxembourg
Luxembourg National Tourist Office
17 Beekman Place
New York, NY 10022
(212) 935-8888
FAX: (212) 935-5896
E-MAIL: luxnto@aol.com
Web Site: http://www.visitluxembourg.com/wlcm_mn.htm

Macau
Macau Tourist Information Bureau
3133 Lake Hollywood Dr
Los Angeles, CA 90078
(213) 851-3402
FAX: (213) 851-3684

Malaysia
Tourism Malaysia
120 East 56th St., Suite 810
New York, NY 10022
(212) 754-1113
(800) KLUMPUR
Fax :(212) 754-1116
E-mail : mtpb@aol.com
Web Site : http://www.tourismmalaysia.gov.my
Portal : http://www.malaysiamydestination.com

Tourism Malaysia
818 W Seventh St.,
Los Angeles, CA 90017
(213) 689-9702
Fax : (213) 689-1530
E-mail : malaysiainfo@aol.com
Web Site : http://www.tourismmalaysia.gov.my
Portal : http://www.malaysiamydestination.com

Malta
Malta National Tourist Organization
350 Fifth Avenue Ste. 4412
New York, NY 10118
(212) 695-2233
FAX: (212) 695-8229
E-MAIL: 104452,2005@compuserve.com
Web Site: http://www.visitmalta.com/

Martinique
Martinique Promotion Bureau
A division of the French Government Tourist Office
444 Madison Ave
New York NY 10022
(212) 838-7800
Martinique@NYO.COM
Web Site: http//www.martinique.org

Mexico
Mexico Government Tourist Office
405 Park Ave Ste. 1401
New York, NY 10022

Gerald Mitchell

(800) 446-3942
Web Site: http://www.visitmexico.com

Mexico Government Tourist Office
10100 Santa Monica Blvd #224
Los Angeles, CA 90067
(800) 446-3942
Web Site: http://www.visitmexico.com

Monaco
Monaco Government Tourist & Convention Bureau
565 Fifth Ave
New York, NY 10022
(800) 753-9696
E-MAIL: mgto@monaco1.com
Web Site: http://www.monaco.mc/usa

Morocco
Moroccan Tourist Office
20 East 46th St #1201
New York, NY 10017
(212) 557-2520
FAX: (212) 949-8148
Web Site: http://www.tourism-in-morocco.com/

Netherlands
NBT New York
355 Lexington Avenue
New York, NY 10017
(212) 557-3500
FAX: (212) 370-9507
Web Site: http://www.holland.com
E-mail: info@goholland.com

New Zealand
New Zealand Tourism Board
501 Santa Monica Blvd #300
Santa Monica, CA 90401
(800) 388-5494, (310) 395-7480
FAX: (310) 395-5453
Web Site: http://www.purenz.com/

Norway
Norwegian Tourist Board
655 Third Avenue
New York, NY 10017
(212) 885-9700
FAX: (212) 983-5260
Web Site: http://www.norway.org/

Panama
IPAT (The Panama Tourist Bureau)
P.O. Box 4421
Zone 5
The Republic of Panama
Telephone: +507 226-7000 or +507 226-3544
Fax: +507 226-3483 or +507 226-6856
Web Site: http://www.ipat.gob.pa/

Philippines
Philippine Department of Tourism
447 Sutter St #507
San Francisco, CA 94108
(415) 956-4060
FAX: (415) 956-2093
E-MAIL: pdotsf@aol.com
Web Site: http://www.tourism.gov.ph/

Poland
Polish National Tourist Office
275 Madison Ave #1711
New York, NY 10016
(212) 338-9412
FAX: (212) 338-9283
E-MAIL: poltrvl@poland.net
Web Site: www.polandtour.org

Portugal
Portuguese National Tourist Office
590 Fifth Ave
New York, NY 10036
(800) PORTUGAL
Web Site: www.portugal-insite.pt

Puerto Rico
Puerto Rican Tourism Company
575 Fifth Ave 23rd Floor
New York, NY 10017
(212) 599-6262
FAX: (212) 818-1866
Web Site: http://www.prhta.org/

Puerto Rico Tourism Company
P.O. Box 5268
Miami, FL 33102
(800) 866-STAR ext 17
Web Site: http://www.prhta.org/

Puerto Rico Tourism Company
3575 West Cahuenga Blvd, Suite 405

Gerald Mitchell
Los Angeles, CA 90068
(800) 874-1230
FAX: (874-7257
Web Site: http://www.prhta.org/

Romania
Romanian Tourist Office
14 East 38th Street, 12th Floor
New York, NY 10016
(212) 545-8484
FAX: (212) 251-0429
Email: onto@erols.com

Russia
The Russian National Tourist Office
130 West 42nd St., Suite 412
New York, NY 10022
(212) 758-1162
FAX: (212) 575-3434
Web Site: http://www.russia-travel.com

Saba & St. Eustatius
Saba & St. Eustatius Tourist Office
c/o Medhurst & Associates, Inc.
271 Main St
Northport, NY 11768
(800) 722-2394

St. Barts
(See French Government Tourist Information)

St. Croix
(See U.S. Virgin Islands)

St. John
(See U.S. Virgin Islands)

St. Kitts & Nevis
St. Kitts & Nevis Tourism Office
414 E. 75th St, 5th Floor
New York, NY 10021
(800) 582-6208
FAX: (212) 734-6511
E-MAIL: skbnev@ix.netcom.com
Web Site: http://www.interknowledge.com/stkitts-nevis

St. Lucia
St. Lucia Tourist Board
820 Second Ave
New York, NY 10017

(800) 456-3984, (212) 867-2950
FAX: (212) 867-2795
Web Site: http://www.st-lucia.com/

St. Marten
Sint Maarten Tourism Office
675 Third Avenue Ste. 1806
New York, NY 10017
(800) 786-2278, (212) 953-2084
FAX: (212) 953-2145
Web Site: http://www.st-maarten.com

St. Thomas
(See U.S. Virgin Islands)

St. Vincent & The Grenadines
St. Vincent & the Grenadines Tourist Office
801 Second Ave, 21st Floor
New York, NY 10017
(800) 729-1726
FAX: (212) 949-5946
Web Site: http://www.stvincentandgrenadines.com

Scandinavia (Iceland, Norway, Sweden, Denmark, Finland)
Scandinavian National Tourist Offices
655 Third Ave
New York, NY 10017
(212) 885-9700
FAX: (212) 983-5260
Web Site: http://www.goscandinavia.com

Scotland
(See Great Britain)

Singapore
Singapore Tourist Promotion Board
590 Fifth Ave 12th Floor
New York, NY 10036
(212) 302-4861
FAX: (212) 302-4801
Web Site: www.singapore-usa.com

Singapore Tourist Promotion Board
8484 Wilshire Blvd #510
Beverly Hills, CA 90211
(323) 852-1901
Web Site: www.singapore-usa.com

Saint Maarten
Saint Maarten Tourism Office

Gerald Mitchell

675 Third Avenue Ste. 1806
New York, NY 10017
(800) 786-2278, (212) 953-2084
FAX: (212) 953-2145
Web Site: http://www.st-maarten.com

Slovenia
Slovenia Tourist Office
345 E. 12th St.
New York, NY 10003
(212) 358-9686
FAX: (212) 358-9025
Email: slotouristboard@sloveniatravel.com
Web site: www.slovenia-tourism.si

Spain
Tourist Office of Spain
666 Fifth Ave 35th Floor
New York, NY 10022
1-888-OKSPAIN
(212) 265-8822
FAX: (212) 265-8864
Web Site http://www.okspain.org

Tourist Office of Spain
8383 Wilshire Blvd #960
Beverly Hills, CA 90211
(213) 658-7188
FAX: (213) 658-1061
Web Site http://www.okspain.org

Sweden
Scandinavian Tourist Board
655 Third Avenue
New York, NY 10017
(212) 885-9700
FAX: (212) 983-5260
Web Site: http://www.gosweden.org/

Switzerland
Switzerland Tourism
608 Fifth Ave
New York, NY 10020
(212) 757-5944
FAX: (212) 262-6116
Web Site: http://www.switzerlandtourism.ch/

Switzerland Tourism
150 N Michigan Avenue, Suite 2930
Chicago, IL 60601

(312) 332-9900
FAX: (312) 630-5848
Web Site: http://www.switzerlandtourism.ch/

Switzerland Tourism
222 N Sepulveda Blvd #1570
El Segundo, CA 90245
(310) 640-8900
FAX: (310) 335 5982
Web Site: http://www.switzerlandtourism.ch/

Syria
Tourist Office of Syria
c/o Syrian Consulate
2215 Wyoming Ave, Northwest DC, 20008
(202) 232-6313
FAX: (202) 265-4585
Web site: www.syriatourism.org

Tahiti
Tahiti Tourist Promotion Board
300 N Continental Blvd #180
El Segundo, CA 90245
(800) 365-4949 (to order brochures only)
(310) 414-8484
FAX: (310) 414-8490
Web Site: http://www.tahiti-tourisme.com

Taiwan
Taiwan Visitors Association
405 Lexington Avenue, 37th Floor
New York, NY 10174
(212) 466-0691
FAX: (212) 432-6436
Web Site: http://www.tbroc.gov.tw

Taiwan Visitors Association
333 N Michigan Ave
Chicago, IL 60601
(312) 346-1038
FAX: (312) 346-1037
Web Site: http://www.tbroc.gov.tw

Taiwan Visitors Association
166 Geary St #1605
San Francisco, CA 94108
(415) 989-8677
FAX: (415) 989-7242
Web Site: http://www.tbroc.gov.tw

Gerald Mitchell

Thailand
Thailand Tourist Authority
1 World Trade Center Suite 3729
New York, NY 10048
(212) 432-0433
FAX: (212) 912-0920
E-MAIL: tatny@aol.com

Thailand Tourist Authority
3440 Wilshire Blvd #1100
Los Angeles, CA 90010
(213) 461-9814
FAX: (213) 461-9834
E-MAIL: tatla@ix.netcom.com

Tonga
Tonga Consulate General
360 Post St #604
San Francisco, CA 94108
(415) 781-0365
FAX: (415) 781-3964

Trinidad & Tobago
Trinidad & Tobago Tourism Development Authority
7000 Boulevard East
Guttenberg, NJ 07093
(800) 748-4224
FAX: (201) 869-7628
Web Site: http://www.visittnt.com/

Turkey
Turkish Tourism & Information Office
821 United Nations Plaza
New York, NY 10017
(212) 687-2194
E-MAIL: tourney@soho.ios.com
Web Site: http://www.turkey.org/turkey

Turks & Caicos
Turks & Caicos Tourist Board
P. O. Box 128
Grand Turk
Turks & Caicos, BWI
(800) 241-0824
FAX: (809) 946-2733
Web Site: http://www.turksandcaicostourism.com/

US Virgin Islands (St. Croix, St. John, St. Thomas)
U.S. Virgin Islands Division of Tourism
1270 Avenue of the Americas #2108

New York, NY 10020
(212) 332-2222
FAX: (212) 332-2223
Web Site: http://www.usvi.net

U.S. Virgin Islands Division of Tourism
3460 Wilshire Blvd #412
Los Angeles, CA 90010
(213) 739-0138
FAX: (213) 739-2096
Web Site: http://www.usvi.net

Wales
(See Great Britain)

> # "Sample"
>
> # Know before you go!
>
> Travelers Welcome to Zambia Kit

Attention: International Tour Director:

"It is impetrative that the International Tour Director, Tour Operator or Destination Management Company (DMC), keep their client informed of what to expect and how to prepare for their trip or cruise. "

SAMPLE-Welcome letter from the International Tour Director

(Dear Client),

Enclosed a complimentary copy Know before you go!

Travelers Welcome to Zambia Kit preparing you for your "Ulendo" (Journey) to Zambia. This manual was produced in cooperation with our travel partners specializing in Zambia and with the Zambian National Tourism Board. It contains a wealth of information to aid you in preparation for your "Ulendo" (Journey) to discover Zambia's hidden treasures. When you visit Zambia, you want to be prepared. With so many things to see and do you may not know where to start. But don't worry; we've got everything you'll need to make your Zambian Journey the trip of a lifetime. The Zambian visitor's information kit will help you plan the perfect trip.

Our complimentary publication provides suggestions on great things to see and do any time of the year. You will find information on Zambia's driving, what to take, dining suggestions, hotels and climate information, links to local tourism organizations, and much more. It's everything you need to know before you go.

Safe journeys,

Agents Name:_____

Gerald Mitchell

Welcome to Zambia,

"Where you'll experience the rich cultures, breathing scenery of Africa's exotic wildlife and the freedom to pursue individual experiences"

Cultural immersion, interaction with locals, outdoor activities

These are just some of the qualities that make exploring Zambia truly special and different. You get an incredibly personal experience…with all; the value and convenience of an escorted tour or safari.

Safe Ulendo (Journey),

TABLE OF CONTENTS

Welcome to Zambia, ... ii
Cultural immersion, interaction with locals, outdoor activities ii
The Zambian Flag 1
Map of Zambia- "The Real Africa" 2
Mwaiseni! (Welcome) to Zambia! 3
History of Zambia 3
The Colonial Period 4
Religious Demography-Zambia 4
Zambian people their cultures and traditions 5
Languages 6
Major vernaculars 6
The Major Tribes 6
Zambia's Customs, cultures and Tradition's 7
Music and Dance 7
Zambian music 7
Traditional Ceremonies 8
Festivals 8
Kazanga 8
Kuomboka 9
Ncwala 9
Kulamba 9
Likumbi Lya Mize (August) 9
Livingstone Cultural & Arts Festival 9
Shimunenga 9
Umutomboko 9
TEN REASONS WHY YOU SHOULD VISIT ZAMBIA 10
Additional sites not to be missed on your "Ulendo" (Journey) to Zambia 11
Passports & Visa Information 11
Current visa prices 11
USA Contact to obtain Visa for Zambia: 12
Immunizations 12
Precautions for travelers 12
International Airlines servicing Zambia 13
Sample South African Airways (SAA) Flight Schedule New York (JFK) - South Africa with regular flight connections to Lusaka 13
Trip insurance-Protect your investment 14
No worries Travel Protection 14
Selecting your "Tour Host" a certified Zambian TAAZ Tour Operator 14
Welcome Message from the Travel Association of Zambian Tour Operator's 14
List of Zambian Tour Operator's 15
Practical Travel Tips-"Things to Know about Zambia" 16
Local times Standard Time Zone: GMT/UTC +02.00 hour 16
Climate-weather conditions 16
Local currency 16
Exchange Rate Indicators 16
Zambian Electrical Service: 17
Banks offering ATM services in Lusaka, Zambia 18
Travel Tips-Caring for your travel documents and Money 18

Public Holidays	19
Discovering exhilarating Lusaka, capital of Zambia	20
Luxury Hotels Lusaka, Zambia:	20
Additional luxury (5 stars) hotels-Zambia	20
Middle Range	20
Livingston-Home to Victor Falls	21
Luxury	21
Kariba and Lower Zambezi	21
Luxury	21
LUSAKA - Places to Visit	21
Local Zambian restaurants; "Experiencing the local cuisine"	22
What is Nshima and who eats it? (A must for the first time traveler)	22
Night Life	23
What's happening in Zambia?	23
Zambia Tourism Board Office, Lusaka	23
Personal hygiene	24
Water and local beverages	24
Auto rentals-Lusaka -For the Independent traveler	24
List of Zambian auto rental companies:	25
Zambia-Shopping	25
Arts & Crafts	26
Don't leave Zambia without your coffee	27
Source for Zambian Coffee:	28
Exploring Zambian National Parks	29
South Luangwa National Park-"Famous Walking Safari"	29
South Lunagwa Wildlife-"Home of the Hippopotamus"	30
North Luangwa Wildlife-"Lion Country"	30
Lower Zambezi National Park-"Fish the Tiger Fish"	31
Kafue National Park-"Fishing Opportunities"	31
Lochinvar National Park- "Home to Candelabra' Tree."	32
Liuwa Plains National Park-"Real Africa"	33
The Bangweulu Floodplains- "Indigenous birds"	34
"Nsumbu National Park- teeming with crocodiles"	35
Mosi -oa- Tunya National Park-"Victoria Falls entrance"	35
"Off the beaten path"	36
North Zambia-Mpulungu and Lake Tanganyika, the world's longest lake	36
Incredible wildlife of Zambia	37
How to prepare for a Zambian Safari	38
Introduction	38
What is a "typical" day on an African Safari?	39
Rule of Safaris:	39
Are the wild animals dangerous?	40
What types of food are served on an African safari?	41
Physical challenges one might encounter while on safari	41
Is there electricity in the camps?	42
Is communication with the "outside world" possible while on an African safari?	42
What laundry facilities are available on an African safari?	42
Can we bring children on our African safari?	42
Keeping Your Children Interested While on Safari	43
Zambian Tour Operator who host"Family Safari Vacations"	43

How to Travel Free as an International Tour Director

Safety Tips & Do's and Don'ts while on Safari 43
Creature encounters 43
Look but Don't Touch, Frighten or Feed 44
What animals will we see on an African safari? 45
Elephant..46
Listing of Luxury Game Lodges and upscale camps 47
Visitors check list-items to take on your trip to Zambia..48
Suggested Luggage List 48
Check list: 48
"Don't forget" items: 48
Photography Equipment for your Photo-Safari 49
Eco-Tourism-Saving the environment 50
Remembering, not forgetting Zambia 51
AFTER-At Home, ...51
Information panels-"Links to Zambian Resources 52
Embassy's located in Lusaka, Zambia: 52
Zambia National Tourist Board Office Lusaka 52
Zambia National Tourist Board Office-North America 52
Lodges...53
Guide Books 53
Wildlife Guides 53
Travel Writers 53
Picture Books 53
General 54
Health Guides 54
Your Personal Custom Trip Inquiry Form 55
We provide much more than a typical African tour! We listen before we speak! 55
Contact Information..56
Your Ideas of Your Trip..56
Visitor's Trip Evaluation 58

Section One- "The Real Africa"

"Welcome to

Mwaiseni! (Welcome) to Zambia!

Why visit Zambia, the "Gem of Africa"-Zambia is a country the size of Texas or France situated in Southern Africa. Zambia, "the Real Africa", is regarded by many as the continent's greatest secret, ranging from the mighty Victoria Falls to the world renowned National Parks of the Luangwa and Zambezi valleys. The fact that the country has, for so long, been largely overlooked as a tourist destination is one of its greatest assets. The wilderness areas are pristine and the country offers its guests views of the African bush that have not changed for centuries

History of Zambia

Zambia's history goes back to the debut of Homo sapiens: evidence of human habitation going back 100,000 years has been found at Kabwe, north of Lusaka. Beginning around 1000 AD, Swahili-Arab slave-traders gradually penetrated the region from their city-states on the eastern coast of Africa. Between the 14th and 16th centuries a Bantu-speaking group known as the Maravi migrated from present-day Congo (Zaïre) and established kingdoms in eastern and southeastern Zambia.

In the 18th century, Portuguese explorers following the routes of Swahili-Arab slavers from the coast into the interior became the first known European visitors. After the Zulu nation to the south began scattering its neighbors, victims of the Difaqane (forced migration) began arriving in Zambia in the early 19th century. Squeezed out of Zimbabwe, the Makalolo people moved into southern Zambia, pushing the Tonga out of the way and grabbing Lozi territory on the upper Zambezi River.

The Colonial Period

The Scottish explorer David Livingstone first came to the area that is now Zambia in 1851; he visited Victoria Falls in 1855, and in 1873 he died near Lake Bangweulu. In 1890 agents of Cecil Rhodes's British South Africa Company signed treaties with several African leaders, including Lewanika, the Lozi king, and proceeded to administer the region. The area was divided into the protectorates of Northwestern and Northeastern Rhodesia until 1911, when the two were joined to form Northern Rhodesia.

The mining of copper and lead began in the early 1900s. By 1909 the central railroad from Livingstone to Ndola had been completed and about 1,500 Europeans had settled in the country. In 1924 the British took over the administration of the protectorate. In the late 1920s extensive copper deposits were discovered in what soon became known as the Copperbelt, and by the late 1930s about 4,000 European skilled workers and some 20,000 African laborers were engaged there.

In 1946 delegates from these groups met in Lusaka and formed the Federation of African Welfare Societies, the first protectorate-wide African movement; in 1948 this organization was transformed into the Northern Rhodesia African Congress. In the early 1950s, under the leadership of Harry Nkumbula, it fought strenuously, if unsuccessfully, against the establishment of the Federation of Rhodesia and Nyasaland (1953–63), which combined Northern Rhodesia (now Zambia), Southern Rhodesia (now

Zimbabwe), and Nyasaland (now Malawi). The booming copper industry had attracted about 72,000 whites to Northern Rhodesia by 1958, and the blacks there experienced increasing white domination.

Zambia joined Great Britain and other countries in applying economic sanctions against white-ruled Rhodesia in 1965. It discontinued transporting goods via rail through Rhodesia to the seaport of Beira in Mozambique. Instead, overseas trade items were transported to and from the seaport of Dar-es-Salaam, Tanzania, by plane and by truck (via the Great North Road). A petroleum pipeline between Dar-es-Salaam and Ndola was opened in 1968 and, with the help of China, the Great Uhuru (Tazara) Railway connecting Dar-es-Salaam and Zambia was opened in 1975. In addition, the country halted imports of coal (used especially in the copper industry) from Rhodesia; mining in southern Zambia increased until it supplied most of the country's needs. The Rhodesian army pressured Zambia to lift the sanctions by destroying parts of Zambia's transportation network. Zimbabwean independence was finally won in 1980.

Religious Demography-Zambia

The country has a total area of 290,586 square miles and its population is estimated at 10,285,631. Approximately 85 percent of the population is Christian; 5 percent are Muslim; 5 percent adhere to other faiths, including Hinduism and the Baha'i Faith; and 5 percent are atheist.

The Christian faith was introduced by foreign missionary groups in the 1890's. The majority of indigenous persons, spread throughout the country, either are Roman Catholic or Protestant. Currently there is an upsurge of new Pentecostal churches, commonly known as the "born again" churches, which have attracted many young persons into their ranks.

Muslims are concentrated in certain parts of the country where citizens of Asian origin have settled along the railroad line from Lusaka to Livingstone, in Chipata, and in the eastern province. Most citizens of Asian origin are Muslims, although Hindus constitute a small percentage. A limited number of indigenous persons also are Muslim.

Foreign missionary groups operate in the country and include the Roman Catholic Church, the Anglican Church, and the Church of God.

Zambian people their cultures and traditions

Zambians are a curious people. To a Western mindset, this might be interpreted as unnecessarily staring at you or talking about you in front of you. Be prepared to be greeted by kids yelling *mazungu, mazungu!* and answer lots of questions about yourself.

Zambians love to shake hands, and you should oblige them. However, Zambians often like to *hold hands* for the duration of a conversation. This should not be interpreted as anything sexual; they are merely trying to "connect" with you. If you feel uncomfortable, simply pull your hand away.

Women should not wear shorts or mini-skirts, especially as they travel away from Lusaka. (Thighs, to Zambian men, are huge turn-ons.) Low-cut tops, however, while discouraged, are not nearly as provocative.

Finally, when meeting a Zambian — even to ask a question — you should always say hello and ask how they are. Properly greeting a Zambian is very important. They are uncomfortable with the Western notion of simply "getting to the point

Languages

English is widely understood and you shouldn't have many difficulties in getting by with this.

Major vernaculars

Bemba, Kaonde, Lozi, Lunda, Luvale, Nyanja, Tonga, and about 70 other indigenous dialects.

Note: The most important thing to remember when speaking to Zambians is to greet them. When you first approach a Zambian, always begin by asking, "How are you?" (*"Muli Bwanji?"* is the most recognized form, or *"Muli Shani?"*) even if you do not care. They will consider you very respectful. While Zambia has a huge number of languages the lingua franca in Lusaka is Nyanja, where it has developed its own style, heavily influenced by the merging of the different peoples in the capital.

Important words are:
Muli bwanji? - How are you?
Ndili bwino - I'm fine.
Zingati? - How much?
Zikomo – Thank you.

The Major Tribes

Zambia's contemporary culture is a blend of values, norms, material and spiritual traditions of more than 70 ethnically diverse people. The Main tribes are the Lozi, the Bemba, the Ngoni, the Tonga, the Luvale and the Kaonde.

Most of the tribes of Zambia moved into the area in a series of migratory waves a few centuries ago. They grew in numbers and many traveled in search of establishing new kingdoms, farming land and pastures.

Before the colonial period, the region now known as Zambia was the home of a number of Free states. The main exports were copper, ivory and slaves in exchange for textiles, jewelry, salt and hardware.

During the colonial period, the process of industrialization and urbanization saw ethnically different people brought together by economic interests. This, as well as the very definite influence of western standards, generated a new culture without conscious effort of politically determined guidelines.

Many of the rural inhabitants however, have retained their indigenous and traditional customs and values. After Independence in 1964, the government recognized the role culture was to play in the overall development of a new nation and began to explore the question of a National identity.

Institutions to protect and promote Zambia's culture were created, including the National Heritage Conservation Commission. Private museums were also founded and cultural villages were established to promote the expression

Zambia's Customs, cultures and Tradition's

Many of the tribal customs are only still practiced in the rural areas as the youth aspire to Western behavior. A greeting is always exchanged before any conversation. If a person approaches you, you should always offer the first greeting. A man should withhold his hand in greeting until the woman offers hers.

Gifts are often offered to a visitor as a sign of honor, friendship or gratitude. One should never refuse a gift and accept it with both hands at the same time expressing thanks.

Music and Dance-Zambian music

Here, music traditional and contemporary is as vital to communication and storytelling as the written word. It is the lifeblood of communities, the solace of the nomad, and the entertainment of choice.

Quiet beauty, bustle, bounding life or brimming joy characterizes many aspects of music and dance in Zambia. Emphasis varies from breathless acrobatic spectacle amid propulsive drumming to fine subtleties of sound and movement.

Many traditional instruments are still played throughout the country, although the desire for western instruments increases. The more common ones are the hand piano, a small instrument with iron keys mounted on a rectangular box and plucked by both thumbs. Or the silimba, a xylophone type instrument with a range of flat wooden keys mounted over gourds. The most common of course is the drum and drumming plays an important part of rituals, ceremonies, celebrations and community communication.

Dance is an important part of musical expression among Africans and along with the ideas they express, serve as reflectors of life and thought over the centuries - of times of turmoil and peace, tension and confidence, retreat and advance, conquest and defeat.

The influence of the west and the rest of Africa is well entrenched in music tastes of the current generation in Zambia. In the big towns, night clubs and shebeens belt the sounds of Kwela and rumba and many local bands play to the increasingly westernized youth

Traditional Ceremonies

There are more than 20 annual traditional ceremonies in Zambia, manifesting customs, social life, rituals, oral history, material and spiritual culture and if you have the opportunity to attend one do. They provide a valuable insight to a traditional culture that has been passed down from generation to generation.

The decline of traditional customs and culture has been brought about by the infiltration of the west and western ways and the melting pot of various tribes living in the same areas. There has recently been a realization of the value of traditions and a conscious effort is being made to preserve them

Most of the ceremonies have a deep meaning, in many cases designed to invoke memories of the transformation from childhood to adulthood. Most tribes in rural areas still practice harmless initiation ceremonies for girls which are generally conducted after puberty. They are intended to help the girls make the transition from childhood to womanhood and prepare them for marriage. Only a few tribes still practice male circumcision initiation ceremonies and those that occur happen in total secrecy.

The open ceremonies that visitors can watch are those that signify ancient times, when new kingdoms were being founded by ancient chiefs and are usually splendid, colorful affairs with much symbolism in their dancing and drumming

Festivals

A highlight of any trip to Zambia is a visit to any of the many traditional festivals held throughout the country. Planning ahead can be tough though, as schedules are variable and not all are held yearly. Also, if you do manage to attend, bring along tolerance for heat, dust and crowds (increasingly drunk as the evening wears on) and patience for endless speeches by local functionaries like the Assistant Vice-Secretary for Fertilizer Co-operatives in Rutungu Sub-Province. On the plus side, any foreigners attending can usually sneak into the VIP stands, although you may get hassled for photo permits.

Kazanga

Kaoma [Central Western Zambia] (June - August). The Kazanga ceremony is considered Zambia's oldest traditional ceremony having been celebrated by the Nkoya people for over 500 years. The ceremony celebrates and maintains Nkoya traditions of music, dance and many other ancient practices.

Kuomboka

Lealui/Limulunga (Western Province, around Easter (March-April). The most famous of Zambia's festivals, this is the ceremonial migration of the Lozi king (*litunga*) from his dry season abode at Lealui to his wet season palace at Limulunga. Wearing an elaborate Victorian ambassador's costume, the *litunga* is taken by a flotilla of barges down the river, with musical accompaniment and, of course, much feasting at the destination.

Ncwala

near Chipata, 24 February. A Ngoni festival to celebrate the first fruit of the season, where the Ngoni chief ceremonially tastes the fruit of the land, then spears a bull and drinks its blood.

Kulamba

near Chipata, August. A Chewa thanksgiving festival known for its *Nyau* secret society dancers.

Likumbi Lya Mize (August)

This is a popular August festival (The Day of Mize). This ceremony takes place at Mize, the official palace of Senior Chief Ndungu, about seven kilometres west of Zambezi Boma. People of the Luvale tribe gather to celebrate their cultural heritage, bringing displays of all types of handicrafts and spicing the event with traditional singing and dancing while the chief holds court. Mize is the official palace of Senior Chief Ndungu. The Makishi dancers recreate famous events from Luvale mythology, and local artists display their work.

Livingstone Cultural & Arts Festival

This was first held in 1994, this festival bring the traditional rulers from all the provinces of Zambia and visitors are also allowed with the knowledge of their culture in their tribe. This festival capture musicians, artist, poets, and dramatist.

Gerald Mitchell

Shimunenga

This is a ceremony to show devotion to ancestors. The ceremony takes place on a full moon on weekends in September and October. The Ba-Ila tribe celebrate this ceremony at Mala on the Kafue Flats.

Umutomboko

The Umutomboko ceremony of the Lunda people in Luapula Province is held at Mwansabombwe to depict the coming to Zambia by the Lunda and Luba people from Kola in now Congo DR. The ceremony is held in July and is graced by Mwata Kazembe who performs a dance to commemorate the occasion.

Section Two

The following are a few guidelines to help you adequately and safely prepare you for your "Ulendo" (Journey) to Zambia

TEN REASONS WHY YOU SHOULD VISIT ZAMBIA

One- Victoria Falls_-Sspectacular in the extreme. One of the most spectacular waterfalls in the world, formed as the wide and entire flow of the Zambezi River dropped from a relatively flat plain into a narrow cataract deepened to 122 meters and zigzagging for 72 kilometers. The Victoria Falls is considered the world's largest curtain of falling water measuring 1,701 meters wide and 111 meters deep. The mist and noise produced by the drop inspired the Kololo people living in the area to name the waterfall Mosi -oa-Tunya ("smoke that thunders"). The waterfall, with its nearby game park is a major attraction for visitors to Zambia.

Two- Home of adventure: Bunji jumping, white water rafting, river boarding, kayaking, abseiling, and many more other water related activities.

Three- South Luangwa National Park, Africa's best kept secret: one of the greatest wildlife sanctuaries in the world. High concentration of wild game and the birthplace of walking safaris.

Four- Kafue National Park is one of the largest game reserves in African and offers viewing of the major species of the continent.

Five- Lochinvar National Park: A bird watcher paradise. More than 400 species are found in this small park.

Six- Our cultural heritage demonstrated through dance and son offering more than ten colorful traditional ceremonies throughout the year.

Seven- Our moderate climate has earned Zambia its nickname – the "air conditioned state."

Eight- Our museums that preserve the long tradition of tribal artifacts are a wonder.

Nine- Proximity to all other countries: Zambia is easily accessed by air from all parts of the world.

Ten- Boast over 43 years of peaceful existence. The friendly and peaceful people of Zambia with their smiling faces are waiting to welcome you to Zambia, the Real Africa. MWAISENI!

Additional sites not to be missed on your "Ulendo" (Journey) to Zambia

- Lake Kariba A lake with a history
- Chimp Sanctuary Africa's sanctuary for Chimps
- Shiwa Ngandu Colonial Manor house in remotest Africa
- **Victoria Falls Mosi -oa- Tunya "smoke that thunders"**

Passports & Visa Information

Obtaining the visa is rarely a problem and a rule of thumb is that most Western visitors could get visas on arrival (bring along a copy of your passport's main page and two photos).

Current visa prices

United Kingdom passport holders: £75 for single entry and £240 for double or multiple entry, valid for 3 months

United States of America passport holders: US$135 for multiple (*single and double not available to US citizens*), valid for 3 years

Other nationalities: US$50 for single entry, US$80 for double entry and US$160 for multiple entry, valid for 3 months

A day entry visa is available to all nationalities at US$10, valid 24 hours

Transit visas carry the same cost as a single entry visa, valid 7 days

Do check with the nearest Zambian embassy for the latest information; the Zambian Embassy to the US has some information on their homepage, and getting the visa before arrival will reduce the uncertainty factor.

Visa can be obtained upon arrival. We strongly recommend that you obtain a visa before arrival. The decision to issue lies with the local immigration officials in the destination country.

USA Contact to obtain Visa for Zambia:

- Visa Systems (TDS) - 925 15th St NW # 300, Washington, DC 20005 Tel: (202) 638-3800; http://www.traveldocs.com/
- CIBT - 2233 Wisconsin Avenue N.W., Suite 215, Washington, D.C. 20007, Tel: (202) 337-2442; http://www.us.cibt.com
- Zierer Visa Services (ZVS); Add: 1625 K Street NW, Suite 102 Washington DC 20006, Tel 1 866-788 1100, http://www.zvs.com
- Perry International; Add: 100 W. Monroe, Chicago, IL 60603; Tel: 312 372-2703; www.perryvisa.com
- G3 - Address: 3300 N. Fairfax Drive, Suite 202, Arlington, VA 22201; Phone: 703 276-8472; https://www.**g3**visas

Immunizations

Malaria- Estimating the risk for infection for various types of travelers is difficult and can be substantially different even for persons who travel or reside temporarily in the same general areas within a country. For example, travelers staying in air-conditioned hotels may be at lower risk than backpackers or adventure travelers). It is recommended they purchase insecticide treated nets from commercial retailers such as Shoprite and Game. There are three Shoprite stores in Lusaka and one in each provincial capital.

Precautions for travelers

Insect Repellent-Use an insect repellent with at least 25% DEET. Effective repellents can also be purchased at Shoprite and most pharmacies (chemists). In addition, using malarial prophylaxis is highly recommended. All travelers should visit either their personal physician prior to departure. *Malaria:* Prophylaxis with Lariam, Malarone, or doxycycline is recommended for all areas.

International Airlines servicing Zambia

All international flights from Europe arrive in Lusaka.

- British Airways: www.british-airways.com
- Kenya Airways: www.kenya-airways.com
- KLM: www.klm.com
- Air Zimbabwe: www.airzim.co.zw
- Air Malawi: www.airmalawi.net
- South African Airways: www.flysaa.com
- Zambian Airways www.zambianairways.co.zm

Trip insurance-Protect your investment

It's vital to ensure that your travel insurance will cover all emergencies that might occur while traveling abroad.

No worries Travel Protection

There are times when unforeseen events will occur. To avoid incurring costly charges should this happen, we strongly urge you to invest in Travel Guard Essential Travel Insurance & Livetravel 24-hour assistance. You choose your coverage;

- Terrorist Incident
- Travel Delay
- Loss of Baggage
- Baggage Delay
- Medical Expense
- Emergency Medical Transportation

www.TrravelGuard.com-1-800-826-`1300

Contact: Mr. Richard Sweet Ext. 13328

Mutual of Omaha Trip Insurance *Worldwide Travel Assistance*
For inquiries within the U.S. call toll free: 1-800-856-9947
Outside the U.S. call Collect: (312) 935-3658

Selecting your "Tour Host" a certified Zambian TAAZ Tour Operator

Welcome Message from the Travel Association of Zambian Tour Operator's

We value our relationship and thank you for your business. We will take the time to make you feel important every step of the way. Above all we are committed to providing your exceptional service. We are your Zambian experts and we are here to share our expertise to ensure you that exploring Zambia will allow you to *escape the ordinary!*

TAAZ Tours specializes in providing custom Safari's and Special Interest Tours to the world's most remarkable destination-Zambia. Have one of our expert trip advisors create the itinerary of your dreams today. Indulge in a travel package to Zambia, take an alluring African safari – just dream of your ultimate trip and we will create the ideal itinerary for you. Our trip advisors distinctively tailor inspiring travel experiences that suit the needs and wants of individual and group travelers.

Call 1-877-899-8747 for a list of certified Zambian Tour Operators to custom create your Zambian itinerary.

- We will respond to your emails by the end of the business day
- We are here to assist you and do all we can to say "yes" to your request. At every step of the booking our aim is to anticipate your needs and go one better.
- Once the tour is paid in full, documents will be sent to you within 48 hours

List of Zambian Tour Operator's

1. The Zambian Safari Company: reservations@zamsaf.co.zm
2. Voyagers: voyagers-travel@voyagers.com.zm
   www.voyageurs.com.zm
3. Cutty Sark Tours: cutysark@zamnet.zm
4. United Touring Company (UTC): utczam@zamnet.zm
   www.utctravelplanner.com

Section Three

Practical Travel Tips-"Things to Know about Zambia"

Local times Standard Time Zone: GMT/UTC +02.00 hour

Climate-weather conditions

If you look at a map, Zambia appears to be squarely in the tropics, but thanks to its landlocked and elevated position it does have distinct seasons that run as follows:

Dry season — May to August. The coolest time of the year, with temperatures 24-28°C during the day, can drop as low as 7°C at night. Probably the best time of year to visit Zambia: come early in the dry season for bird watching or to see Vic Falls at their biggest, or later when the bush has dried up for good game-spotting on safari.

Hot season — September to November. Temperatures rocket up to a scorching 38-42°C and clouds of swirling dust make driving on dirt roads an asthmatic's nightmare. If you can take the heat, though, it's a good time for safaris as wildlife clusters around the few remaining watering holes.

Wet season — December to April. Temperatures cool down to 32°C or so and, true to the name, there is a lot of rain — sometimes just an hour or two, sometimes for days on end. Unsealed roads become impassable muddy nightmares, and many safari lodges close.

All temperatures above are given for the lowland valleys that house most of Zambia's population and national parks. If you're heading up to the plateaus, temperatures will be around 5°C lower.

Local currency

The Zambian Kwacha Recent historical exchange rates are as follows:

Exchange Rate Indicators

Date Apr 08

  £1.00= ZMK6,993.86
  $1.00= ZMK3,530.00
  €1.00= ZMK5,487.48

Example: $100.00 USA converts to 342,542.96 Kwacha's (6/08)

If you want to **sound like a local**, refer to 1000 kwacha as a **pin**, so for example 10,000K is "ten pin". In the '90's, the kwacha devalued so rapidly that the government didn't have time to produce new, larger bank notes. To pay for things, Zambians often had to bundle — or "pin" together — large numbers of small bills.

Zambian Electrical Service:

Zambia uses both the round 3-pronged and the British flat 3-pronged plugs.

It is recommended you will need to buy at least one adapter. Zambia's voltage is 230V. U.S. outlets are 120V. Most new devices (phones and laptops) can handle the different voltage rates, but some devices only work on the U.S. standard of 120V. Check your device to see what voltage range it handles. Most transformer blocks will have an "Input" line that defines its voltage capacity. For example, "Input: 100 - 240V" means that it will work on voltages from 100V to 240V. If your transformer can't handle the different voltage, you'll need to purchase a voltage converter. You can find world regional voltage converters power packs at various vendors. For example, on the Teledapt site, you can click on the Regional Phone and Power link.

Laptops- Most laptops have both wifi (802.11) and wired Ethernet ports that can be used in many hotels and convention centers around the world. There are basic instructions for configuring wireless networking for Windows XP, Windows ME and Apple Macintosh computers. While this information is targeted towards UW networks, it is applicable to other wifi networks as well.

There are other alternatives if neither wireless nor Ethernet service is available.

- Hot spots
- Aircard
- Dial-up

Hot Spots: A number of service providers offer hot spots; you can use their hot spots as part of your service. Check your provider for service area availability (Cingular, T-Mobile) href="https://selfcare.hotspot.tmobile.com/locations/viewGlobalLocations.do">

Hot-Spot service is available at many retail locations. Many airports also offer wireless services, usually pay as you go.

Aircard: Most cellular service providers now support aircards from one or more vendors. An aircard fits into a laptop's PC card slot, and provides internet access via the cellular phone network. You can get current information by calling a cellular provider (Cingular, Sprint, T-Mobile, Verizon) or by searching their web site for the terms "aircard", "pc card" or "cellular pc".

The country code for Zambia is "260." The city code for Lusaka is "211." For the city code for other towns check the directory." However, **phone service** both within Zambia and into Zambia is very hit-or-miss. In large cities, you are more likely to get regular, dependable phone service, but it is by no means a guarantee. The farther you travel from Lusaka, the less likely you are to maintain a good connection. International calling rates can be as high as $3 per minute.

Cell phones have been booming in recent years, and Zambia has a highly competitive market with three main operators: **Cell Z** (0955), **MTN** (0966) and **Celtel** (0977). Generally speaking, Celtel has the largest network, while **Cell Z** and **MTN** are the cheapest. You can pick up a local SIM card for as little as 5,000K ($1.5). Prepaid time is sold in Kwacha denominated "units": figure on 0.4 units for an SMS or up to 1,000K minute for calls, although as always the precise tariffs are bewilderingly complex. If you plan on roaming with your non-Zambian SIM, check first to see if your home operator has made any roaming agreements — Zambia is usually not on the top of their list. Also note that coverage in rural areas can be spotty.

By local phone-Booths labeled "public telephone" these days consist, more often than not, of a guy renting out his cellphone. Typical rates are 5000K/min ($1) for domestic and 15000K/min ($3) for international calls.

Internet cafes are springing up in Zambia, but again, connections can be sporadic and *very* slow. Moreover, because constant electricity is not a guarantee, some Internet cafes operate backup generators, which can be extremely costly. Be prepared to see Internet cafe charges as high as 25 cents per minute. Some hotels might offer Internet connections to their guests.

Banks offering ATM services in Lusaka, Zambia

ATMs may be found in major cities, but you should not depend on them to be functional. Most of the ATM's accept international credit cards (VISA and MASTERCARD, AMEX is a problem).Some shops and restaurants might accept **debit** or **credit cards**, as do practically all high-end hotels and safari lodges, but surcharges of 5-10% are common.

- African Commercial Bank, Lusaka
- Barclays Bank of Zambia, Lusaka
- Capital Bank, Lusaka
- Citibank Zambia, Lusaka
- Standard Chartered Bank (Zambia Limited) – Lusaka
- Stanbic Bank Zambia Limited – Lusaka
- Zambia National Commercial Bank - Lusaka

Travel Tips-Caring for your travel documents and Money

- Always have a photo copy of your passport and required visas
- Make a list of traveler's checks numbers (**packed *separately* from** the originals)
- Never carry large amounts of cash; credit cards are widely welcomed
- If you need cash handy for purchases at local markets – keep it in a travel wallet or a zip pocket

Public Holidays

- 01 January - New Year's Day
- 12 March - Youth Day
- Good Friday (Easter weekend) - April (variable date)
- Holy Saturday (Easter weekend) - April (variable date)
- 01 May - Labour day
- 25 May - African Freedom Day
- Heroes Day - 1st Monday in July
- Unity Day - 1st Tuesday in July
- Farmers Day - 1st Monday in August
- Christmas Day - 25th December

Section Four

Discovering exhilarating Lusaka, capital of Zambia

Lusaka is the capital of Zambia, so you are sure to end up here at some stage. It is situated in the southern part of the country, about 100km from the Zimbabwe border. Lusaka is as much a part of "the real Africa" as the rich national parks and stunning scenery.

Art Galleries: Some great galleries here that you should visit, the Henry Tayali Visual Arts Gallery, the Mpapa Gallery, the sculpture garden at the Garden House Hotel and the Zintu Community Museum.

The other **major attraction in Lusaka** is the busy open-air Kamwala Market. Here you will encounter the "real Africa" are the markets, a hive of activity; the thousands of stalls are filled and cleared every day. A myriad of motor parts dealers, restaurants, hairdressers, fishmongers, fruit sellers and rows and rows of "salaula" - discarded clothing from the West sold to Africa by the bale.

Luxury Hotels Lusaka, Zambia:

The Taj Pamodzi is a 5-star hotel situated in a somewhat inconvenient location in Lusaka. The hotel has everything that a business/pleasure travel or needs - in-room internet access, two nice restaurants, a decent bar, health club, and good service; good service.www.tajhotels.com

Holiday Inn-Lusaka: The hotel is superbly located in the business district of Lusaka. It is in close proximity to most government offices and embassies. The hotel is 4 kilometers from the city centre and 27 km from the Lusaka International Airport. Shopping and entertainment areas are close by. For sports enthusiasts, the golf course, tennis, squash and bowling courts are only 1.5 miles away. Each of the tasteful 155 rooms has en-suite bathroom. www.holidayinn.zambia.zm

Inter-Continental Hotel –Located in the Diplomatic district, l Lusaka is the preferred destination for businesspeople as well as those who want a leisurely escape. Embassies and government buildings are just across the street and the main shopping and commercial districts are within a 10-minute drive. Of interest are the Lusaka Museum, Kabwata Cultural Village and Mundawanga Botanical Gardens. www.ichotelsgroup.com

Additional luxury (5 stars) hotels-Zambia

- Chaminuka Nature Reserve: www.chaminuka.com
- Chrismar Hotel: www.chrismar.co.za
- Lilayi Lodge: www.zambiz.co.zm/lilayi

Middle Range

- Lusaka Hotel: www.lusakahotel.za
- Mulungushi Village: mcv@zamnet.zm
- Palmwood lodge: www.pearl@zamnet.zm

Livingston-Home to Victor Falls

Luxury

- The Islands of Siankaba: www.siankaba.net
- The river Club: www.riverclubzam.com
- The Royal Livingston: www.suninternaitonal.com
- Songwe Point Village: www.kwando.co.za
- Stanley Safari Lodge: www.stanleysafaris.com
- Sussi & Chuma: star@starofafarica.co.zm
- Taita Falcon Lodge: www.taita-falcon.com
- Tongabezi: www.tongabezi.com
- Zambezi Royal Chundu: www.royalchundu.com
- The Zambezi Sun: www.suninternaitonal.com

Kariba and Lower Zambezi

Luxury

- Chete Island Safari Lodge: www.cheteisland.com
- Chiawa Camp: www.chiawa.com
- Kanyemba Lodge: www.kanyemba.com
- Kasakasaka Luxury Tented Camp: www.kasakasaka.com
- Kayila Lodge: www.zambezisafari.com
- Kiambi Safari Lodge: www.karibu.co.za
- Kulefu Game Lodge: www.star-of-africa.com
- Mvuu Lodge: www.mvuulodge.com
- Mwambashi River Lodge: www.zambezisafari.com
- Royal Zambezi Lodge: www.lionroars.com
- The River House: www.zambezia.com
- Sausage Tree Camp-www.sausagetreecamp.com

LUSAKA - *Places to Visit*

Zambia's Munda Wanga Environmental Park has blossomed into a functional educational and recreational center catering for the needs of Zambians and the country's visitors. The excitement and interest of the lions, tigers, elephant, painted dogs and primates in the Wildlife Park and sanctuary is complemented uniquely by the tranquility and atmosphere of the beautiful botanical gardens. The terrace bar and café, braaii stands, jungle gyms and playground, swimming pool and recreational area provide additional fun for the whole family. Drop in today and see for yourself. Open 365 days of the year, 09 hrs until 17 hrs. For further details of what is available and the entrance costs, contact us on Tel. 278 456/529, e-mail us on biopark@zamnet.zm.

Kalimba Reptile Park has an impressive collection of snakes, all found in the surrounding area, crocodiles, tortoises and some of the most unusual chameleons found in Africa. The park is set in a lush garden with a kid's playground, putt putt course and a verandah where refreshments are served.

Gerald Mitchell

Head out of town on the Great East Road towards the airport and turn left at the last Caltex garage before the airport turnoff. Follow the signs for about 11km. The park, which is part of a fish farm, also sells fresh frozen fish and crocodile tails, as well as a range of crocodile bags, purses, belts, etc.

A good place for locally hand-crafted curios is the Kabwata Cultural Village, which is in the suburb of Kabwata along Burma Road. The residents are carving all day and a wide variety of items are for sale at reasonable prices. Test your bargaining skills.

Adventure City is a water theme park located two kilometers off Leopards Hill Rd near the American International School. The Park offers three different attractions and these are the Botanical World, featuring desert, tropical and indigenous plants, picnic spots, braaii areas and green lawns for fun and games. Water World consists of curved swimming pools for all ages, one of which has a water volleyball court, and Jungle Monkey. Tel: 287751/4

Lusaka National Museum on Independence Avenue is undoubtedly one of the most attractive public buildings in the city. This cultural history museum tells the story of Zambia in four main sections; ethnography, witchcraft, history and contemporary art. The ground floor presents the works of artists from Zambia's independence (1964) to date: contemporary paintings, sculpture and ceramics. With no national art gallery, this provides the visitors with a rare opportunity to sample Zambian Art. The upper floor houses historical and cultural artifacts. Particularly fascinating is the witchcraft exhibit which will give the visitor the opportunity to learn about a part of Zambian life that is rarely discussed, but is deeply imbedded in every sphere of daily life. Facilities: The museum has a small library, a small conference room and a snack shop. Opening hours: 9am-4. 30pm daily; closed public holidays. Admission: US$2 adults, US$1 children. Guided tours possible. Parking available.

Nembo Scenic Park is located 11 kilometers from the city centre at Ngwerere. This scenic park is designed to scale over 47 000 square meter area depicting a model of the map of Zambia featuring the waterfalls and lakes of in the country. It's ideal for individuals, school children and environmental groups. Open from 10:00 to 17:00 on weekend and public holidays by special arrangement by phoning 01 250152

Bente Lorens Ceramic Studio in Longacres has a fine collection of bowls, plates and ornaments which are also for sale. The Henry Tayali Visual Arts Centre at the showgrounds has a fine selection of works by Zambian artists. Single-exhibitor and group shows are held every

Local Zambian restaurants; "Experiencing the local cuisine"

What is Nshima and who eats it? (A must for the first time traveler)

Nshima is the staple food eaten by not only Zambians but Malawians and many other African neighbors. Almost all indigenous African languages in Zambia probably call *nshima* by a different name according to the specific area language and dialect variation. The *Chewa*, *Tumbuka*, and *Ngoni* of Eastern Zambia and Malawi call it *sima or nsima*, the Bemba of Northern Zambia call it *ubwali*, the Tonga of Southern Zambia call it *Insima* and Lozi of Western Zambia call it *Buhobe* It is a food cooked from plain maize or corn meal or maize flour known as mealie-meal among Zambians. Zambians are generally raised to believe that only *nshima* constitutes a full and complete meal.

Any other foods eaten in between are regarded either as snacks or a temporary less filling or inadequate substitute or a mere appetizer. Lets say you meet a Zambian late in the afternoon and ask him if he or she has eaten. Most likely they will tell you that they haven't eaten all day although they might have eaten a sandwich, peanuts, milk, and a few other non-*nshima* foods. *Nshima* is such a key factor loaded with such emotional investment in the diet that many rituals, expectations, expressions, customs, beliefs, and songs have developed in the culture around working for, cooking, and eating of *nshima*. For example, *nshima* is best when eaten steaming hot. A *Chewa* speaking man in Eastern Zambia, in moments of great masculine exuberance might say: *"Ndine mwamuna ine, yikapola ndi ya mwana!"* "I am a man who eats only hot *nshima*, if its cold I give it to children

- **Chit Chat Restaurant** -The menu consists of many items that you might find at a standard Americana restaurant -- wraps, sandwiches, pizza, but also has a surprising list of Pan-Asian cuisine, including stir fry, etc.
- **Cafe D'Afrique:** Delicious food and excellent cultural entertainment. Thurs-Fri - Saturdays. Lufubu Rd, 237745
- **Green Ethiopian Restaurant:** A wonderful spicy experience. Tel: 01 - 291578
- **Le Soleil:** Authentic Zambian dishes in an outside Boma 212437. Roma Ext.

Night Life

Venture out to a nightclub or roadside shebeen and "get in the groove", so to speak, of the local people. Dance the night away to the sounds of rhumba, kwela, techno or good old rock 'n roll.

All over Zambia, you will find so many things to do, see and experience, you may not have enough time to do everything. Zambia is full of interesting places, where one can easily pass many hours enjoying the entertainment that can be found in Zambia.

Night Spots:

- Brown Frog-Kabelenga Rd. – British style pub
- Johnny's-9Lagos Rd- Local pub
- Chez -Ntemba-Kafue Rd. – Great rumba music

What's happening in Zambia?

For the lowdown on Clubs, Shows, Restaurants and other "happenings" go to www.lowdown.co.zm

Zambia Tourism Board Office, Lusaka

PO Box 30017, Century House, Cairo Road. **Tel :**(260 211)229087/90 **Telex:** 41780 **Fax:** (260 211)225174 **E-Mail:** zntb@zamnet.zm

Note: Tourist offices in Zambia publish an annual and monthly diary of events.

Personal hygiene

Outside the major cities, you are unlikely to find a proper washroom with running water. You will probably be given a bowl of water, a piece of soap, and a (damp) towel. Therefore, some travelers bring small bottles of anti-bacterial hand soap with them.

Water and local beverages

Tap water in Zambia is generally not drinkable, at least unless boiled. Bottled water is widely available in cities, but not necessarily in rural areas.

Maheu-A traditional local drink worth trying is *maheu*, a somewhat gritty and vaguely yogurty but refreshing beverage made from maize meal. Factory-produced maheu is sweet, comes in plastic bottles and is available in a variety of flavors including banana, chocolate and orange, while homemade versions are usually unflavored and less sweet.

Soft drinks-Coke products are accessible and cheap at less than a quarter a bottle, but beware of the deposit system: in rural areas, you may have to return an empty bottle before they'll sell you a new one!

Beer: Zambia's best-known brew is **Mosi**, a clear 4% lager available everywhere. **Eagle** has more taste and more kick at 5.5%, while **Zambezi Lager** is a microbrew worth sampling if you run into it. The South African brand **Castle** is also bottled locally, and all of the above run around $0.35 in a store or $1-2 in a bar.

If you are near the borders, you are likely to find **Carlsberg** (good, from Malawi), **Simba** (excellent, from the Democratic Republic of the Congo), **Kilimanjaro** (nice lager, from Tanzania), and **Tusker** (strong, from Kenya). Other imports can be found in larger markets but will also cost more.

Local alcohol: The locals' drink of choice is masese (muh-SE-say) or ucwala (uch-WALA), also known as Chibuku after the biggest brand, made from maize, millet, or cassava and resembling sour porridge in texture and taste. If you want to try this, it's best to look out for the factory-made kind in milk-carton-like containers.

In rural areas, there are opportunities to drink local "homebrews." A wide variety of homebrews exist in Zambia, from beers made from honey (in the Southern province of the country), to wine made from tea leaves (in the Eastern portion of the country).

Auto rentals-Lusaka -For the Independent traveler

What You Get: There are many car hire companies in **Lusaka** and **Livingstone** with a few in **Ndola**. They all offer a range of vehicles. Some offer a flat weekly rate, but most charge a daily rate plus mileage, insurance and petrol. Cars are available on both **self-drive** and **chauffeur driven basis**.

Chauffeur-driven cars are, of course, expensive. Self-drive customers should hold valid international driver's license or one from the SADC region (that is to say a southern African region driving license). Most car rental companies will accept credit cards such as **MasterCard, Visa,** and **Diners Club**. And how has this been possible? Simply... Zambia has seamlessly embraced all cultures and races and created an environment conducive to foreign travelers and tourists. Zambia is considered one of Africa's peace havens...and car rental Zambia is part of it

List of Zambian auto rental companies:

- Juls Car Hire: Hire-julscar@zamnet.zm
- Taiwo Car Hire: taiwo@zamnet.zm
- Voyagers Rentals/Imperial Car: Hire-voytrav@zamnet.zm
- Zungulila Zambia: zung@zamnet.zm
- Zambian Safari Company: reservations@zamsaf.co.zm

Note: Traffic drives on the left. There is a fairly good network of roads (38,763km/24,087 miles in total, of which 8200km/5095 miles is tarred), although they are often in poor condition. There are many ways to get into Zambia by car, but the most popular include:

- through Livingstone (in the south) from Zimbabwe
- via the Chirundu Bridge (in the south) from Zimbabwe
- via the Kariba Dam (in the south) from Zimbabwe
- through Chipata (in the east) from Malawi
- through Chingola (in the Copperbelt) from the Democratic Republic of the Congo
- via the Katima Mulilo Bridge from Namibia
- via the Kazungula Ferry from Botswana
- through Tunduma and Nakonde from Tanzania

Crossing international borders by car will incur a tax.

Zambia-Shopping

If not for shopping, but just for the experience of how the local masses shop, a visit to one of Lusaka's markets is a must.

It's an interesting experience and well worth a visit, if just for the colourful and lively atmosphere. The Soweto Market is two roads west of Cairo Road, and the other opposite the Tazara building in Independence Ave. A new, smarter, roofed market has just been built along Freedom Way.

Arts & Crafts-

Zambian Tribal Textiles produce unique hand-painted traditional and contemporary fabrics in Zambia-Tribal Textiles all made with 100% cotton fabric, designed and painted individually, includes cushion covers, bed linen, table linen, wall hangings, aprons, fabric material, home accessories, Christmas and children's products.

Zambian Art-You can acquire the hand-made exotic drawings embossed on copper plates, otherwise known as "copper pictures". The copper pictures are made from copper sheets on which the drawings are hand pressed or embossed by the use of hand chisels and hammers. This is exciting stuff because it requires real craftsmen, even if I do say so myself. The copper pictures show exotic Zambia African art with African flavor and artwork of Zambia. These copper pictures depict a variety of art, ideas, or even life in Africa. You can choose whatever you wish to see depicted on the copper pictures such as;

- Wild animals,
- Exotic African village life,
- African landscape,
- A hunting party,
- African dance,

These experienced craftsmen will put together whatever work of African art you like. They have been doing this for a long time, from time immemorial. They have knowledge and skills handed down from master craftsman to master craftsman.

What is even more exciting is that these "copper pictures" alias copper-plate-embossed drawings can be seen being made on the roadsides. A picture measuring one square meter (3 feet by 3 feet) will take just a few days to make.

"Canvas seed drawings": The artist glues colored seeds individually on canvas to make a drawing of anything such as wild animals, landscape, people, etc. Since they require an artist's total concentrations the outcome is lovely. Again you may ask for a picture of your choice. You can also see these "canvas seed drawings" being made on the roadsides.

Artifacts, curios, figurines or carvings. They are made from many materials such as stone, wood or metal. Yet others are made from the malachite mineral, a stone with a beautiful deep green color.

Decorative ornaments and hand-made jewelry from malachite and metals such as copper or brass. These are a real value to have. They range from trinkets, necklace, bracelets; rings to even earrings, all of course, are hand-made with an African art theme.

Basketry, practiced by both the men and the women is widespread. The many forms and raw materials used reflect the environment in which they are made: bamboo, liana vines, roots, reeds, grasses, rushes, papyrus palm leaves, bark and sisal. They are decorated with symbolic designs using traditional dyes made from different colored soils, roots, bark and leaves. The variety of uses for basketry is wide; carrying and storage, fishing traps, beer strainers, flour sieves, sleeping and eating mats and a variety of tableware. The Lozi and Mbunda people in the Western Province are particularly skilled in this field.

Woodwork: It is the men that usually do the woodwork and carving and produce canoes, furniture, walking sticks, utensils and food bowls as well as masks, drums and a variety of animal forms. The potters are usually, though not always women, who work the clay and then fire them on open fires or pitsbags,

Don't leave Zambia without your coffee

The Zambian coffee growers are true pioneers: Before 1981 there was virtually no coffee grown in Zambia. Today there are 4,000 hectares of coffee, providing employment to some 2,100 permanent staff.

Seasonal employment during the harvest season (July through October) provides a further 18,000 jobs. There are now 75 large scale and 520 small-scale farmers who grow coffee in Zambia.

Most coffee farmers belong the Zambia Coffee Growers Association (ZCGA). The association provides growers with expert advice on the growing, on-farm processing and export processing of coffee through a team of permanent extension officers. The Lusaka based liquoring department provides quality control and feedback to growers - all Zambian coffee is liquored (tasted) by expert liquorers before being exported. ZCGA is the specialty coffee distributor for green coffee in Zambia.

Source for Zambian Coffee:

In the Zambian village of Mazabuka, the Terranova Coffee Estate has helped to build a community within itself. Here a self sustained farm supports a village, where over 300 people live and work year round. This coffee estate also provides work for over 2,500 temporary workers during peak coffee season www.street@terranovacoffe.com

Munali Coffee-MUBUYU FARM, Zambia, Perched in the little Munali Hills of southern Zambia, the Mubuyu coffee farm is carving a name for itself. www.munalicoffee.com

Section Five

Exploring Zambian National Parks

Zambia has a relatively undeveloped tourism infrastructure and a small but sophisticated safari industry with excellent lodges and seasonal bush camps and some of Africa's best safari guides. Safaris in Zambia are ideally suited for "old Africa hands" or those seeking a remote and more exclusive safari.

South Luangwa National Park-"Famous Walking Safari"

Experts have dubbed South Luangwa National Park as one of the greatest wildlife sanctuaries in the world, and not without reason. The concentration of game around the Luangwa River and it's oxbow lagoons is among the most intense in Africa.

The Luangwa River is the most intact major river system in Africa and is the life blood of the park's 5,624. The Park hosts a wide variety of wildlife birds and vegetation. The now famous 'walking safari' originated in this park and is still one of the finest ways to experience this pristine wilderness first hand. The changing seasons add to the Park's richness ranging from dry, bare bushveld in the winter to a lush green wonderland in the summer months. There are 60 different animal species and over 400 different bird species found in the park. The rainy season lasts up until the end of March and the migrant birds arrive in droves. Each lodge stays open for as long as access is possible, depending on its location in the area.

South Lunagwa Wildlife-"Home of the Hippopotamus"

The hippopotamus is one animal you won't miss. As you cross over the bridge into the park there are usually between 30 and 70 hippos lounging in the river below and most of the dambos and lagoons will reveal many. There is estimated to be at least 50 hippos per kilometre of the Luangwa River.

Thornicroft's Giraffe (Giraffa Camelopardalis thorncrofti) is unique to Luangwa Valley and therefore a specialty of the region. Also seen, but not common are Cookson's wildebeest (Connochaetes taurines cooksoni) - a subspecies of the Blue Wildebeest.

South Luangwa has 14 different antelope species, most of which are easily seen on day and night drives. Watch out for the elusive bushbuck, preferring to inhabit densely covered areas.

Perhaps the most beautiful is the Kudu, with its majestic spiral horns and delicate face. Although fairly common, they're not always easy to find due to their retiring habits and preference for dense bush. Reedbuck, roan, sable, hartebeest, grysbok, klipspringer and oribi are all here but not prolific in the central tourist area of the Park. They tend to stay deeper in the remote parts towards the Muchinga escarpment. Hyenas are fairly common throughout the valley and their plaintive, eerie cry, so characteristic of the African bush can be heard on most nights.

South Luangwa also has a good population of leopard but they are not easily seen and tend to retreat when they hear vehicles. Many of the Lodge's game trackers are skilled in finding leopards on night drives however, and often visitors are rewarded with a full view of a kill.

Lions are as plentiful in the Luangwa as anywhere else in Africa, but when a kill is made away from the central tourist area, the pride may stay away for several days and may not be seen by visitors on a short stay. Very often they roam in prides of up to thirty.

The Luangwa River also has an extraordinarily high number of crocodiles. It is not uncommon to see several basking on the riverbanks or even floating down the river tearing at a dead animal. Night drives are fascinating in the Luangwa. Not only for the chance of seeing a leopard but for the many interesting animals that only come to life at night. Genets, civets, servals, hyenas, and bush babies as well as owls, nightjars, the foraging hippos, honey badgers and lion.

Bird watching is superb in the Valley. Near the end of the dry season, when the river and oxbow lagoons begin to recede, hundreds of large water birds can be seen wading through the shallows With about 400 of Zambia's 732 species of birds appearing in the Valley, including 39 birds of prey and 47 migrant species, there is plenty for the birdwatcher to spot, whatever the season.

North Luangwa Wildlife-"Lion Country"

The park is noted for its massive herds of buffalo, a spectacular sight if they're seen on the run, kicking up dust for miles behind them. Large prides of lion inhabit the territory and it is not uncommon to witness a kill. Other common mammals are hyena, Cookson's wildebeest (Connochaetes taurines cooksoni) - a subspecies of the Blue Wildebeest, bushbuck, Crawshay's zebra, warthog, baboon, vervet monkey, puku and impala.

Elephant and leopard are also seen, but not as frequently as in the South Park; however, you are more likely to see hartebeest, reedbuck and eland here. All the birds in the South Luangwa have been recorded here as well. Sighted regularly are the crowned cranes, purple crested louries, broad billed roller, Lilian's lovebird, the carmine bee-eater, giant eagle owl and Pel's fishing owl. Occasionally seen are the bathawk, black coucal and osprey.

Lower Zambezi National Park-"Fish the Tiger Fish"

Lower Zambezi National Park is Zambia's newest Park and as such is still relatively undeveloped, but it's beauty lies in it's absolute wilderness state. The diversity of animals is not as wide as the other big parks, but the opportunities to get close to game wandering in and out of the Zambezi channels are spectacular. The Park lies opposite the famous Mana Pools Reserve in Zimbabwe, so the whole area on both sides of the river is a massive wildlife sanctuary. Enormous herds of elephant, some up to 100 strong, are often seen at the river's edge. 'Island hopping' buffalo and waterbuck are quite common. The park also hosts good populations of lion and leopard and listen too for the ubiquitous cry of the fish eagle.

Fishing is good along the Zambezi River and healthy Tiger fish and bream catches are common as well as vundu, a member of the catfish family, weighing up to 50 kilograms. Strangely, cheap, strong smelling soap is an excellent bait.

Canoeing is a must. The lodges in the park provide day long canoeing trips. Float down the river at your leisure and they'll pick you up in a speedboat at the end of the day to bring you back.

The river guides will take you down remote channels between the islands where your opportunities to get close to game are very high. Hippos are always in sight, and elephant, zebra, puku, impala, buffalo; kudu and baboons can be seen browsing on the banks from the laid back comfort of your canoe.

The valley floor, although a small area, is host to many of the bigger mammals, including elephant, buffalo, hippo, waterbuck, kudu, zebra, and crocodiles, impala and warthog. Occasionally, roan, eland and the Samango monkey are seen. Nocturnal animals here are hyena, porcupine, civet, genet and honey badger.

The birdlife along the riverbanks is exceptional. Many a fish eagle can be seen and heard for miles around. Nesting along the cliffs are white fronted and carmine bee eaters. Other species include the red winged pratincole, the elegant crested guinea fowl, black eagle, and vast swarms of quelea. In summer the stunning narina trogon makes its home here. Other specialties are the trumpeter hornbill, Meyer's parrot and Lilian's lovebird.

The best time is mid season from June to September, but all lodges and canoeing operators are open from April to November. Fishing is at its best in September / October.

Kafue National Park- "Fishing Opportunities"

Kafue is Zambia's oldest national park and by far the largest. It was proclaimed in 1950 and is spread over 16,000 square miles - the second largest national park in the world and about the size of Wales.

From the astounding Busanga Plains in the North-western section of the Park to the tree-choked wilderness, and the lush dambos of the south, and fed by the emerald green Lunga, Lufupa and Kafue Rivers, the park sustains huge herds of a great diversity of wildlife. The lush grasslands are grazed by red lechwe in their thousands. Fifty years ago, lechwe were almost extinct in this area; however, the establishment of the national park has seen a phenomenal recovery in their numbers and it is a sight of great beauty to see them wandering in such vast herds across the golden plains. During the wet season they splash about in the shallow waters, and, interestingly enough, lion, who usually dislike water, can be seen chasing them through water at least a half a meter deep.

The wealth of game on the plains are a big attraction for lions and prides of up to twenty are spotted regularly. Cheetah and Leopard also roam the plains, the cheetah being able to exercise their famous turn of speed. There is also a host of smaller carnivores from the side-striped jackal, civet, genet and various mongooses.

Bird watching - especially on the rivers and the dambos, is superb. Notables include the wattled crane, purple crested lourie and Pel's fishing owl. Over 400 species of birds have been recorded throughout the park.

The Kafue and Lunga Rivers offer superb fishing opportunities, especially good bream, barbell and fresh water pike. Most lodges have fishing tackle, rods, boats and bait available. Musungwa Lodge in the south hosts an annual fishing competition in September on Lake Itezhi Tezhi.

Lochinvar National Park- "Home to Candelabra' Tree.".

Hundreds of wattled cranes can be seen feeding on vegetable matter dug from the soft mud and the large marabou stork can be seen scavenging for stranded fish. Around Chunga Lagoon you'll find the greater and lesser flamingo, the pink backed and white pelicans, African skimmer, Caspian tern, baillon's crake and the red knobbed coot.

It is particularly well known for the large herds of Kafue lechwe, unique to the Kafue flats. Other antelope are the blue wildebeest, kudu, oribi and buffalo. Water birds are especially abundant. At high water, massive herds may be seen along the upper flood line and in the open grassland further south. As the floods recede the herds move north into the grassy floodplain. They feed on grasses and herbs in water up to a meter deep and are often seen wading or swimming in the Chunga Lagoon. Mating takes place mainly between December and January. Males fight over small territories known as leks and then mate with several females

In the Termitaria Zone, trees and shrubs grow only on the large termite mounds with grasses and herbs covering the rest of the area, which often becomes waterlogged during the rainy season. There are also many small grey mounds which are always unvegetated. The magpie shrike is one of the birds to be seen in the scattered trees of this zone and the surrounding grassy plains are grazed by buffalo, zebra, wildebeest and oribi. Very much in evidence is the 'candelabra' tree.

Sebanzi Hill is an archaeological site which has been excavated. It was the site of an Iron Age village, inhabited for most of the last century. Look out for The Baobab Tree with a hollow trunk large enough for several people to sleep in. Historically the tree was said to boast special powers which would protect passing travellers from wild animals.

There is a curious rocky outcrop called Drum Rocks not far from the lodge, which produces a resonant sound when tapped. They are also part of local superstition in former times and passers-by had to stop and greet the rocks before proceeding.

Around Chunga Lagoon you'll find the greater and lesser flamingo, the pink backed and white pelicans, African skimmer, Caspian tern, Baillon's crake and the red knobbed coot. Many species of duck are abundant in this environment; the black duck, fulvous duck, whistling duck, pintail, garganey, southern pochard, pygmy goose, yellow billed duck and the Cape and European shovellers. Waders include avocet, the Mongolian, Caspian and Pacific golden plovers, whimbrel, turnstone, sanderling, little stint, spotted redshank, black tailed and bar tailed godwits and six species of sandpiper. Movement of the animals between the park and the GMA and allowing access to the Zambezi River. The Park and surrounding GMA form an important link in the migratory route of elephants from the bordering national parks of Botswana and Namibia.

Liuwa Plains National Park- "Real Africa"

This remote park in the far west of Zambia is pristine wilderness, which to the ardent bush lover, makes it a huge attraction and the rewards are great. Liuwa Plain is best accessed with licensed tour operators offering mobile safaris.

This is not a park one should tackle without a guide as there are no visitor facilities or roads and it is very easy to get lost. Going with a licensed tour operator to see the best this Park has to offer is highly recommended.

If you do tackle it alone, make sure you take an armed scout/guide from the Parks office in Kalabo. One can camp anywhere in the park but don't attempt it unless there are at least two vehicles and you are fully self sufficient and prepared for all eventualities. This is the 'real' Africa, and help is a long way away. In November, with the onset of the rains, the massive herds of blue wildebeest arrive from Angola, traversing the plains in their thousands, very often mingling with zebra along the way or gathering around water holes and pans.

Other unusual antelope found in Liuwa Plains include oribi, red lechwe, steenbuck, duiker, tsessebe and roan. The Jackal, serval, wildcat, wild dog as well as lion and hyena are the predators of the area. Many birds migrate here during the rains and massive flocks of birds can be seen as they migrate south. Some of the more notables are the white bellied bustards, secretary bird, red billed and hottentot teals, crowned and wattled cranes, long tailed whydah, sooty chat, yellow throated longclaw, large flocks of black winged pratincoles around the pans, fish eagle, tawny eagle, marshall eagle, woodland kingfisher, pink throated longclaw. The plains are dotted with woodlands which also make excellent birding opportunities

Mweru Wantipa National Park, adjacent to the lake, used to harbour vast herds of elephant but poaching has depleted most of the wildlife, although there are still some small herds of buffalo. There are no tourist facilities but it is possible to camp along the lakeshore.

The Bangweulu Floodplains- "Indigenous birds"

One of the best reasons for coming to this unusual watery wilderness is the remarkable experience of this infinite flat expanse. The views to the horizon seem endless and one imagines one can almost see the curve of the planet. The birdlife is just magnificent and the sight of thousands upon thousands of the endemic black lechwe, unforgettable.

Vast open floodplains, several kilometres wide exist at the periphery of the permanent swamps. White and pink backed pelicans, wattled cranes, white storks, saddlebilled storks, spoonbills and ibises in flocks numbering in the hundreds, as well as many species of the smaller waders, are a common but dramatic sight when the waters are rich in small fish, shrimps and snails.

One of the most rare and elusive birds in Africa, the shoebill stork, Balaeniceps rex, which is in fact closer to the pelican family than a stork, favors the Bangweulu swamps as one of its last remaining habitats and during the early months following the rains, this strange looking bird can regularly be seen on the fringe between the permanent swamps and the floodplains.

"Nsumbu National Park- teeming with crocodiles"

Lying on the southern shores of Lake Tanganyika, in the northern most tip of Zambia, Nsumbu National Park covers an area of just over 2,000 square kilometers and encompasses 100kms of some of the most pristine shores of this vast Lake. Its beauty ranges from sandy beaches, vertical cliffs, rocky coves and natural bays to the rugged hills and deep valleys of the interior. The Lufubu River winds its way through a valley flanked by 300 meter escarpments on either side.

Although wildlife numbers have declined, there is still a wide range of species present in the park and numbers are recovering, although sightings are not guaranteed. Roan, sable, eland, hartebeest, and buffalo are commonly seen, with zebra and occasionally elephant, lion and leopard also present. Bushbuck, warthog and puku often frequent the beaches. The rare blue duiker, a small forest antelope, is one of the Park's specialties along with the shy swamp dwelling sitatunga.

Other species seen here are the spotted hyena, side-striped jackal, serval, impala, waterbuck and reedbuck. The lake bordering on the park is teeming with crocodiles, so swimming is obviously not advisable. Some of these crocs reach up to six meters in length. Hippos often emerge at night around the lodges to 'mow' the green grass.

Birdlife in the park is still prolific with many migrants coming down from East Africa and up from South African regions. The flamingo is one of the more spectacular migrants while some of the lakeshore inhabitants include the skimmer, spoonbill, whiskered tern along with many different storks, ducks and herons. Commonly encountered species around the lake include the grey-headed gull, lesser black-backed gull, white-winged black tern, whiskered tern, African skimmer, and of course the ubiquitous fish eagle. The palmnut vulture and Pel's fishing owl are also occasionally seen.

Mosi -oa- Tunya National Park- "Victoria Falls entrance"

Mosi-oa-Tunya National Park is divided into two sections; a game park along the riverbank and the staggering Victoria Falls, each with separate entrances. The immense and awe-inspiring Victoria Falls are known to the local people as Mosi -oa- Tunya - "Smoke Which Thunders", and is the greatest known curtain of falling water in the world.

However you describe them, the falls are a breathtaking spectacle which, "roar as if possessed", and spew vast clouds of mist from a dark and seething cauldron." They are one of the greatest natural wonders in the world.

This is a small wildlife sanctuary (only 25.5 square miles (66 square kilometres) running along the north bank of the Zambezi, encompassed in Mosi -oa- Tunya National Park. It is worth a short visit not only for the sight of what are probably Zambia's only remaining rhino, but also for some other common species.

Within this park is the Old Drift cemetery where the first European settlers were buried. They made camp by the river, but kept succumbing to a strange and fatal illness.

They blamed the yellow/green-barked 'Fever Trees' for this incurable malady, while all the time it was the malarial mosquito causing their demise. Before long the community moved to higher ground and the town of Livingstone emerged.

Livingstone's main street is dotted with classic colonial buildings, and while some are decaying, many others have been restored. Victorian tin roofed houses with wooden verandas are a typical example of the English settler architecture and there is also a distinct art-deco influence. Livingstone is a quiet lazy little town with much charm and a feeling of optimism in the air.

Baboons are frequently seen on the paths leading to the falls and small antelopes and warthogs inhabit the rainforests that hug the edge of the falls. In the wildlife reserve, the pastures and tall riverine forests contain plenty of birds and a scattering of animals including some white rhino, elephants, giraffe, zebra, sable, eland, buffalo and impala.

"Off the beaten path"

North Zambia-Mpulungu and Lake Tanganyika, the world's longest lake

Zambia's Lake Tanganyika shoreline is only just being discovered. The coastline is a mixture of sandy beaches, rocky coves, cliffs and marshes. The water is clear and full of vibrantly coloured fish. The angling is superb. You can even have the odd scuba dive. Not bad for this tiny corner of the country. Lake Tanganyika is the world's longest lake and its second deepest. It is part of a string of lakes along the Rift Valley that fascinate scientists, who come from all over the world to study their endemic fish species. You can join them in their studies and wonder at the tropical colours as long as you've got a snorkel (or scuba-diving equipment). If you're an angler you are probably more interested in size and that's where the **goliath tigerfish** comes in. Your best chance of catching them is between November and March when their numbers are greatest. Otherwise, you are likely to see game coming to drink from the lake shore in the dry season.

Gerald Mitchell

The Nsumbu National Park is nearby. Although sadly depleted by poaching it still contains herds of antelope and buffalo and a few elephant. Like most of the parks in the north of Zambia it is totally undeveloped, so you will have it to yourself if you do visit and explore its beautiful coves and wooded valleys.

Another attraction nearby is the Kalambo Falls, the second highest waterfall in Africa and the 12th highest in the world. You can rent a boat for the day and row up the shore of the lake (17km from Mpulungu) to watch them plunge 221m from the plateau above. They are at their most impressive in the rainy season (November- April).

Mpulungu is the main port on the lake and the gateway to the few guest lodges. Most of them require a short boat ride from the town. The lodges are the places to base your expeditions and to find out about how to hire boats and guides, or to get hold of snorkelling equipment. Several of them also offer water-skiing, windsurfing and scuba-diving as well. You should also check with them about precautions on the lake. Crocodiles are sometimes found where rivers flow into it and there are a couple of areas where there is bilharzia.

Section Six

Incredible wildlife of Zambia

Zambia has an incredible wildlife asset, a natural heritage with many unique species of wild game. The superb wild animals are found in pristine wilderness. This ensures that the finest safaris are available. The safaris may be arranged from our theme-designed hotels, lodges and safari companies. Travel agents will help too.

You needn't worry yourself about how you'll travel. The travel agents and safari operators will take you on tours of your choice. Either on bush walks or safari drives, either at night or during daylight, either way you'll be able to enjoy a wildlife safari of your choice. Think of whatever wild animal or a group of animals you would like to see… You still have options of safaris to choose from.

If your wish is to watch the graceful lechwe antelopes filling the vast plains of Busanga and Bangweulu in their tens of thousands, this is within your reach. But again you may wish to see the unique annual wildebeest migration in the Liuwa Plains which rivals the Serengeti. Or simply go fishing…

If you're more adventurous go for the big five. **Elephant, lion, leopard, rhino and buffalo.** Your safari tour operators will advise you where to go. There are well known wildlife safari routes which will ensure common sightings of large animals such as **elephant, hippo (hippopotami), buffalo, giraffe, zebra, warthog, primates, antelope** and various reptiles and rodents. It is all up to you, only your choice counts!

As for the predators there are many to see in action. The **cheetah** (fastest animal on land), the **leopard** (shy lone hunter), the **lion** (the legendary king of the jungle), the **spotted hyena** (the "wild strongest" teeth), a pack of **wild dog**, etc. There are also smaller carnivores such as the **honey badger, African wildcat, mongoose jackal**, etc. All these predators help to keep in check the populations of various wildlife species. **The crocodile**, "the undisputed king of river predators", stalk its prey. Legend beholds that a single meal will keep the crocodile for several months, perhaps even half a year. This is the reason for the croc's patience. It will wait for its prey to come and drink water at the river's bank. With its powerful tail and incredible strength the croc will beat the animal into the water and with its bite pull the prey under water to drown it. Keeping well away from croc infested water bodies is good advice.

Fishing for the "Tiger" Most Zambian rivers and lakes including swamps and wetlands support fish life. Take the southern tip of Africa's oldest and deepest Lake Tanganyika. More than three hundred fish species have been logged there. This is the site for the annual fishing completion. Another place great for tiger fishing is Lake Kariba and the Zambezi River. Zambia is named after the Zambezi, a river reserve for **giant carp fish, tiger, vudu, bream,** etc.

Birding- Zambia's wildlife supports good birding. She is a birders' paradise too! Ornithologically speaking, a whopping 749 bird species have been recorded so far! The common bird sightings include doves, pigeons, parrots, cuckoos, owls, nightjars, kingfishers, hornbills and the broad-billed roller, barbets, honey guides, woodpeckers, swallows, the fork-tailed drongo and flycatchers, red-necked falcon, crested guinea fowl, African broadbill, black-breasted snake eagle, and the lesser spotted eagle.

Section Seven

How to prepare for a Zambian Safari

Take the challenge and sample the rhythms of southern African safari in the most majestic settings and exotic parks. You'll have a delightful visit and, forever, a memorable stay in Zambia!

Ask yourself the following questions before you begin planning your African safari or Africa vacation:

- When would I like to go on an African safari and for how long?
- Would I go on African safari alone or with friends in a group?
- What are my main interests and activities other than the game viewing while I'm on my African safari?
- When is a good time to go on African safari?
- What is my budget for my African safari?
- What travel style would I be most comfortable with on my African safari?
- Would I like the services of a private/specialist guide familiar with my specific African safari?
- What do I want out of my African safari experience?

Introduction

Up until the 1970's, Zambia was considered to have had some of the highest game populations in Africa; unfortunately, over-hunting and poaching have since decimated the game in many areas. Recently however, the Zambia safari industry has been steadily recovering, with fresh government controls and new safari camps being built in the Luangwa and Kafue. Today almost 30% of Zambia is under game management, making a safari to Zambia one of Africa's best.

The Zambia safari and tourism infrastructure are still relatively undeveloped; however, there is a small but sophisticated safari industry with excellent safari lodges and seasonal bush camps and some of the best African safari guides. African safaris in Zambia are ideally suited for "old Africa hands" or those seeking a remote and more exclusive African safari.

A vast grassy plateau dominates the country, with the prime wildlife regions being concentrated around the Luangwa, Kafue and Zambezi water systems. While not sharing the game diversity of some of its neighbors, Zambia's wildlife concentrations are impressive and a safari to Zambia is ideal for specialists seeking specific African game species or birdlife on a brilliant scale.

Zambia is the home of the modern walking safari and it offers some of Africa's best traditional walking safaris, particularly in the Luangwa Valley. Night drives are another specialty of the Zambia safari and they provide arguably the best means for seeing some of the Zambia's elusive nocturnal safari species, including leopard.

How does a safari operate? A safari is a trip on land, usually in "the bush" or savanna environments, which is engaged in for the purpose of viewing or hunting animals. Most often, the modern safari involves viewing, photographing, and experiencing animals in their natural habitats. With greater laws for the preservation of many animal species, fewer people undertake a safari to hunt animals.

What is a "typical" day on an African Safari?

Every camp and safari location will differ in terms of its activities and schedules, but in general, safaris follow a general pattern which is consistent throughout southern Africa.

Typically, a safari day includes two major activities per day - one which begins early in the morning and the second which occurs in the mid- to late-afternoon and continues until dark or sometimes up until 2 hours after sunset.

A safari activity may include game drives in Land Rovers (or other safari vehicle), water activities like canoeing, mekoroing or motor boating, and also game walks. Most safaris are predominantly game drives as this is usually the best way to see wildlife unless your safari is on a river or in a permanent water area.

Morning activities begin with tea or coffee and a light morning snack before sunrise with the drive or activity beginning at or just after sunrise. The mornings are really the BEST opportunities to see good wildlife and interactions as it is still cool and the nocturnal animals are still quite active. There is usually a break to get out and stretch and have another coffee and snack.

Rule of Safaris:

NEVER miss a morning game drive. Skip an afternoon drive if you're worn out or need a break, but the mornings are usually far more productive for game sightings.

Morning activities are usually over by late morning and guests return to camp for a full breakfast / brunch.

The middle of the day is your own. Because Zambian climate is warm, midday's are typically very warm to hot and the animals are therefore quite inactive for the most part and seek shelter in the shade to wait out the heat.

Guests may relax at the camp swimming pool, in a hammock; take a nap, read, etc. For the intrepid, most camps will allow a short midday activity like a game walk or a visit to a hide.

After the siesta, guests return to the main area for tea (drinks, snacks, etc) before heading out on the afternoon safari activity. This activity typically starts at 3:30 or 4:00pm and the weather at this time is usually quite warm. The activity will carry on until sunset or afterwards for a night drive. Guests return to camp, freshen up, come down for drinks at the bar and sit for a full dinner. Drinks around the camp fire are always offered but most find that they are tired from all the fresh air and are in bed by 10pm.

The next day begins again before sunrise and you're out in the bush exploring again. It's addicting!

Are the wild animals dangerous?

Most of the regions visited in Zambia are in areas where you are within the natural habitat of the wildlife and so there are no fences surrounding the camps. In South Africa you will find that most of the private reserves are fenced, but within the confines the animals roam freely and you still need to be cautious.

The best advice to be given here is to listen to your guide's instruction while in camp, ensure that your tent flaps are not left open and doors are closed etc. At almost all the camps the guides walk you to and from your tents and they are trained to handle any situation, should it arise. Keep in mind that animals do wander through the camps during the day and at night, so at all times just be aware of your surroundings

Gerald Mitchell

and you will be fine. Having wild animals in such close proximity is one of the main reasons people visit the area – enjoying them in their natural habitat is what makes the experience all the more special.

The game drives are conducted in open-air vehicles which really allows you to get up close and to see that animals from an unimpaired viewpoint. Many people argue that animals only see the vehicle as it would a tree (albeit, a tree that moves") and not the people in it.

This point is debatable but, personally, with hundreds upon hundreds of hours spent on game drives, we feel that most of the animals, and certainly the primates like Baboons and Monkeys and most likely the larger cats like Lions, are keenly aware of human presence.

But they do not, for the most part except if you are in an area that has seen poaching from a vehicle, view a Land Rover with people in it as a threat. The animals actually become habituated to the vehicles and eventually ignore them for the most part - this allows guests to view animals exhibiting their natural behavior. It is truly a pleasure, I can assure you.

Occasionally an Elephant, especially the females in the breeding herds, become annoyed and their protective, motherly instincts take hold and they chase a vehicle off, but this is rare. Also, the guides at the camps are very good with reading an Elephant's moods and will avoid situations which could be potentially dangerous. Mostly, you are in no danger whatsoever if you listen to the guides and keep aware of your surroundings - always remember that you are in a wild place, with wild animals. After all, this is Africa's allure!

What types of food are served on an African safari?

Top class Zambian and European cuisine as well as some local dishes are served in the hotels, lodges, camps and restaurants. Most foreign visitors are very impressed with the quality and quantity of food provided while on an African safari. Some of the more up-scale camps provide food, presentation and service which rivals that of a 5 star hotel in any top city. The tables are elegantly set under the stars, under thatch or even in a boma - and you will never go hungry.

The standard 3 meals a day is done away with in the bush as the meals are geared around the game viewing times and activities. Typically one starts off with a light continental breakfast upon waking before heading out on the early morning activity. Guests usually return at about 10/11 am for a large brunch, which incorporates meals from both the breakfast and lunch menus. A light tea and snack is offered before the afternoon activity and upon returning to camp in the early evening, a hearty three-course dinner is enjoyed followed by after dinner drinks around the campfire.

The camps are able to cater for all food types as long as they are made aware at the time of booking so as to ensure sufficient time to fly in the necessary supplies.

Physical challenges one might encounter while on safari

When traveling in Zambia you will encounter full days of sightseeing frequently in warm temperatures. In order to most fully experience the wildlife, you will be traveling by custom built safari vehicle which requires climbing in and out frequently and sometimes travel on bumpy roads.

To experience Zambia fully, it is recommended that all travelers be in reasonably good health and prepare properly. Unfortunately, wheelchairs cannot be accommodated on most tours. In addition, passengers who require assistance walking or who travel with oxygen tanks should consider having a tour designed to accommodate their travel need.

Is there electricity in the camps?

Camps and safaris in the remote wildlife regions of Zambia have no access to electrical power due to the remote nature of their locations. Most camps have generators on site with 220v electricity or they make use of solar panels. The generators are not normally heard by guests as they are run for a couple of hours at a time in the morning and afternoon while guests are enjoying their activities.

The electricity is used to power ice machines, fridges and freezers that keep the food and drinks cool and fresh. The generator charges batteries that provide the power for the bedroom lights and overhead fans in the rooms. There is plenty of power available to charge batteries for cameras and video cameras, but not for hairdryers and the likes.

For most mobile tented camps there is no electricity; lighting is by paraffin lamp and campfires in the true traditional style of Africa. For any lodges in Zambia there is ample electrical power.

Is communication with the "outside world" possible while on an African safari?

For most people wishing to visit the remote parts of Southern Africa, getting away from civilization so to speak, is the major attraction and reason for going. As with electrical power, communication by phone, fax, etc. is out of the question given the remote locations of the camps. All camps do however have radio communications with their town/city offices in case of any emergencies. Most lodges in South Africa offer full telephone and internet services for those who do not wish to detach from the world completely.

What laundry facilities are available on an African safari?

Most safari camps in Southern Africa offer a laundry facility, but there are a few where given water restrictions and the location this is not possible. Please check with us to make sure. This service is included in the accommodation cost for most African safari camps. Hotels in the cities as well as some lodges charge a nominal fee for it. Most underwear and delicates are not washed by the local people due to their traditions and so washing up powder is supplied in most of the rooms/tents for this purpose.

Can we bring children on our African safari?

Most African safari camps welcome children over the age of eight. There are few exceptions, so please check with us when making an enquiry. These rules can be waived by booking out smaller camps for exclusive use by parties with young children. Families with children between the ages of 8 and 12 will have to book private activities so as not to disturb other guests. Depending on the size of the family, this may necessitate additional costs at certain camps or at certain times of the year.

Some camps have family tents where families are able to have their children in the adjoining tent (sometimes sharing the same bathroom). Children staying in the family tents get a discount for this type of accommodation.

Traditionally, there is no age limit at African safari camps. On some cross country and camping safaris, suppliers set an upper age limit due to the active nature of some of the African safaris. Please advise ages your Zambian Tour Operator to check if in doubt and check with us for any possible restrictions.

Keeping Your Children Interested While on Safari

Game drives can be long and a little dull since spotting wildlife can be tricky (they like to wear camouflage). Here are some tips to help keep your little ones interested:

- Buy them a camera.
- Let them use binoculars.
- Award points or a prizes for spotting birds, insects, wildlife.
- Give them a bird or animal checklist to mark off what they see (every wildlife park will have these available).

Zambian Tour Operator who host "Family Safari Vacations"

The Zambian Safari Company: reservations@zamsaf.co.zm Central Park, Cairo Rd, Lusaka, Zambia -Telephone (260 211) 231450 -Fax No 224915

Safety Tips & Do's and Don'ts while on Safari

Creature encounters

Although a multitude of potentially dangerous species like snakes, scorpions, spiders, and insects are indigenous to Africa, very few visitors are adversely affected if common sense is used. Snakes are typically shy and generally stay away from highly populated areas. Safari lodges and camps usually have insect (especially mosquito) proofing. If you go on a walk, a good rule of thumb is to always wear **enclosed walking shoes**, socks, and long trousers.

In the interest of Wildlife Conservation and eco-tourism we ask that you do not purchase any shells, corals, animal skins, and ivory or wildlife products. These may be confiscated by customs. Please be aware that the purchase of large wooden carvings places a strain on forest resources. Rather purchase smaller items.

Please do not give money, sweets, pens and so forth to children, as it encourages begging and demeans the child. A more constructive and respectful way to help to give a donation to a health centre or school is.

Some safari trips are done mostly by motor transport. It may simply be too dangerous to be walking around lions, tigers, and bears, or other possibly deadly animals. It can also be dangerous to the animals to closely interact with humans. Watching animals from the security of a vehicle allows one to come more closely to the animals with less danger to both animals and humans.

Other safari trips are walking trips, and armed guides usually lead them. They may take place on wildlife preserves. People might camp out for a night on the African Savannah, for example, in tent cabins or semi-permanent camps. These are usually the cheapest way to take a safari, but they do have their privations. For example, access to toilets and ability to bathe or shower may be quite limited.

If you are considering taking a guided Zambian safari, your chances of encountering difficulties are minimal. Due to inaccurate media representation, people often harbor unfounded concerns about the dangers of going on safari, including an exaggerated fear of civil unrest and crime. In fact, tour operators make it their business to be intimately familiar with the areas in which they travel, thus minimizing risk for travelers. Nevertheless, it is sensible to take customary precautions on your Zambian safari, especially when traveling through urban areas.

Look but Don't Touch, Frighten or Feed

Your safari guide will typically discuss safety and safari etiquette with you prior to your safari, whether your game viewing is to be done from a vehicle or on foot. Although all wildlife can be potentially dangerous, if you follow the instructions your guide gives you, there is little need for concern. At viewpoints, hides, camps and other more heavily populated areas, wildlife is more accustomed to people and will usually be less threatened by your presence. A general guideline is to refrain from teasing or cornering wild animals as it may cause a potentially dangerous reaction. In addition, feeding or calling animals should be avoided, as this can cause them to lose their fear of humans.

will we see animals on an African safari?

The variety of animals found in the Southern African Sub region is incredible. For example, there are 337 different species of mammal and 480 different reptile species currently known to occur here. As for bird species, the number is difficult to give with certainty because the known total is constantly changing as new species (usually visitors) are often recorded. However, a recently compiled list of birds in Southern Africa gives a total of over 900, with all doubtful species not included.

Of course, most visitors want to see **"The Big Five"**. The big five is a term originally used by the "Great White Hunters" in Africa to refer to the five most dangerous prey animals to hunt: ***Lion, Leopard, Elephant, Buffalo, and Rhinoceros***. Today, these animals are thankfully more often hunted by those with a camera than by those with a rifle (although legal and illegal hunting is still possible for all of these animals). It is possible to see all five of the Big Five in certain areas in Zambia.

Elephant

Zambian Bush Camps and Lodges

Many camps and game lodges are built near animal reservations. Lodges can also vary in price. Some of the most expensive can cost over 500 US dollars (USD) a night. They usually include meals in the price, and one can experience some fantastic meals if one is willing to fork over quite a bit of money for the more expensive lodges.

With sufficient funds, one can take a vast variety of transport on a safari. Some lodges offer air balloon or helicopter rides. Others may provide boat trips down rivers, or even journeys on elephants, or camels. Many safari lodges also provide additional activities and luxuries to keep guests amused when not viewing animals.

It is recommended that you consult with your Zambian Tour Operator in selecting a Rustic Zambian safari, walking between bush camps or luxury Zambia safari, relaxing in comfort at our safari lodge and our more sophisticated camps? It's your choice.

- Lower Zambezi - MVUU Lodge:
- Kafue National Park - Mukambi Safari Lodge:
- Kafue National Park - Kaingu Safari Lodge:

- <u>Kafue National Park - Hippo lodge</u>:
- <u>South Luangwa - Kafunta River Lodge</u>:

Listing of Luxury Game Lodges and upscale camps

- Chete Island Safari Lodge: www.cheteisland.com
- Chiawa Camp: www.chiawa.com
- Kanyemba Lodge: www.kanyemba.com
- Kasakasaka Luxury Tented Camp: www.kasakasaka.com
- Kayila lodge: www.zambezisafari.com
- Kiambi Safari Lodge: www.karibu.co.za
- Kulefu Game Lodge: www.sar-of-africa.com
- Mvuu Lodge: www.mvuulodge.com
- Mwambashi River Lodge: www.zambezisafari.com
- Royal Zambezi Lodge: www.linonroars.com
- The River House: www.zambezia.com
- Sausage Tree Camp: www.sausagetreecamp.com

Section Eight

Visitors check list-items to take on your trip to Zambia

Suggested Luggage List

Check list:

1. Good quality sunglasses - preferably polarized. Tinted fashion glasses are not good in strong light.
2. Sun hat.
3. Golf-shirts, T-shirts and long-sleeved cotton shirts.
4. Shorts/skirts.
5. Long trousers/slacks.
6. Sweat pants/sweat shirt.
7. More formal attire for your stay at prestigious city hotels or on one of the luxury trains.
8. Underwear and socks.
9. Good walking shoes (running/tennis shoes are fine).
10. Sandals.
11. Swimming costume.
12. Warm winter sweater.
13. Warm Anorak or Parka and scarf / gloves for the cold winter months (May to September).
14. Light rain gear for summer months (late November to April).
15. Camera equipment and plenty of film (or digital storage) - see more photography information under the Photography Link at left.
16. If you wear contact lenses, we recommend that you bring along a pair of glasses in case you get irritation from the dust or pollen.
17. BINOCULARS - ESSENTIAL (and Newman's bird book if you are keen).
18. Personal toiletries (basic amenities supplied by most establishments).
19. Malaria tablets (if you choose).
20. Moisturizing cream & suntan lotion.
21. Insect repellent e.g. Tabard, Rid, Jungle Juice, etc.
22. Basic medical kit (aspirins, plasters, Imodium, antiseptic cream and Anti-histamine cream etc).
23. Tissues/"Wet Ones".
24. Visas, tickets, passports, money, etc.
25. Waterproof/dust-proof Ziploc bags/cover for your cameras.

"Don't forget" items:

- **Imodium or other anti-diarrhea:** For those who suffer from hay fever and/or "itchy eyes" - Allergy Relief Eye Drops and/or antihistamine medication - Especially if you are traveling during the months of November through March.
- **Hydrocortisone cream/ointment**: This is helpful for any mosquito bites or scratches.

Personal note: Please note that bright colors and white are NOT advised while on an African safari.

Photography Equipment for your Photo-Safari

Take all the equipment you will need for your camera system (flash, filters, etc), as well as supplies such as cleaning paper and fluid. Bring plenty of film (if you are not shooting digital) and extra batteries since their availability will be limited on your itinerary and prices will be higher than at home. Also, carry your camera's instruction manual in case problems arise.

To avoid disappointment, pack too much film, or digital accessories, instead of too little. If you are using film you may want to take a variety of film speeds for the various conditions you will encounter. It is recommended taking one roll per day, plus extra roll for every event or location highlighted on the itinerary. Despite the bright light of the region, for which ASA 564 or 100 is most appropriate, dense day, to the lower 70s at night. It can be cool at night or an overcast day.

Section Nine

Eco-Tourism-Saving the environment

(During your journey)

- Remain on trails, keep far from wildlife, be silent, wear natural colours, do not take or introduce anything to the environment.
- In protected or archaeological areas, do not disrupt scientists at work.
- Be appreciative and genuinely interested to learn new things, do not try to outsmart local guides or impress them with your vast knowledge and travel experience.
- Stop your guide if they try to do something inappropriate to wildlife for your amusement, and politely explain why tourists are no longer interested in such gimmicks. Do not insist on watching wildlife in case your guides go overboard to satisfy you.
- Do not constantly compare your country with your destination, relax!
- Try to immerse and pace yourself - keep a balance between Museums, cultural events, meeting people, visiting protected areas, monuments.
- Support traditional, locally-made crafts when buying gifts for loved ones back at home.
- Observe violations of environmental laws, human rights (abuse to women, children, and minorities), and animal rights (cruelty to animals). Speak up only when it will not put you in an unsafe situation, or better report to an appropriate local or international organisation. Take a picture if possible to substantiate your claims.
- Similarly do not barge into the homes of locals in tourist sites, respect their privacy.
- Do not photograph locals without asking, and don't overdo it when they accept. Offer to delete a photo you have taken if the person was for some reason offended or changed his/her mind. Be sensitive about religious, cultural or security sites.
- If the destination you are visiting does not have suitable recycling facilities, take your rubbish (plastic, batteries) with you. For the same purpose prefer reusable items - razors, rechargeable batteries, thermos instead of plastic bottles.
- Do not encourage children to expect sweets, money or presents from foreigners, nor their parents to use the children so as to sell products or services to tourists. Child labour in Tourism is not a sacred local tradition or custom that you necessarily need to respect.
- If you promise something to people you meet (sending a picture, a letter), make sure you can keep your word!

Remembering, not forgetting Zambia

AFTER-At Home,

- Consider organizing a slide-show for good friends and relatives to increase interest knowledge and dispel misconceptions about the wonderful place you have just been to.
- Keep your promises to people you have met.
- Send a thank you note by e-mail or a postcard to your hosts.
- If you were satisfied, recommend these hosts to your friends.
- Try linking up with people from the country you have just visited and happen to live in your city. Visit an ethnic restaurant, a cultural centre, a shop. Tell them how much you liked their home, and they will love yours.
- Send in your comments to the Zambian National Tourism Board-USA

Section Ten

Information panels-"Links to Zambian Resources

Embassy's located in Lusaka, Zambia:

- UNITED KINGDOM
  Independence Ave,
  Tel: 251133
  Fax: 253798
- UNITED STATES
  United Nations Ave,
  Tel: 250955
  Fax: 252225
- CANADA
  5119 United Nations Ave
  Tel: 250833
  Fax: 254176

Zambia National Tourist Board Office Lusaka

PO Box 30017, Century House, Cairo Road
Tel :(260 211)229087/90 **Telex:** 41780 **Fax:** (260 211)225174
E-Mail: zntb@zamnet.zm

Zambia National Tourist Board Office-North America

2419 Massachusetts Avenue, NW, Washington, DC 20008
Tel: (202) 265 9717/8/9 Toll FREE-1-877-899-8747.

Center for disease control and prevention: *www.cdc.gov/travel*

- **Source for** an insanely diverse selection of outdoor performance and casual apparel to help you feed your habit. Shop brands from The North Face to Icebreaker, Arc'teryx to Oakley, Patagonia Chaco. www.backcountry.com
- Families run business serving the world travelers. Known for equipment for safari's and expeditions. Mosquito protection-First aid and health, Clothing, footwear and camping equipment. www.gearzone.co.uk
- Offering an extensive range of entirely natural Welcome to *Blue Turtle Remedial Sciences* where you may select from an extensive range of entirely natural and highly effective homeopathic prophylactics / treatments for many tropical diseases including; malaria, dengue fever, typhoid & hepatitis. www.blueturtlegroup.com
- Trip health and cancellation insurance. www.travelguard.com
- www.oanda.com
- Currency conversion
- Zambia-Zambia National Tourist Board:

Lodges

- Lower Zambezi - MVUU Lodge:
- Kafue National Park - Mukambi Safari Lodge:
- Kafue National Park - Kaingu Safari Lodge:
- Kafue National Park - Hippo lodge:
- Livingstone - Natural Mystic Lodge:
- South Luangwa - Flat Dogs Camp:
- South Luangwa - Kafunta River Lodge:

Guide Books

- Lonely planet, Zambia
- Brendan Dooley & Nicholas Plewman : African Adventurer's Guide to Zambia - Bradt Travel Guide Zambia
- Wildlife Guides
- Tracks and Signs, Chris & Tilde Stuart
- Southern, Central & East African Mammals, Chris & Tilde Stuart.
- Common Wild Mammals of Zambia, Wildlife Conservation Society, Zambia
- Guide to Reptiles, Amphibians & Fishes, WCS
- Common Birds of Zambia, WCS
- Guide to the Common Wild Flowers of Zambia, Doreen Bolnick
- Southern African Trees-a Photographic Guide, Piet van Wyk
- Birds of Southern Africa, Kenneth Newman
- Piet van wijk – Southern African Trees
- Chris & Tilde Stuart – Mammals
- Bill Branch – Snakes and other Reptiles
- Elliot Pinhey & Ian Coe – Butterflies of Zambia
- Insects of Zambia
- Grasses of Southern Africa
- Keith Coates Palgrave – Trees of Southern Africa

Travel Writers

- In Quest of Livingstone, Colum Wilson & Aisling Irwin.
- Mr. Bigstuff and the Goddess of Charm, Fiona Sax Ledger
- The Africa House, Christina Lamb

Picture Books

- Photobook Zambia by Ian Murphy
- Zambia Landscapes by David Rogers
- Spirit of the Zambezi, Jeff & Fiona Sutchbury
- The Bush & Eye, Francois d'Elbee
- Busanga, Francois d'Elbee

General

- Kakuli, Norman Carr

- Return to the wild, Norman Carr
- The Long African Day, Norman Myers
- Zambezi, Journey of a River, Mike Main

Health Guides

- Staying healthy in Asia, Africa and Latin-America, Dirk Schroeder
- Healthy Travel Africa, Lonely Planet

Section Eleven

Your Personal Custom Trip Inquiry Form

We provide much more than a typical African tour! We listen before we speak!

If none of our pre-designed tour packages satisfy you, and if you would like to plan a custom China trip to just about anywhere, this is the place to start.

Since we know every traveler's interests and requirements are **UNIQUE**, we will provide personalized travel service to you, whether you are an individual traveler, couple, family, or a group of people from an organization. Here are the easy steps for us to work out a perfect itinerary at a reasonable price:

1) Decide how many **days** you have to travel in Africa; and when you want to begin;

2) Decide what **places** or areas you want to go. Simply give us a list of places you would like to visit, or we can make some suggestions.

3) Tell us **the number of travelers**. The bigger the size of the group, the better the discount you can get.

4) Tell us the class of the **hotel** you want to stay in and what kind of **room** you need (twin beds, king-size bed, non-smoking, etc.)

5) Tell us if you have any other **special requirements** (e.g., **vegetarian**)

Just tell us what kind of trip you have in mind, and let us take care of the details. We are experienced in giving professional tour proposals that will fit your individual needs. Please send us an inquiry by filling an online inquiry form here.

This is an inquiry form, not a reservation form. **No deposit is needed** for tour designing! We will get back to you with a full itinerary and a quotation on it within 24 hours, (weekends might require 48 hours). The more information you provide in this inquiry form, the quicker we can help you design the perfect personalized tour proposal.

Once you submit an inquiry form, a Zambian Tours staff member will email or phone you to give you a tour proposal. Our goal is to work out a perfect trip for you, not just a standardized trip such as 90% of the other tourists who come to China receive, but a special life-time experience that will leave you with memories that will last a lifetime!

Section Twelve

Visitor's Trip Evaluation

"We value your comments" When you return home, we hope you will complete this evaluation and send it to us. Your comments and suggestions are extremely valuable to us, and eagerly read by the Travel Agents Association of Zambia and the Zambian Minister of Tourism.

"Sample Tour Evaluation Form"
Note: e-mail or send to you clients upon their return

Name: Date(s) of travel

Name: _____200_

*

Trip/Destination: _____(Name tour/cruise)

Trip/Destination:

Please rate the following aspects of your trip and trip planning experience:

Travel Offices:

	Poor	Below Average	Average	Above Average	Excellent
Trip preparation materials:	Please rate the following aspects of your trip and trip planning experience:	Below Average	Average	Above Average	Excellent
Communications with: Zambian Tourism Office	Travel Offices: Trip preparation materials: Poor Communications with ZNTB Poor	Below Average	Average	Above Average	Excellent
Communications with/from the tour or operator:	Communications with/from the tour operator: Poor	Below Average	Average	Above Average	Excellent

Tour Program:

	Poor	Below Average	Average	Above Average	Excellent
The tour itinerary and sites visited were:	Tour Program: The tour itinerary and sites visited were: Poor	Below Average	Average	Above Average	Excellent
The birding and wildlife was:	The birding and wildlife was: Poor	Below Average	Average	Above Average	Excellent
The accommodations were:	The accommodations were: Poor	Below Average	Average	Above Average	Excellent
The meals were:	The meals were: Poor	Below Average	Average	Above Average	Excellent

Personnel and Operators:

	Poor	Below Average	Average	Above Average	Excellent
The local guides and naturalists were:	Personnel and Operators: The local guides and naturalists were: Poor	Below Average	Average	Above Average	Excellent
The Tour Leader was:	The Tour Leader was: Poor	Below Average	Average	Above Average	Excellent
Drivers and people who handled transfers were:	Drivers and people who handled transfers were: Poor	Below Average	Average	Above Average	Excellent

Overall Tour:

	Poor	Below Average	Average	Above Average	Excellent
Overall, I would rate this tour as:	Overall Tour: Overall, I would rate this tour as: Poor	Below Average	Average	Above Average	Excellent

Zambian Travelers kit written by,

g.e Mitchell
Author, Tour Designer & Lecturer

7/2008

TAKE OFF!

For a Hospitality and Tourism Career

With the GEM Group

Learn How to Start a Tour Guiding Business©

Your Complete Tour Guide Career and Starting Your Own Tour Guiding Business Manual Included in this manual is everything you need to know about starting your own tour guiding business and tour guide career. Being tour guide career can give one a most rewarding life and lifestyle (accomplished Tour Guides earn over $2000 a day). Tour guides provide a very valuable service. They serve as a link between the visitor and an area and its people.

They try to ensure that their tours will be enjoyable and a safe as possible. Tour guides are the source of interesting information about the area visited. They serve as a source of answers to questions covering local history, flora, fishing, golf, wildlife and where best to dine.

Anyone with an interest in people and places and things is a candidate to be a tour guide. A college degree is not necessary, but can be helpful when leading tours to foreign countries which are conducted in native languages. Courses in history, the arts, as well as local native cultural and historical activities, are very helpful.

A tour guide can work from home or office, part time or full time. You are in charge. The only requisite is that you be, and remain, customer focused. You job will be to provide value to your customers by providing that link between them and the area you are introducing them to.

How to Start a Tour Guiding Business is a comprehensive manual that takes you in detail through the eight steps for starting a tour guide career and your tour guiding business. Here are the steps:

- Hospitality Test & Assessment
- Writing a Successful Business Plan
- Introduction to Tour Design
- Marketing Your Tours
- Designing Tour Brochures
- Tour Site Inspection
- Pricing & Processing Your Tours
- Introduction to the Tour Guiding Profession

The manual is supplemented by the staff and services provided by The GEM Group and its Institute of Tourism Career Development. The GEM team is dedicated to proving unique and innovative materials in support of the travel market. The GEM Group is dedicated to helping those who choosing a Tour Guide Career the materials and support to be the very best in the profession.

Discover Careers in the Hospitality Tourism Industry©

Get packed for the Life-enhancing experience of your lifetime!

Table of contents:

- Learn inside Secrets to where the high paying jobs are
- Turn you hopes into action
- Learn How to turn your avocation into vocation
- Learn How to write a "Resume" for success
- Learn How to start your own business in the travel-tourism industry
- How exporting Travel-Tourism creates jobs and new business opportunities for you
- The 7 essential "pulling Powers" a country or community has to export to create tours, jobs and business opportunities
- How to overcome the lack of experience in the Travel-Tourism Industry
- Benefit of entering the Travel-Tourism Industry as a front line worker
- Personality characteristics of a Travel-Tourism professional
- Hours and working conditions of typical Travel-Tourism occupations
- What does the future hold for employment opportunities in the travel-tourism industry?

Introduction to the Seven Major Sectors of the Travel-Tourism Industry to assist you in finding a career and employment:

- Adventure Guide, Heritage Tour Guide & Interpreter
- Events and Conference Planners
- Tour Operator
- Travel Writer-Photographer
- Government-State Tourism Offices
- Exciting Career Choices in the Cruise Line Industry
- Airline career and employment opportunities
- Theme Parks & Attractions
- Ride Operations
- Park Maintenance
- entertainment security
- Wardrobe Department
- Park superintendent
- Park Naturalist
- Park Ranger
- Recreation Leader
- Organized Camping Coordinator
- Yacht Crew
- Beach Resort Staff
- Airport Management
- Ski & spas
- Survival School Trainer
- Plus…other career opportunities
- Professional Associations & Certifications
- How to "sell" yourself for to get the job of your dreams
- What prospective employers are looking for in your resume

- Listing of employment firms servicing the hospitality, tourism, travel industry
- List of International Trade Shows - Career Fairs for networking and employment opportunities
- List of training and educational opportunities
- List of professional organizations and associations

The GEM Group Consulting Services

We are here to help you succeed!

Need Help?

Contact the author "Gerry" Mitchell

The GEM Group is now offering "Direct Contact and Consulting Services" with the author and founder of The GEM Tour Guide System.© Gerald Mitchell furnishes solid consulting with refreshing informality. Gerald enriches his advice with his own experience as a tour guide, lecturer, educator and consultant to clients from around the world. With contagious enthusiasm, you will be guided by Gerald's Consulting Services with Gerald Mitchell, founder of Tour Guides USA ©

Tour Guiding, like all enterprises, is likely to benefit you in proportion to your investment in it. If in addition to a fair profit and the professional tour guides' pride, you can reap from it the satisfaction of having done a professional service to your clients, you will experience the magical glow prized by those for whom tour guiding has become a unique joy and life's vocation. Good Guiding!

How the Gem Group Ltd. Can Help You

- What is your purpose for purchasing this book?
- What are your Objectives?
- What are your interest/Hobbies?
- What are your strengths?

Do You Require Assistance On The Following Subjects?

- Sales, Marketing & Promotional Assistance
- Tour Designing
- Guide Training
- Brochure Development
- Advertising
- Web Site Design
- Upcoming Training Workshops
- Other

If the GEM Group can assist you in starting your own tour guide business, please complete the form on the following page and e-mail –gem39@bellsouth.net t to the attention of Gerry Mitchell.

Confidential Client Profile- Consulting Service Form

Name: _____

Address: (Residence) _____

_____State: _____

Country: _____ e-mail: _____

Phone: _____

Present Occupation: _____

Title: _____

Formal Education: _____

Hospitality – Tourism experience (s):

_____
_____
_____

List your goals Objectives and Comments: _____

_____
_____
_____
_____
_____
_____

How can The GEM Group HELP YOU develop your Tourism Business?

#1_____
_____
_____

#2_____
_____
_____

#3_____
_____

#4_____
_____

Please e-mail your request(s) for assistance to the GEM Group @ gem39@bellsouth.net

Thank you

Workshop & Seminar Testimonials

Over 7,000 participants…150,000 hours of training provided
The GEM Group takes your there…we push your vision to the limits!

"Gerald E. Mitchell is one of the best speakers I have heard. He keeps the class interested and makes learning fun and interesting."

- Dr.Russell Backardt, Western Carolina University

"A dynamic speaker and instructor. Should be used on a continuous basis in our Tourism industry to teach and educate various sectors of the industry on the whole."

- Laurie McConnell, Travel Away Tours

"All I can really say is "thank God" you sponsored this workshop. It is the real program to come along and I know with your caring feeling that there's more to come."

- Justine Clinton, St. Lucia

"This is the first time I have attended a seminar on this topic that has been conducted with so much focus towards achieving real practical objectives."

Richard Spei, Toronto, Canada

"We wish to express our most sincere appreciation for your tremendous contribution to the Business Management for Women tourism session for the delegates from the former Soviet Union. We are confident that the delegates took home practical information needed to upgrade their tour companies and establish useful future relationships with U.S. companies as a result of the excellent program you provided."

- Liesel Duhon, Director, Sabit United States Depart. Of Commerce, International Trade Administration, Washington, D.C.

"Extremely informative, and educational, and I feel that I learned a great deal to apply and hopefully turn these hours into profits."

- Lester Winston, Trinidad West Indies

"Gerald E. Mitchell is one of the best speakers I have heard. He keeps the class interested and makes learning fun."

- Dr. Joe Manjone, University of Alabama, Huntsville

"The Tour Guide manual made it possible for me to start my own business. I read all your books, made notes that I needed to refer to often, highlighted other topics, and then reread the book. It has become a real workbook for my staff. Thank you for helping me gain financial freedom and be my own boss. "

- Maria Jackson, US Army Recreational Services

"The author, Gerry Mitchell, has provided practical advice, and models to follow. This is the best book I've seen on the subject. "

- Aura J. Carter, Hotel Manager, Barbados, West Indies

"Mr. Mitchell exceeded our expectations in every aspect of the training and significantly contributed to our tourism industry development programs. It was very easy communication, smooth process of shaping up the training and effective and interesting lectures and workshops during the training."

Siniša Bronić, Tourism and Hospitality Industries Team Leader USAID - ESP project

"I would highly recommend the GEM Tour Manuals. The author, Mr. Mitchell, makes sharp analysis of what it takes to bring tour components together for a finished product, a quality tour package. This wonderfully insightful, to-the-point manual will be of great help to travel professionals."

-Michael Pinchbeck, B.Ed., Executive Director, Bahamas Hotel Training College

This manual presents a paradigm of the tourism industry. "In the How to travel FREE as an International Tour Director, Gerry's positive influence on the career of so many potential tourism agents is encapsulated for all to enjoy and utilize."

Tim Ham-International USAID Advisor

Anyone who wants to turn their life into a highly successful business must understand the fundamental models that drive the best Tour Director's and Tour Guides in the industry. Gerry's books represent the culmination of decades of tourism experience, research, and consulting.

"Chuck" Fast, Global Tours and Cruise, Michigan

Gerry's books are not about quick money. It is about the innovative application of proven business techniques in the tourism industry. Isn't it about time you consider becoming a member of the Hospitality and Tourism industry?

Sally-Majors Wood, Consultant to the National Eco-Society

> **Guaranteed Results!**
>
> All of the GEM Group Workshops and Seminars are 100% SATIFISFACTION GUARANTEED Thirty Days full refund upon receipt of any GEM manual or Workshop.
>
> **Tax Credits**: The Federal government offers tax credits "up to 20% of your first $5000 in expenses for tuition and other fees." This can reduce your GEM fees by as much as $195.00. These are referred to as "Lifetime Learning Credits." For more information

Center for Women's Travel - Tourism

Since 1976 The GEM Group has provided training for women around the globe in how to start their own business within the Travel &Tourism industry.

Women's Groups: UAW, Women's Association-Surnime, Amazon- Inuit Women Tour Guide/ Destination Managers, Canadian Artic (NWT,) -Desk & Derrick,-Activities Coordinator's for the National Parks and Recreation,-US Military- Moral Welfare and Recreation (MWR), Caribbean Basin, Association of Business Owners (Hospitality & Tourism),- her Majesty Queen Noor of Jordan ,National Parks Society Program

Women's Role in the Tourism Industry. Examples of women and women's groups starting their own income generating businesses are plentiful. Increasingly appealing to women, these businesses help to create financial independence for local women and challenge them to develop the necessary skills and support opportunities to increase their education. Research has shown that financial independence and good education lead to improved self-esteem of women and more equitable relationships in families and communities.

Both Women's Rights: The United Nations Convention on the Elimination of all Forms of Discrimination Against Women (CEDAW, 1979), and the Universal Declaration of Human Rights (1948) form the basis of addressing human rights and women's rights issues in the tourism industries. Case studies show that women can find a voice and independence through getting involved in tourism activities by becoming part of decision-making processes and carving out new roles in their families, in their homes and communities, and within local power structures. Source: www.theearthsummit.org 2004

Gerald E. Mitchell, president of the GEM Group, Ltd. brings his expertise as an educator, tour operator, author, and lecturer, providing an insider's view of the travel industry. He has traveled worldwide promoting tourism in emerging countries and demonstrates a special talent for showing experienced and first-time tourists alike the beauty of the natural and cultural heritage of the destinations they visit.

Gerald's breadth of experience in developing tour programs provides a travel experience to destinations throughout the world that few can equal. He is renowned as a lecturer for both government and private industries, bringing to his audiences a depth of knowledge about the customs and indigenous populations of countries around the world that enlightens and entertains.

As an educator, Gerald Mitchell has served as adjunct professor at four U.S. universities and lectured on sustainable travel-tourism development for the Organization of American States, Canada, Russia, the Bahamas, and at the nation's military academies at West Point and Annapolis. He has served as a special advisor to the U. S. Naval Command, the U.S. Department of Commerce, and the U.S. Agency for International Development. In this last capacity, Gerald worked with the kingdom of Jordan to develop certification standards for the nation's Royal Society of Conservation, funded by Queen Noor of Jordan.

Gerald Mitchell formed the GEM Group over two decades ago to provide a quality experience for tourists to international destinations, including those in Europe, Asia, South America, Canada, and the Arctic, where he trained the Inuit tribes to conduct tours for whale watching expeditions, and along historic Native American trails. He is as much at home conducting tours in remote corners of the world as he is on the lecture podium providing training and insight into the adventure of travel for all audiences.

Mitchell is the author of a number of books on tourism and careers for those in the travel industry, including the recently published *Global Travel Tourism Career Opportunities* this is a "must read" fundamental text book for anyone considering tourism as a career. His book *Travel the World Free as an International Tour Director* has just been released in its fourth edition and provides all the fundamentals of the requirements for entering the travel industry on the international scene. Both books are now available at http://www.tour-guiding.com. Gerald Mitchell's talent and experience in the tourism industry have made him an international leader in the profession. His greatest joy over the years has been to show others the joys of travel and bring about greater understanding among the peoples of different cultures. He is truly a citizen of the world.

"Make Detours your Destination"